QUESTIONS & ANSWERS:
Evidence

Multiple Choice and Short Answer
Questions and Answers

REVISED FIRST EDITION

By

David P. Leonard
Professor of Law and
William M. Rains Fellow
Loyola Law School, Los Angeles

LexisNexis™

ISBN#: 0820562432

Editorial Offices
744 Broad Street, Newark, NJ 07102 (973) 820-2000
201 Mission St., San Francisco, CA 94105-1831 (415) 908-3200
701 East Water Street, Charlottesville, VA 22902-7587 (804) 972-7600
www.lexis.com

(Pub.3177)

ABOUT THE AUTHOR

David P. Leonard is Professor of Law and William M. Rains Fellow at Loyola Law School, Los Angeles. Prior to joining the Loyola faculty in 1991, Professor Leonard was Professor of Law at Indiana University School of Law—Indianapolis. He has taught Evidence for more than twenty years.

Professor Leonard is author of numerous law review articles as well as *Selected Rules of Limited Admissibility,* a volume of *The New Wigmore: A Treatise on Evidence.* Along with Roger C. Park and Steven H. Goldberg, he is co-author of the hornbook *Evidence Law: A Student's Guide to the Law of Evidence as Applied in American Trials.*

PREFACE

The law of evidence is complex, but if you work hard at it, you can develop an understanding of the individual rules and of the way the rules interact to form a system. The key to learning evidence law is to ask several questions about each problem:

(1) What is the questioned evidence? (This is a very important step; isolating the exact evidence at issue often provides clues to the rules that must be satisfied.)

(2) What is it offered to prove?

(3) Is it relevant when offered for that purpose?

(4) If it is relevant, are there any other rules of evidence that might lead to its exclusion?

These simple steps will always get you off to a good start. You can also develop a series of more specific questions for each area of evidence law. For example, if you suspect that the problem might deal with witness impeachment, you might ask the following questions:

(1) What is the questioned evidence?

(2) Is it offered to impeach or support the credibility of a witness? If so, what method of impeachment is involved?

(3) Are there any specific rules that govern the use of the evidence for that method of impeachment? If so, have those rules been followed? To determine whether the rules have been followed, ask:

(a) Is the evidence admissible only after the opposite party has offered evidence to the contrary?

(b) Are there limits on the form the evidence may take?

(4) If there are no rules that specifically govern this method of impeachment, would admission of the evidence violate any other rules, such as FRE 403?

(5) Do any foundational requirements, such as giving the witness an opportunity to explain or deny the statement or showing the evidence to the witness, apply? If so, have those rules been followed?

If you work methodically through each problem, and if you *read the rules* with care, you will succeed.

Though the explanations in this book contain a good deal of information you will find useful, the purpose of this book is not to teach you the rules of evidence. The main purpose is to test your knowledge of the individual rules and of how the rules work together. It is therefore a supplement to the primary casebook you will use in your class. In this book, you will find questions and answers in sixteen main subject areas that correspond to the basic topics you are likely to cover in an evidence course. There is also a practice final exam that samples issues from most of these subject areas. Though the book is organized in roughly the same way as some of the popular texts, it will work for you even if your class covers the material in a different order.

The problems in this book are based almost entirely on the Federal Rules of Evidence. The Federal Rules have been extremely influential in the development of state evidence codes, and where there are differences between federal practice and the law of particular states, those differences are usually quite easy to learn once you have mastered the Federal Rules. And because the Multistate Bar Examination tests federal evidence law, you need to learn the Federal Rules in any event. Throughout the book, "Federal Rules of Evidence" is abbreviated "FRE."

One final thought: Take the time to answer every question as carefully as possible. If the question calls for a short answer, write out the entire answer. It is easy to look at a problem, think briefly about the answer, and then read the answer printed in the book. It is a much better test of your understanding, and much more beneficial to the learning process, for you to do all you can with each question before you look at the response printed in the book.

I want to acknowledge the assistance of my students over more than twenty years, whose comments on many of the questions contained in this book have helped to sharpen and improve them.

Professor David P. Leonard
Los Angeles, California
January 2003

TABLE OF CONTENTS

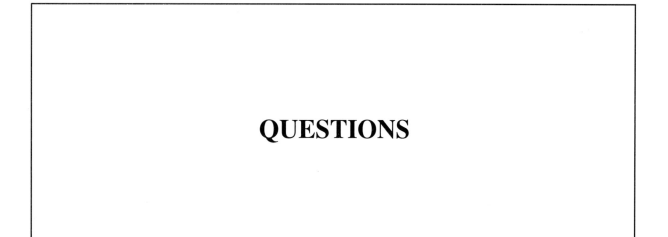

QUESTIONS

Civil action by P against D. During the direct examination of one of P's witnesses who claims to have seen the crucial event, D's attorney raises a specific objection to a question asking the witness to relate what she saw. After extensive argument on the evidentiary point, the court sustains the objection.

 Which of the following best reflects what P's lawyer should do next?

(A) P's lawyer should move on to the next question.

(B) P's lawyer should ask the court to have the record reflect P's disagreement with the court's ruling, and move on to the next question.

(C) P's lawyer should cease his examination of the witness because continuing with the examination will create a risk that an appellate court would find that P impliedly waived his right to appeal the court's ruling.

(D) P's lawyer should place in the trial record a statement of what the witness would have testified if permitted to answer the question.

At the trial of a civil action between P and D following an intersection collision between their cars, P calls W, the only other witness to the accident. Just after P's attorney asks W a question, D's attorney says, "I object, your honor. That question is clearly improper." The court overrules the objection. D loses the case, and appeals the judgment on the basis of the court's ruling on the objection.

 Which of the following statements is most accurate?

(A) Because D objected at the appropriate time, the appellate court will reverse as long as any error in the court's ruling affected a substantial right of D.

(B) If the record clearly reflects the nature of the error, the appellate court will reverse because W's testimony was crucial to P's case.

(C) Unless the record clearly reflects both the nature of the error and that it affected a substantial right of D, the appellate court will not reverse.

(D) Because D did not state a ground for the objection, the appellate court will not reverse. *can't reverse on plain error*

Prosecution of D for murder. D denies involvement. During its case-in-chief, the prosecution calls W, who has lived in the same community as D for many years, and asks W to testify about D's community reputation for violence or peacefulness. D's attorney does not object, and W testifies that D has a community reputation for being a very violent person. D is convicted, and appeals, claiming that this evidence should have been excluded under FRE 404(a).

3. Which of the following statements is most accurate?

(A) Because the record clearly reflects that the court violated FRE 404(a) by admitting the evidence, the appellate court will reverse.

(B) Because the record clearly reflects that the court violated FRE 404(a) by admitting the evidence, the appellate court will reverse if the error affected a substantial right of D.

(C) Because the trial court has discretion to admit character evidence that has substantial probative value, the trial court's error, if any, is not plain error. Because D did not make a specific objection, the appellate court will not reverse.

(D) Because D did not state a ground for the objection, the appellate court will not reverse.

Prosecution of D for the murder of V. At trial, the prosecution offered into evidence a series of gruesome photographs of V's body. D objected on FRE 403 grounds: that the probative value of the photos was substantially outweighed by the danger of unfair prejudice. The court overruled the objection and admitted the photos after stating that the probative value of the evidence was substantial under the circumstances, and that the danger of unfair prejudice was not too great to warrant exclusion. D was convicted, and appeals on the ground that the court erred by admitting the photos.

4. Which of the following statements is most accurate?

(A) Because rulings based on FRE 403 are solely committed to the discretion of the trial court, the appellate court will not review this alleged error.

(B) Because rulings based on FRE 403 involve the exercise of discretion that partly concerns matters that the trial court is in a better position to evaluate than is the appellate court, the appellate court will only find error if it determines that the trial court abused its discretion.

(C) Because the test set forth in FRE 403 is a legal standard that does not involve the exercise of discretion, the appellate court will review the alleged error *de novo*.

(D) Because the trial court applied the wrong standard to its ruling on the FRE 403 objection, the appellate court will reverse and remand for a new trial.

Prosecution of D for assault and battery on V. During its case-in-chief, the prosecution called W, a long-time acquaintance of D, and sought to elicit W's opinion about D's character for violence. D objected on the ground that this question sought inadmissible character evidence pursuant to FRE 404(a). The court overruled D's objection and permitted W to answer the question. W testified that in her opinion, D was a violent person. D was convicted, and appeals on the ground that the court should have excluded this testimony.

5. Which of the following statements is most accurate?

(A) Because rulings based on the exclusionary provision of FRE 404(a) are solely committed to the discretion of the trial court, the appellate court will not review this alleged error.

(B) Because rulings based on the exclusionary provision of FRE 404(a) involve the exercise of discretion that partly concerns matters that the trial court is in a better position to evaluate than is the appellate court, the appellate court will only find error if it determines that the trial court abused its discretion.

(C) Because the exclusionary provision of FRE 404(a) is a legal standard that does not involve the exercise of discretion, the appellate court will review the alleged error *de novo*.

(D) Because the trial court applied the wrong standard to its ruling on the FRE 404(a) objection, the appellate court will reverse and remand for a new trial.

Slander action by P against D. P alleges that in a speech at the American Bar Association convention, D called P a "damned liar." D claims he said P was a "kind lawyer." At trial, P calls W, who attended D's speech. W testifies that D called P a "damned liar." On cross-examination, D's attorney asks W, "Isn't it correct that you were sitting near the back of the auditorium?"

6. Which of the following statements is most accurate?

(A) The question is unobjectionable.

(B) If P makes a relevance objection, the court will sustain the objection.

(C) If P objects to the question as leading, the court will sustain the objection.

(D) If P objects to the question on the ground that the question assumes a fact not in evidence, the court will sustain the objection.

Prosecution of D for assault and battery on V, a law professor. The attack took place at the corner of First and Main Streets. At trial, the prosecutor calls W, who witnessed the attack. After a few preliminary questions, the prosecutor asks W where he was late on the evening the crime occurred. W says he cannot remember. The prosecutor then asks if W was standing on the corner of First and Main Streets.

7. Which of the following statements is most accurate?

(A) The question is unobjectionable. ← _correct._

(B) If D's attorney objects to the question as assuming a fact not in evidence, the court will sustain the objection.

(C) If D's attorney objects to the question as leading, the court will sustain the objection. _ok if W trouble remembering?_

(D) If D's attorney objects on the basis that the question has already been asked and answered, the court will sustain the objection.

Negligence action by P against D arising from a collision between the two in-line skaters. At trial, P testifies that she suffered permanent damage to her knee in the collision. On cross-examination, D asks P if it isn't true that P injured her knee playing basketball about a year before the accident in question. P objects to the question on the ground that it goes beyond the scope of the direct examination.

8. How should the court rule? Why?   _overrule. opened door by claiming collision caused damage_

ANSWER:

Prosecution of D for burglarizing a rare coin shop. To prove D's involvement, the prosecution calls W, who testifies that she saw D leaving the shop about an our after it closed on the night the crime took place. On cross-examination, D asks W if it isn't true that W and D were former business partners who had a falling out about a month before the crime was committed. The prosecutor objects to the question on the ground that it goes beyond the scope of the direct examination.

9. How should the court rule? Why?

ANSWER:

Prosecution of D for the murder of V. The prosecution calls W, a close friend of V. W testifies that she spoke with V's husband the day after the killing. The prosecutor then asks, "What did V's husband say?" W answers, "V's husband told me he saw D kill V." Assume the testimony concerning the husband's statement is inadmissible hearsay.

10. What should D do?

    (A)   D should object to the question on the ground that it calls for inadmissible hearsay.

    (B)   D should move to strike the testimony on hearsay grounds.

    (C)   D should move to strike the testimony on hearsay grounds, and ask the court to instruct the jury to ignore W's answer.

    (D)   There is nothing D can do because W has already answered the question.

Negligence action by P against D arising from an intersection collision. P calls W, and after some introductory questions establishing that W was near the scene, P's attorney asks, "Where exactly were you at the time of the collision, and what happened?"

11. Discuss two possible objections to this question, and how P's attorney can correct any problems.

ANSWER:

Negligence action by P against D arising from an intersection collision. As her first witness, P's attorney calls W, and after some introductory questions establishing that W was near the scene, P's attorney asks, "Did you see D's car run the red light?"

12. What objection should D make to this question, and how should P's attorney correct any problems?

ANSWER:

Prosecution of D for assault and battery. The prosecution calls W, who was present when the altercation took place. W is six years old. D objects on the ground that W is not competent to be a witness.

13. How should the court rule, and why?

ANSWER: *allow testimony, take precaution*

Action by P against the estate of X for non-payment of a promissory note. P filed the action in federal court under its diversity jurisdiction. The estate claims that X paid the note in full before her death. The state in which the federal court sits maintains a "dead man statute." At trial, P wishes to testify that shortly before her death, X acknowledged that the debt remained unpaid. The estate objects.

14. Which of the following statements is true?

 (A) The court should sustain the objection because of the dead man statute.

(B) The court should sustain the objection because P's testimony constitutes inadmissible hearsay.

(C) The court should sustain the objection both because of the dead man statute and because of the hearsay rule.

(D) The court should overrule the objection because there is no federal dead man statute and FRE 601 removes such a ground of witness incompetency.

During the trial of a case, a prospective witness refuses to take the oath or affirmation in the words prescribed by the court, claiming that "honesty" is superior to "truth" and proposing to affirm, instead, that she will testify with "fully integrated honesty." The opponent objects, and asks the court to refuse to permit the person to testify.

15. How should the court rule, and why?

ANSWER:

During the trial of a civil action, the judge decides to take the stand to testify about certain relevant facts of which she is personally aware. The party against whom the judge testifies does not object. After losing, that party appeals on the ground that it was error for the judge to testify.

16. Which of the following statements is correct?

   (A) The court should hold that the judge erred by testifying, reverse the judgment, and order a new trial.

   (B) The court should hold that the judge erred by testifying, determine whether the error affected a substantial right of the aggrieved party, and reverse and order a new trial if it did.

   (C) Because the party did not object at the time the judge testified, the error is not preserved for appeal and the court will affirm.

   (D) Because this is a civil action, the trial judge did not commit error by testifying.

Product liability action by P, a ten-year-old child, against D, the manufacturer of a bicycle that P alleges was defectively designed, causing him to lose control and crash, suffering serious injuries. Specifically, P claims the bike's frame was not strong enough to handle even the weight of a ten-year-old, and that it collapsed under him while he was riding. Although the actual bike was accidentally destroyed before trial, P produces another bike of the same model and exhibits it to the jury during the trial. The judge allows the jury to take the bike to the jury room. After the jury renders a verdict for D, the bailiff tells P's lawyer that when he entered the jury room to deliver some water, he saw the jurors taking apart the bike and examining its suspension system, something that was not done in open court. Based on this information, P moves for a new trial and asks the court to hold a hearing so the bailiff can testify about what he saw.

17. How should the court rule?

   (A) The court should hold the hearing because if true, the jury's conduct amounted to the taking of new testimony without the parties present.

   (B) The court should hold the hearing because the jurors are not allowed to handle exhibits.

   (C) The court should not hold the hearing because the bailiff may not testify to impeach the verdict.

   (D) The court should not hold the hearing because it is improper for a party to inquire about, or receive information about, the factors that motivated the jurors to render their verdict.

Following her murder conviction, a juror approaches defendant's attorney and complains about several things that occurred during deliberations.

18. If defendant makes a motion for a new trial, and asks the court to hold a hearing at which the juror may testify, which of the following would the court permit the juror to describe at the hearing?

   (A) Several of the jurors announced at the beginning of deliberations that they made up their minds right at the end of the prosecution's case-in-chief that the defendant was guilty, and that they paid little attention to the defendant's case.

(B)   During a lunch break while the trial was still going on, several of the jurors drank beer to the point of obvious intoxication.

(C)   One of the jurors told the other jurors that a publisher had approached her about a book deal if the jury voted to convict.

(D)   One of the jurors made a disparaging remark about the defendant's racial background, and stated that people of that race "just commit these crimes like it was nothing."

State court prosecution of D for assault and battery. The charge arises from an altercation that left both D and the alleged victim severely injured. D wishes to testify at trial. The prosecution objects on the ground that prior to testifying, D was hypnotized to help her remember the facts better, and that this makes her incompetent under the state's rule forbidding a previously hypnotized witness from testifying.

19.   How should the court rule?

(A)   The court should sustain the objection because the rule forbids D from testifying.

(B)   The court should sustain the objection if it finds that there is an equally good alternative to D's testimony.

(C)   The court must overrule the objection unless it finds that under the circumstances, the evidence is so untrustworthy as to overcome D's constitutional right to testify in her own behalf.

(D)   The court must overrule the objection because D has a constitutional right to testify at her own trial.

Prosecution of D for the murder of V. D admits killing V, but claims she acted in self-defense. To prove V started the fight, D offers evidence that V had committed numerous acts of violence in the months prior to the killing. D was unaware of these acts when the killing occurred. The prosecution objects on relevance grounds.

20. How should the court rule? Why? If you believe the evidence is relevant, set forth the chain of inferences that demonstrates its relevance, and include the generalizations that show how the inferences are linked.

ANSWER:

Prosecution of D for conspiracy to murder a well-known political figure. At trial, the prosecution calls W to testify that a week before the killing, W saw D talking to X, the confessed trigger-person, in a nightclub. D objects on relevance grounds.

21. How should the court rule? Why? If you believe the evidence is relevant, set forth the chain of inferences that demonstrates its relevance, and include the generalizations that show how the inferences are linked.

ANSWER:

Prosecution of D for burglary. D claims she never left home on the day the crime took place. To prove she was home all day, D testifies that she reads her horoscope every morning in order to help her decide what to do that day, and that on the day in question her horoscope said that she should not "undertake any risky endeavors." The prosecution objects on relevance grounds.

22. How should the court rule? Why? If you believe the evidence is relevant, set forth the chain of inferences that demonstrates its relevance, and include the generalizations that show how the inferences are linked.

ANSWER:

Civil rights action by P against D police department for using excessive force in arresting P at P's home. The officers went to P's home to execute an arrest warrant resulting from P's failure to pay fifty parking tickets. It is undisputed that as soon as P opened her front door, the officers grabbed P and beat her with their night sticks until she lost consciousness. D claims its officers acted in the reasonable belief that such force was necessary. To prove this, D wishes to offer evidence that on two occasions not long before this incident, P had acted violently when confronted with police officers. The two officers involved in this incident were not aware of these previous confrontations. P objects on relevance grounds.

23. How should the court rule? Why? If you believe the evidence is relevant, set forth the chain of inferences that demonstrates its relevance, and include the generalizations that show how the inferences are linked.

ANSWER:

Prosecution of D for the murder of V, D's ex-wife. D denies involvement. To prove that D committed the crime, the prosecution wishes to call W, a friend of D's, to testify that a few days after the killing occurred, D told W, "I dreamed last night that I killed V." D objects on relevance grounds.

24. How should the court rule? If you believe the evidence is relevant, set forth the chain of inferences that demonstrates its relevance, and include the generalizations that show how the inferences are linked.

ANSWER:

Prosecution of D for the murder of V in V's home. D claims she was on vacation in another state when the crime took place. To prove that D could have been in V's home at the time of the murder, the prosecution wishes to offer evidence that D was a federal inmate on work-release who worked for V as a housekeeper.

25. Which of the following statements is most accurate?

(A) The evidence is relevant and because it goes to a central issue in the case, its probative value cannot be substantially outweighed by the danger of unfair prejudice.

(B) The evidence concerning D's job as a housekeeper is relevant but her status as an inmate on work-release is not. Because the probative value of that aspect of the evidence is zero, the court must not allow the jury to hear that D was an inmate on work-release.

  (C) The evidence is relevant, but if the court finds that its probative value is substantially outweighed by the danger of unfair prejudice, the court may exclude the evidence.

  (D) The evidence is irrelevant.

Prosecution of D for first degree murder of V. D admits shooting V but claims she acted in self-defense when V attacked her. At trial, the prosecution calls W, a forensic pathologist who conducted the autopsy on V. W testifies that she found three entry wounds on the back of V's head. The prosecution then shows W a series of photographs, which W states were taken of V's upper body and head during the autopsy. The photographs clearly show the bullet wounds to the back of V's head that W had testified about. The prosecution offers the photographs into evidence. D objects.

 26. Which of the following statements is most likely correct?

  (A) Because the photographs are cumulative, they are irrelevant and must be excluded.

  (B) Although the photographs are relevant, the fact that they merely corroborate W's testimony deprives them of all but minimal probative value, and they must be excluded.

  (C) Although the photographs are relevant, the court may exclude them if it finds that they are less reliable evidence of the condition of V's body than is W's oral testimony.

  (D) Although the photographs are relevant, the court may exclude them if it finds that their probative value is substantially outweighed by the danger that the jury will convict D for the wrong reasons.

Wrongful death action by P against D arising from a horrible head-on automobile collision that killed P's deceased. To prove that D was traveling considerably above the speed limit of 25 miles per hour at the time of the crash, P wishes to offer into evidence several photographs taken at the scene. The photographs show P's mangled car, reduced to half its original size. Blood stains can be seen through the windshield. D offers to stipulate that she was traveling at least 60 miles per hour, and asks the court to exclude the photographs. P refuses to accept D's stipulation and insists on offering the photographs.

 27. How should the court rule?

  (A) Because the photographs would provide the jury with a greater understanding of the accident, the court should deny D's motion and allow P to offer the photographs.

  (B) Because D's stipulation would give P everything the photographs would have shown, the court should grant D's motion and exclude the photographs.

  (C) Because a party may prove its case with any otherwise admissible evidence, and may never be forced to accept a stipulation, the court should deny D's motion and allow P to offer the photographs into evidence.

(D)   Because trial courts generally exclude gory photographs, which tend to invite unfair prejudice by inflaming the jury's passions against the opponent, the court would exclude them even without D's offered stipulation.

Action by P, who was struck in a crosswalk by driver D. P wishes to offer evidence that D is a wealthy person.

28.   Which of the following statements is most likely correct?

(A)   The evidence might be relevant if P's action is brought on an intentional tort theory and P seeks punitive damages.

(B)   Because a wealthy person is not likely to be concerned about the potential financial impact of a tort judgment against her, the evidence is relevant if P's action is brought on a negligence theory.

(C)   Regardless of the substantive theory supporting P's action, the evidence is relevant.

(D)   Regardless of the substantive theory supporting P's action, the evidence is irrelevant.

Prosecution of D for bank robbery. The bank is next door to a multiplex movie theater. Prosecution witness W has testified that she was standing in line to buy tickets for the movie "Bar Wars: Episode 2" when she saw D emerging from the bank with a gun in one hand and a large sack in the other. On cross-examination D wishes to ask W if it isn't true that W was standing in line to buy tickets to "Bar Wars: Episode 3," not Episode 2. The prosecution objects on relevance grounds.

29.   Discuss whether the evidence is relevant.

ANSWER:

Prosecution of D for murder. D denies committing the crime. The prosecution calls an eyewitness who describes the killer as a "white male with blond hair." The prosecution then calls a police officer who testifies that she collected blood samples from the scene. The prosecutor then calls an expert who testifies that she conducted DNA tests on the blood samples, separated the victim's blood from blood assumed to be from the perpetrator, tested a sample of blood from D, found a "match," and calculated that only one in 500,000 white men could have produced the sample found at the scene. D does not dispute the validity of the DNA tests, nor does he call his own DNA expert. During final argument, the prosecutor makes the following statement to the jury: "Based on the expert's testimony, which was uncontradicted, there would only be a one in 500,000 chance that you would be wrong if you convicted D. That is certainly 'beyond a reasonable doubt.' "

30.   Discuss the validity of this argument.

ANSWER:

Same case as in the previous question. Assume D offers evidence that over 5 million people live in the metropolitan area in which the crime was committed. During final argument, D's attorney makes the following statement to the jury: "Based on the expert's testimony, there are at least ten people in this metropolitan area who could have produced the sample found at the crime scene. That means there is only a one in ten chance you would be correct if you convicted D of the crime. There is more than reasonable doubt of D's guilt in this case, and so you must acquit."

31. Discuss the validity of this argument.

ANSWER:

Negligence action by P against D arising from a skateboard collision. P claims D skated into P's path, causing the collision. D denies doing this, and claims it was just the other way around. To prove D skated into P's path, P calls W, who will testify that immediately after the collision, W heard someone scream, "D just got in P's way!" Assume this statement is hearsay, but that it will be admissible as an "excited utterance" if the declarant (the person who made the statement) was speaking under the "stress of excitement" caused by a "startling event or condition" (FRE 803(2)). D admits that the accident was a "startling event or condition," but claims that it has not been sufficiently established that the declarant was still under the stress of excitement when making the statement.

32. How should the court rule?

(A) The court should overrule the objection if it finds that there is sufficient evidence to support the jury's conclusion that the declarant was speaking under the stress of excitement caused by the accident.

(B) The court should overrule the objection if it finds by a preponderance of the evidence that the declarant was speaking under the stress of excitement caused by the accident.

(C) The court must admit the evidence because whether the declarant was speaking under the stress of excitement caused by the accident is a question of fact, which the jury must decide.

(D) The court must exclude the evidence because, as a matter of law, it is not possible to conclude that the declarant was speaking under the stress of excitement caused by the accident without identifying the declarant and having him or her testify at trial.

Prosecution of D for murder. The prosecution wishes to offer into evidence a confession D admittedly signed. At trial, D moves to suppress the confession, however, claiming that the police did not read her the Miranda rights before beginning the questioning that led to the confession. A police officer testifies that he did read D her Miranda rights.

33. How should the court rule?

(A) The court should deny D's motion if it finds by a preponderance of the evidence that the officer read D her Miranda rights.

(B) The court should deny D's motion if it finds by clear and convincing evidence that the officer read D her Miranda rights.

(C)   The court should deny D's motion if it finds beyond a reasonable doubt that the officer read D her Miranda rights.

(D)   The court should deny D's motion if it finds that there is evidence sufficient to support a finding that the officer read D her Miranda rights.

34.   Assume D's claim is that she confessed only after 24 hours of non-stop torture, including infliction of physical pain, threats against D's family, and sleep deprivation. D claims she would have signed anything to end the torture. The police deny categorically that any torture took place, and claim D confessed quickly and willingly. How should the court rule on D's suppression motion?

(A)   The court should grant D's motion if it finds by a preponderance of the evidence that D's story is true.

(B)   The court should grant D's motion if it finds that there is evidence sufficient to support a finding that D's story is true.

(C)   The court should let the jury decide the question because the voluntariness of a confession is a question of fact that is always for the jury.

(D)   The court should decide the question because the admissibility of evidence is always a decision for the court.

Negligence action by P against D arising from a skateboard accident. P claims D, owner of a small skateboard shop, improperly fixed the wheels on P's skateboard, causing P to crash. D denies negligence, and claims P assumed the risk by riding a defective skateboard. To prove assumption of risk, D wishes to testify that when P showed D the skateboard and asked her to fix it, D told D, "all I can do is tighten the wheel trucks, but it won't do any good. If you don't replace the trucks, the wheels will fall off when you're riding." D will testify that after she said this, P gave her an angry look and took back the skateboard. Assume this statement would only be admissible to prove assumption of risk if P "adopted" D's statement as true, making it a party admission under FRE 801(d)(2)(B). P claims D has not proven adoption.

35.   How should the court rule?

(A)   The court should overrule the objection if it finds that there is sufficient evidence to support the jury's conclusion that P adopted D's statement as true.

(B)   The court should overrule the objection if it finds, by a preponderance of the evidence, that P adopted D's statement as true.

(C)   The court must admit the evidence because P's purported adoption of D's statement is a question of fact that the jury must decide.

(D)   The answer depends on the approach taken by the jurisdiction.

36.   Explain why questions of preliminary fact that do not involve "conditional relevancy" should be decided by the court rather than the jury.

ANSWER:

Negligence action by P against D arising from an automobile collision. P calls W, who testifies that she was standing at the intersection waiting to cross the street when D ran a red light and struck P's car broadside. On cross-examination, D establishes that W was toward the back of a large crowd on the sidewalk before the crash, and had only a partial view of the street, that W was looking in the direction of the bright sun, that W has poor eyesight and was not wearing her glasses at the time, and that just after the crash, someone told W that D had run the red light. D moves to strike W's testimony due to lack of personal knowledge, and asks the court to instruct the jury to disregard W's testimony.

37. Which of the following statements is correct?

  (A) The court should deny the motion if it concludes that W had first-hand knowledge of the accident.

  (B) The court should deny the motion if it finds that there is evidence sufficient to support a finding that W had first-hand knowledge of the accident.

  (C) The court should deny the motion because whether W had first-hand knowledge is always a question for the jury.

  (D) The court should deny the motion regardless of whether W had first hand knowledge because W has already testified about the crash.

38. Using the facts of this problem, explain why the conditional relevancy doctrine might be illogical.

ANSWER:

Prosecution of D for the murder of V. To prove she did not commit the crime, D wishes to testify that after the murder was committed, X, a member of the Jets, a violent street gang, told her the Jets had "whacked" V. D is not a member of the Jets.

39. Which of the following statements is most likely correct?

    (A)   Because D's testimony concerning X's statement would be highly self-serving, the court should exclude it as a waste of time.

    (B)   Although X's statement is relevant to D's innocence, it is hearsay when offered for that purpose.

    (C)   X's statement is not hearsay when offered to prove D's innocence, but it must be excluded because its probative value is substantially outweighed by the danger of unfair prejudice.

    (D)   X's statement is relevant non-hearsay when offered to prove D's innocence.

Prosecution of D for the murder of V. D claims X committed the crime. To prove X killed V, D calls W to testify that just after the killing, which took place in a secluded area, and before V's body was discovered, X told her he had just killed a person, and described in detail the exact manner of killing (which was very unusual) and where the body could be found. All details given by X were accurate.

hearsay
excited utterance.

40. Which of the following statements is most likely correct?

    (A)   X's statement to W is only relevant to prove that X killed V, and is hearsay when considered for that purpose.

    (B)   X's statement to W is relevant both to prove that X killed V and to prove that X had knowledge of certain key details, but is hearsay when offered for either purpose.

    (C)   X's statement to W is relevant both to prove that X killed V and to prove that X had knowledge of certain key details. The statement is hearsay when offered for the first purpose, but not hearsay when offered for the second.

    (D)   X's statement is relevant both to prove that X killed V and to prove that X had knowledge of certain key details. However, because the testimony concerning X's statement is so self-serving and because D did not call X, the court should exclude it.

Personal injury action by P against D following a slip-and-fall in D's store. P calls W to testify that shortly before the fall, W told D that there was a big puddle of liquid on the floor.

41.   Which of the following statements is most accurate?

(A)   W's testimony is hearsay if offered to prove the floor was slippery, but not hearsay if offered to prove that D knew the floor was slippery.

(B)   W's testimony is not hearsay if offered to prove the floor was slippery (because W didn't say the floor was slippery), but is hearsay when offered to prove that D knew the floor was slippery.

(C)   W's testimony is hearsay when offered for either purpose.

(D)   W's testimony is not hearsay when offered for either purpose.

Prosecution of D for burglary of V's home. To prove that D committed the crime, the prosecution wishes to offer evidence that as D was being led through the police station, V, who was at the station giving a statement, saw D and screamed, "You are the scum of the Earth." D objects on hearsay grounds.

42.   Which of the following statements is most likely correct?

(A)   The statement is more likely hearsay under an assertion-based definition of hearsay than under a declarant-based definition.

(B)   The statement is more likely hearsay under a declarant-based definition of hearsay than under an assertion-based definition.

(C)   The statement would be hearsay under either definition.

(D)   Without further information, it is not possible to predict whether the statement is more likely to be admitted under one definition than the other.

Prosecution of D for assault and battery on V. D admits striking V but claims self-defense. To prove her self-defense claim, D testifies that the day before the altercation, X told D that V was planning to kill D the next time they saw each other.

43.   Discuss the hearsay implications of X's statement to V.
ANSWER: *admissible to D statement mind*
inadmissible to V planning kill

Libel action by P, a prominent philanthropist, against D, a newspaper, alleging that D published a false story stating that P supported neo-Nazi organizations. D wishes to present evidence that it received the information from X, a reliable source. Assume two defenses are (1) that the story is true; and (2) that even if false, D acted in good faith because it did not know the story was false and did not act in reckless disregard for the truth.

44. Which of the following statements is most accurate?

    (A) The evidence is relevant and not hearsay both to prove the story is true and to prove that D published the story in good faith.

    (B) The evidence is hearsay for either purpose.

    (C) The evidence is hearsay if offered to prove the story was true but not hearsay if offered to prove D's good faith in publishing the story.

    (D) This question cannot be answered without more information.

Prosecution of D for assault and battery on V. To prove she acted in self-defense, D calls W to testify that V had a reputation for being violent. D did not know V's reputation at the time of the altercation.

45. The evidence of V's reputation is

    (A) irrelevant if D's theory is that D acted in reasonable fear of V, and relevant non-hearsay if D's theory is that V attacked first.

    (B) irrelevant if D's theory is that D acted in reasonable fear of V, and relevant but hearsay if D's theory is that V attacked first.

    (C) relevant under either theory but hearsay under both.

    (D) irrelevant under either theory.

Breach of contract action by P against D. To prove a contract existed, P wishes to call W, her friend, to testify that the night the negotiations ended, P called him and said, "I just accepted D's offer!"

46. Is P's statement hearsay? Why or why not?

ANSWER:

Will contest. To prove the testator lacked testamentary capacity when she signed her will leaving everything to her law school alma mater, P calls W, the testator's former servant, to testify that on the day the testator signed her will, she asked the servant to make her a "Moon sandwich with Jupiter cheese on Martian brain bread" for lunch.

47. The evidence of the testator's statement to W is

    (A) more likely hearsay under a declarant-based definition than under an assertion-based definition.

    (B) more likely hearsay under an assertion-based definition than under a declarant-based definition.

(C) clearly hearsay under both definitions.

(D) clearly non-hearsay under both definitions.

Libel action by P against D, a well-known entertainer. P alleges that in front of a comedy club audience, D called P a "slimy, scum-sucking bottom-feeder who wouldn't free his own mother if she was tied to a railroad track." D denies saying this. To prove D uttered the words, P wishes to offer in evidence two things: (1) the testimony of a person who was in the audience that night, who will state that D spoke the words; and (2) a newspaper review of D's performance mentioning what D said.

48. Discuss the hearsay implications of each item of evidence.

ANSWER:

For the following questions, indicate whether each utterance or act is hearsay for the purpose for which it is offered, and explain why. Apply the Federal Rules of Evidence. If something would not be hearsay under the Federal Rules, call it non-hearsay. Also, do not assume that a declarant is a party unless the facts indicate such.

49. To prove P has become the owner of a piece of land by adverse possession, P calls W to testify that one day, X approached her and said, "P's going around saying she owns the lot."

ANSWER:

50. Slander action by P against D. To prove he suffered significant harm to his reputation when D called him an "airhead" in front of a large audience, P testifies that prior to this incident, he was known in the community as a brilliant corporate leader.

ANSWER:

51. Civil rights action by P against D, a police officer. P claims that D shot her without reason during a confrontation before a sporting event. D claims she acted in self-defense. To prove she acted reasonably, D testifies that while en route to the sports arena, the dispatcher told D that P was armed.

ANSWER:

52. Negligence action against D, the builders of a suspended pedestrian bridge that collapsed. To prove that the bridge was sturdy, D offers testimony that a day before the accident, X, a structural engineer, walked onto the bridge in front of a large crowd, said "Observe!", and proceeded to jump up and down and shake the bridge.

ANSWER:

53. Personal injury action by P against D arising from a skateboard collision. To prove that D was at fault, P testifies that just after the collision, D said to P, "Sorry I cut you off, dude."

ANSWER:

54. Prosecution of D for the murder of V. At trial, the prosecution calls W, who claims to have witnessed the killing. When asked who killed V, W points to D.

ANSWER:

55. To prove that the weather at the beach on a certain day was very sunny, W testifies that most people at the beach put on sunscreen.

ANSWER:

56. To prove that it was raining at a certain time, W testifies that at that time, a weather reporter on a local news program said, "Dust off those umbrellas!"

ANSWER:

57. To prove that P and D entered into a contract, P calls W, her secretary, to testify that after P and D completed a negotiation session, and while D's back was turned, P whispered to W, "I just sold those leftover Sugar Boys CDs."

ANSWER:

58. To prove that a physician feared contracting AIDS from X, the physician's nurse testifies that before examining X, the physician put on latex gloves.

ANSWER:

59. To prove that D liked X, W testifies that D introduced X to her as "my favorite person in the whole world."

ANSWER:

60. To prove that X was W's mother, W testifies, "X is my mom."

ANSWER:

61. To prove that X was the owner of a certain dog, W testifies that she saw the dog run up to X wagging its big bushy tail.

ANSWER:

62. To prove that a certain event occurred at 5:10 p.m. W testifies that she was sitting in Professor Wigmore's evidence class one day when the professor looked in the direction of the clock and said, "I see our time is up." The class ended at 5:10.

ANSWER:

63. To prove that P, a big-screen TV store owner, was a sales leader in the business, P calls W to testify that she heard P say at the end of a radio advertisement, "I *am* the king."

ANSWER:

64. To prove that Elvis is dead, W testifies that she visited Graceland and saw a tombstone with the name "Elvis Aaron Presley" chiseled on it.

ANSWER:

65. To prove that D's red car hit P's blue car, P testifies that just after the accident, she turned to her companion and said, "that red car just rammed right into us."

ANSWER:

66. Personal injury action by P against D following an automobile collision. D calls W, who testifies that D had the green light. To impeach W's credibility, P calls X to testify that shortly after the accident, W told her that *P* had the green light.

ANSWER:

67. To prove that X was close to Y's car, W testifies that as X walked past Y's car, an automated voice from Y's car stated, "Back off! You are too close to the vehicle."

ANSWER:

68. Negligence action by P against D arising out of an automobile collision. To prove that he suffered emotional distress as a result of the accident, P calls W to testify that at the scene just after the accident, P was sobbing.

ANSWER:

69. Slander action by P, a film director, against D arising out of a speech D gave to an audience of film critics. To prove that the slander was uttered, P testifies that in the speech, D said that P was the illegitimate offspring of the unholy mating of a pig and a wolf and that he possessed the morality of a buzzard hovering over a corpse.

ANSWER:

70. Prosecution of D for the murder of V. To prove D's guilt, the prosecution offers testimony that while being transported to the police station following her arrest, D said, "that creep I just killed deserved to die."

ANSWER:

71. Negligence action by P against D after the two roller skaters collided on a beach sidewalk. To prove that D was responsible, P calls W, who came on the scene shortly after the collision. P wishes to have W testify that as soon as she saw what had happened, she asked a bystander which skater was responsible, and that the bystander pointed to D. D lodges a hearsay objection to W's testimony about the bystander's pointing motion.

ANSWER:

72. Civil action by P against D bank for wrongful discharge. P alleges that D's president fired P for improper reasons. Assume a valid defense is that the employee has been convicted of a crime involving dishonesty, and that D raises such a defense. To prove its defense, D wishes to call its president to testify that before firing P, she heard that before coming to work for the bank, P had been convicted of embezzlement.

ANSWER:

73. Will contest initiated by P, who claims to have been the deceased's best friend but who was granted nothing in the will. To prove that the deceased intentionally left P out of the will, the deceased's executor calls W to testify that on the day she made her will, the deceased called P "a bloody leech who would con a homeless baby out of her spot on a steam grate on a cold winter night."

ANSWER:

74. Negligence action by P against D arising out of an intersection collision between their cars. Both drivers claim they had the green light. To prove she had the green light, D testifies that a few moments before the collision, the driver in front of D, who had been stopped at the intersection, began to move forward.

ANSWER:

75. Breach of contract action by P, a music wholesaler, against D, a record store owner. P alleges that in a telephone conversation, P and D entered an oral contract for the sale of two cartons of "Sneezer" CDs at a specified price, but that D failed to pay for the CDs after they were delivered. D denies that a contract existed. To prove a contract existed, P offers to testify that after D offered to purchase the CDs, P responded, "I accept your offer."

ANSWER:

76. Prosecution of D for willful neglect of his pet fish. To prove that D had not been feeding his fish, the prosecution wishes to offer evidence that when the police came to D's home to arrest him and approached the tank in which the poor fish lived, all the fish immediately swam to the surface and began moving about wildly.

ANSWER:

77. Prosecution of D for the murder of V, her husband. D admits killing V, but claims she was provoked. To prove provocation, D wishes to testify that just before the killing, X told her that V had been arrested for engaging in lewd conduct with a prostitute.

ANSWER:

78. Wrongful death action by P against Taikachanz Airlines (D) following a fatal crash that killed P's deceased. P alleges that the plane in which P's deceased was riding was not airworthy. To prove the plane was airworthy, D calls W to testify that D's pilot visually inspected the outside of the plane just before she went aboard.

ANSWER:

79. Civil action by P against D bank for wrongful discharge. P alleges that D's president fired P for improper reasons. Assume a valid defense to the action is that D acted in good faith in firing the employee, and that D raises such a defense. To prove good faith, D calls Y, its president, to testify that before firing P, she heard that P had been convicted of embezzlement a year earlier.

ANSWER:

80. Prosecution of D for the murder of V. In order to establish that the killing took place at noon, the prosecution calls W, who witnessed the killing, to testify that just after the killing occurred, he turned to his friend, asked her what time it was, and that the friend then looked at her watch and said, "12:00 sharp." D objects to the evidence of the friend's statement.

ANSWER:

81. Prosecution of D for a murder that took place in State X. D claims she was a thousand miles away in State Y when the killing took place. At trial, D testifies that she remembers the day well because in State Y on that day, the temperature was unbearably hot. To corroborate her testimony, D wishes to offer in evidence a newspaper article from State Y dated the following day. The article states that the temperature on the previous day had hit a record high of 112 degrees.

ANSWER:

82. Action for civil commitment of a law professor due to insanity. To prove insanity, plaintiff offers evidence that right in the middle of an evidence class, the professor jumped on the podium and shouted, "I am the king of the Federal Rules!"

ANSWER:

83. To prove an accident happened at dawn, a farmer testifies that just before the crash, her husband poked her and said, "rooster's crowing. Time to get up."

ANSWER:

84. To prove that X is dead, a party offers into evidence the original death certificate, obtained from the county recorder's office.

ANSWER:

85. To prove that A and B, two companies, had agreed to merge, a party calls W to testify that X, a corporate officer, told W that she heard A's president said to B's president,

"I propose that we merge our companies," and that B's president responded, "I accept your offer."

ANSWER:

86. To prove that X had conveyed a piece of land to Y, a party offers in evidence a deed signed by X conveying X's interest in the property to Y.

ANSWER:

87. To prove that X is a blond, W testifies that at a party, Y pointed to X and said, "Have you ever seen such blond hair in all your life?"

ANSWER:

88. Negligence action by P against D arising from an automobile accident. To prove that P was in pain following the accident, W testifies that she saw P sitting alone on the sidewalk crying.

ANSWER:

89. Prosecution of D for passing counterfeit money. To prove that D was aware that the notes she passed were not genuine, a prosecution witness testifies that before D passed the notes, X told D that they were "bogus."

ANSWER:

90. Prosecution of D for the murder of V. To prove her innocence, D calls W to testify that X confessed to the crime.

ANSWER:

91. Prosecution of D for a murder committed in a supermarket at 8:00 p.m. on a Sunday night. To prove that she did not commit the crime, D calls W to testify that at 7:45

on the night of the murder, D said to W, " 'The Shrimptons' is my favorite television program." It is undisputed that "The Shrimptons" is televised at 8:00 on Sunday evenings, including the evening in question.

ANSWER:

92.   Prosecution of D for burglary. To prove D committed the crime, a prosecution witness testifies that D confessed to the police.

ANSWER:

93.   Negligence action by P against D arising from an automobile accident. To prove that P did not suffer a broken arm in the accident, W testifies that a few minutes after the accident, she saw P playing catch using the arm in question.

ANSWER:

94.   During a criminal trial, X, sitting in the audience, rises and proclaims that she, rather than D, committed the crime.

ANSWER:

95.   To prove that Y, a law student, understood evidence law well, Y testifies that X, Y's evidence teacher, wrote a note on Y's final exam stating, "excellent work."

ANSWER:

96.   To prove X hated Y, W testifies that when X saw Y at a party, X said, "Y is a stupid person."

ANSWER:

97.   To prove that X is dead, W testifies that she saw officials of the coroner's office placing X's body into their van.

ANSWER:

98. Sexual harassment action by P against D Corp., her employer. To prove the harassment occurred, P testifies that one of D's managers, who served as P's boss, cornered P one evening after everyone else had left and said, "You have the most amazing eyes I've ever seen."

ANSWER: *not hearsay.*

99. To prove X liked Y, W testifies that X said to Y, "I hope you'll go out with me some time."

ANSWER: *not hearsay?*
                 but admissible

100. To prove that a prototype automobile was working satisfactorily, W testifies that after taking the car for a test drive, the driver looked toward the control booth and raised one thumb.

ANSWER: *Hearsay*

Note: To answer many of the following questions, you must have covered the material on preliminary questions of fact (FRE 104), the exceptions to the hearsay rule (FRE 803, 804, and 807), and exemptions from the hearsay rule (FRE 801(d)).

Prosecution of D for the murder of V. To prove that D committed the murder, the prosecution calls W, who was with V when he died. The prosecution wishes to have W testify that just before V died, W said to him, "Where did this happen?", and that V pointed to D, who was standing in a corner of the room, and said, "his house." D lodges a hearsay objection to W's proposed testimony.

101. Which of the following statements is most accurate?

(A) Because W's out of court statement is hearsay for which no exception applies, it is inadmissible.

(B) Because neither W nor V have made statements as defined in the hearsay rule, W will be permitted to testify both to what he said to V and to V's nodding conduct.

(C) If V is found to have adopted W's assertion as his own, both W's statement and V's response will be admissible.

(D) If V heard W's statement and if V believed he was about to die, W's question and V's pointing will be admissible.

Prosecution of D for the murder of V in a city plaza. It is undisputed that at the time of the killing, D was standing in a grassy area on the east side of the plaza, about 50 feet from V. D claims, however, that she had nothing to do with the killing. At trial, a critical issue is the direction from which the shots were fired. The prosecution claims the shots came from the grassy area, while D claims they came from a six-story building on the west side of the plaza. To prove that the shots issued from the grassy area, the prosecution calls W, and wishes to have her testify that she was in the plaza at the time of the killing, that she heard the sound of gunfire, and that moments later, she saw X, a bystander who she'd noticed had been in the plaza for several minutes, raise her arm and point toward the grassy area. D lodges a hearsay objection to W's testimony about X's actions.

102. Which of the following statements is most accurate?

(A) The judge must decide whether X was asserting the direction from which the shots were fired. If the judge decides that she was, the evidence will be hearsay but admissible as a present sense impression.

(B) The judge must decide whether there is sufficient evidence to support the conclusion that X was asserting the direction from which the shots were fired. If the judge makes that finding, she will allow the jury to hear the evidence of X's conduct.

(C) Because the foundational elements for the excited utterance exception are clearly satisfied, the court must admit the evidence.

(D) Because X's conduct is irrelevant if he was not asserting the place from which the shots were fired, and inadmissible hearsay if X was in fact asserting the place from which the shots were fired, the judge must exclude the evidence.

Breach of contract action by the P Opinion Survey Co. (P) against D, an unsuccessful presidential candidate. P claims that D failed to pay a large bill for political polling P had performed. D claims that she never hired P to do any work for her. At trial, P calls W, a news reporter, and wishes to have W testify that during the campaign, he attended a press conference conducted by X, D's husband, and that at that press conference, X said, "according to figures put together for us by the P Opinion Survey Co., we have a 19 percentage point lead over our closest rival."

103. Which of the following constitutes P's strongest argument that the evidence of X's statement is admissible?

(A) Because the making of X's statement constitutes the very fact in issue, it is an act of independent legal significance, and is thus admissible as non-hearsay.

(B) Because X's statement does not assert that D hired P, it is admissible non-hearsay.

(C) Because X was probably authorized to speak for D, X's statement is admissible as an authorized admission under FRE 801(d)(2)(C).

(D) Because X was speaking about a matter within the scope of his employment, X's statement is admissible as an agency admission under FRE 801(d)(2)(D).

Prosecution of D for conspiracy to sell illicit drugs. D denies that he was involved in any conspiracy. The prosecution calls one witness who testifies that she was a part of the conspiracy but backed out before the drug sales took place. To prove D's involvement in the conspiracy, the prosecution wishes to call PO, an undercover officer, to testify that she infiltrated the organization which allegedly planned the crime, and that on the day before the "big deal" was going to "go down," X, a member of the organization, said to PO, "D and I need a driver for tomorrow's big buy. Can you help out?" D lodges a hearsay objection to PO's testimony concerning X's statement.

104. Which of the following statements is most accurate?

(A) The existence of a conspiracy is a preliminary fact which must be found in order for X's statement to be admissible. It is also a fact which the jury must ultimately decide in order to convict D. As a result, the jury should decide the preliminary fact.

(B) The existence of a conspiracy is a preliminary fact which must be found in order for X's statement to be admissible. It is also a fact which the jury must ultimately decide in order to convict D. Therefore, although the existence of the preliminary fact will be for the court to decide, the court must apply the reasonable doubt standard in making that determination.

(C) Because the statement asserts that a conspiracy existed, which is the very thing the court must decide in order to determine the admissibility of the statement, it would be improper "bootstrapping" to allow the court to consider the statement as evidence of the existence of the conspiracy.

(D) Even though the statement asserts that a conspiracy existed, which is the very thing the court must decide in order to admit the statement, the court may consider the statement as it determines the preliminary fact question.

105. Assume X's statement was the only evidence the prosecution offers to prove that a conspiracy existed. Will the trial court be acting properly if it decides as a preliminary fact that a conspiracy existed and allows the case to go to the jury? (Assume that the other preliminary facts necessary to the admissibility of the statement have been found to exist.) Explain.

ANSWER: *Yes. discretion. preponderance*

Prosecution of D for assault and battery on V, a hitchhiker who was driven by his attacker to a remote location and brutally assaulted before being dumped in an alley. D denies that he was the attacker. At trial, the prosecution calls V to testify about the incident, and then calls PO, a police officer, to testify that while V was recuperating in the hospital the day after the attack, V told her that he expected to die and then described the inside of the van in which he was attacked, saying that the interior was upholstered with red and white striped leather, and that the walls of the van were covered with "gang-style" graffiti and photographs of a well-known political figure. It is undisputed that D owns a van meeting the description given by V. D lodges a hearsay objection to PO's testimony concerning V's out of court statement.

106. Which of the following constitutes the prosecution's strongest argument in favor of admissibility?

(A) Although the statement is hearsay because it is offered to prove the appearance of the interior of the attacker's van, there are sufficient indications of trustworthiness to warrant admission.

(B) Although the statement is hearsay because it is offered to prove the appearance of the interior of the attacker's van, the statement is admissible as a present sense impression.

(C) Although the statement is hearsay because it is offered to prove the appearance of the interior of the attacker's van, the statement is admissible as a dying declaration.

(D)   The statement is not offered to prove the appearance of the interior of the attacker's van, but to demonstrate V's knowledge of its quite unique interior under circumstances indicating that V must have been inside the van.

Prosecution of D, a woman, for assault and battery following a fight with V, a man, in a bar. The primary issue is whether it was D or V who started the fight. At trial, to prove that D started the fight, the prosecution calls W to testify that moments after the fight began, X screamed, "that woman just ran up and slugged that guy!" D lodges an objection to the testimony concerning X's statement on both hearsay and personal knowledge bases. The prosecution responds that the statement is admissible as an excited utterance and that X did in fact have personal knowledge of the facts.

107.   Which of the following best describes the procedure the court should follow?

(A)   The court should decide by a preponderance of the evidence whether X had personal knowledge of the fight and whether the foundational requirements for the excited utterance exception have been satisfied.

(B)   The court should decide beyond a reasonable doubt whether X had personal knowledge of the fight and whether the foundational requirements for the excited utterance exception have been satisfied.

(C)   The court should decide whether there is sufficient evidence to support a jury finding that X had personal knowledge of the fight, and should then decide by a preponderance of the evidence whether the foundational requirements for the excited utterance exception have been satisfied.

(D)   The court should decide whether there is sufficient evidence to support a jury finding that X had personal knowledge of the fight, and whether there is sufficient evidence to support a jury finding that the foundational requirements for the excited utterance exception have been satisfied.

Breach of contract action by P against D. P claims that D promised to hire P to work for her law firm, that P turned down another job offer in reliance on this promise, and that D then failed to hire P. Assume it is given that D's firm planned to hire only one new person. At trial, D calls W, her secretary, and wishes to have him testify that just after P completed his interview with the law firm, D said to W, "I think I'll go downstairs to start the paperwork to hire Q for the job." P lodges a hearsay objection to W's testimony concerning D's statement.

108.   Which of the following arguments has the greatest chance of succeeding?

(A)   Because D's statement tends to make it more likely that D did not promise to hire P, it is relevant. Because the statement only circumstantially indicates his state of mind, it is not hearsay. It is therefore admissible.

(B)   Because D's statement tends to make it more likely that D did not promise to hire P, it is relevant. Though the statement asserts D's state of mind, and is therefore hearsay, it fits within the exception for statements of then existing state of mind. It is therefore admissible.

(C) Because D's statement tends to make it more likely that D did not promise to hire P, it is relevant. However, because the statement asserts D's state of mind, it is hearsay, and it does not fit within the state of mind exception because it refers to the future status of a third person.

(D) Because D's statement does not make it more likely that D did not promise to hire P, it is irrelevant and therefore inadmissible.

Prosecution of D, a law student, for vandalizing the offices of Bigue Biggere & Biggeste, a law firm which denied her a summer clerkship. At trial, the prosecution wishes to call W to testify that the day before the crime was committed, she overheard X, who had also been denied an offer, mumbling the following to himself: "I think I'll go with D tomorrow night to the offices of Bigue Biggere and leave those creeps a message even they will understand." X has already been convicted of this crime and now resides in the state penitentiary. D lodges a hearsay objection to W's testimony concerning X's statement.

 109. Which of the following constitutes the prosecution's strongest response?

(A) The statement is not hearsay because it is not offered to prove the truth of what it asserts.

(B) The statement is admissible as a co-conspirator statement.

(C) The statement is hearsay but admissible as a declaration against interest.

(D) The statement is hearsay but admissible under the state of mind exception.

110. Which of the following constitutes D's strongest policy argument against admitting W's testimony concerning X's statement?

(A) Admission of the statement violated the defendants' right to confront the witnesses against them.

(B) Because the main purpose for admitting the statement was to establish the intent (and by implication the future conduct) of a third person, the foundation which makes state of mind statements reliable drops away, and we are left with an arguably unreliable statement the credibility of which cannot be tested contemporaneously with its making.

 (C) The probative value of the evidence in establishing D's intentions and future conduct was greatly outweighed by the danger of unfair prejudice arising from the jury's inability or unwillingness to abide by an instruction that the evidence is to be considered only for that purpose.

(D) Because the statement did not directly assert the declarant's state of mind, the state of mind doctrine does not apply at all to the case, and the evidence should have been excluded.

Prosecution of D, a blond man, for bank robbery. The prosecution alleges that D participated with X in committing the crime. At trial, the prosecution calls PO, a police officer, and wishes to have PO testify that two days after the crime, she arrested X, and that on the way to be booked, X said, "Yeah, me and some blond guy did it. So what?" Two days later, X died of food poisoning while he was being held in the county jail. D lodges a hearsay objection to PO's testimony concerning X's statement.

111.   Which of the following rulings would be most supportable?

(A)   The court should admit the evidence as an admission.

(B)   The court should admit the evidence as a declaration against interest.

(C)   The court should admit the evidence as a dying declaration.

(D)   The court should exclude the evidence as irrelevant.

Prosecution of D for assault and battery on V. V was attacked in a dimly lit alley late one night, with the perpetrator jumping V from behind. A struggle ensued, during which V got a glimpse of the perpetrator. The day after the assault, while V was recuperating in the hospital from serious head injuries, he described his attacker to PO, a police officer, as a white male between 25 and 35, medium height, with long brown hair. PO then showed V some photographs of men generally meeting the description V gave. V picked D's photograph out of this group. At trial, V testifies generally about the crime, but is unable to provide much detail because, he claims, he remembers little. V remembers looking through some photographs, but does not remember who, if anybody, he selected. The prosecutor then calls PO and wishes to have PO testify that V chose D's photograph. D lodges a hearsay objection to PO's testimony insofar as it relates that V selected D's photograph.

112.   Which of the followings statements is most accurate?

(A)   PO's testimony concerning V's selection of D's photograph is admissible under the prior identification rule.

(B)   Because V remembers so little about both the attack and identification procedure, admitting PO's testimony would violate D's right to confront the witnesses against him.

(C)   Because PO did not know whether V chose the correct person when he selected D's photograph from the book, PO's testimony is inadmissible.

(D)   Because V could not have gotten a good look at the attacker, V did not have personal knowledge. Thus, V would not have been allowed to testify about who attacked him. If V could not have testified to this fact, neither can PO.

Wrongful discharge action by P, a law professor, against D University, his employer. P claims he was fired without cause. D claims it fired P because rather than teaching Evidence, P taught quantum mechanics. P denies this. To prove that P was teaching quantum mechanics, D calls

W, a student in P's class, to testify about the contents of a certain class session. Despite efforts to refresh W's recollection, she cannot recall what took place on that day. D then asks W if she took notes during the class on that day and whether the notes accurately reflected what took place in the classroom. W answers "yes" to both questions. D then asks W to read aloud a page of her notes. The notes state that D discussed Schroedinger's cat, a quantum mechanics thought experiment. P makes a hearsay objection.

113. Which of the following statements is most accurate?

(A) W's notes are not hearsay because they are not offered to prove the truth of P's statements about quantum mechanics. The notes may be read into the record.

(B) W's notes are hearsay and because W had no legal duty to record P's words accurately, no hearsay exception applies.

(C) W's notes are hearsay but admissible under the doctrine of past recollection recorded.

(D) W's notes are not hearsay because D is merely using them to refresh the witness's recollection. They may therefore be read into the record.

Negligence action by P against D arising out of a collision between the two skateboarders. At trial, to prove damages, P calls W to testify that she saw the collision, and ran over to P (who was lying on the ground) immediately after it. P then wishes to have W testify that when he saw W, P said, in an anguished tone, "My leg is all twisted the wrong way and I don't have any feeling in it at all." D lodges a hearsay objection to the evidence concerning P's response.

114. Which of the following statements is most accurate?

(A) The statement is not hearsay because it is an admission. *physu*

(B) The statement is hearsay, and it is admissible only under the exceptions for excited utterances and present sense impressions.

(C) The statement is hearsay, and it is admissible only under the exceptions for statements of then existing physical condition.

(D) The statement is hearsay, and it is probably admissible under the exceptions for excited utterances, present sense impressions, statements of then existing physical condition, and statements made for purposes of medical diagnosis or treatment.

Prosecution of D for the murder of V in a barroom brawl. D claims she was attending a World Series game when the murder took place. The prosecutor calls W, who testifies that he was in the bar when the killing occurred and clearly saw the killer's face. The prosecutor then wishes to have W testify that the day after the killing, W was shopping with his girlfriend at a supermarket when W saw D coming down the same aisle; that W walked up to D and said, "You're the woman who killed that old man"; and that D continued walking down the aisle. D lodges a hearsay objection to the testimony about W's statement to D, and a relevancy objection to the evidence concerning D's failure to respond.

115. Which of the following constitutes the prosecution's best response?

(A) W's statement to D is hearsay but admissible as an excited utterance. The court should then admit the evidence of D's silence if it finds that by her conduct, D admitted the truth of W's accusation.

(B) W's statement to D is not hearsay because it constitutes a prior identification. The court should then admit the evidence of D's silence if it finds that by her conduct, D admitted the truth of W's accusation.

(C) W's statement to D is not hearsay because it constitutes a prior identification. The court should then permit the jury to decide whether by her conduct, D admitted the truth of W's accusation.

(D) The court should allow the jury to decide whether W's statement to D constitutes a prior identification. The court should then permit the jury to decide whether by her conduct, D admitted the truth of W's accusation.

Prosecution of D for arson arising out of a fire that destroyed D's insured building. Earlier, D had sued her fire insurer after it refused to pay. At the trial of that action, the insurer called W, D's friend, who testified that he saw D place an incendiary device in the shop just before the fire. D cross-examined W at that time, trying to shake his story. W is now dead, killed in a fire in another store. In D's criminal trial, the prosecution offers the transcript of W's testimony under the former testimony exception.

116. Which of the following statements is most accurate?

(A) The transcript is inadmissible because in the criminal action, D has much to lose and thus a strong motive to more vigorously cross-examine W.

(B) The transcript is inadmissible because the civil trial came first.

(C) The transcript is inadmissible because its admission would violate D's constitutional right to confront the witnesses against him.

(D) The transcript is admissible.

117. Assume that in this criminal trial, the state has also named X as a defendant. X is the person from whom D had bought the store a few months before the fire. X was not a party in D's civil action against the insurance company. X bases his defense on the same theory as D—that the fire was accidental. At trial, the prosecution wishes to offer against X the transcript of W's testimony from the previous civil action. Which of the following statements is most accurate?

(A) The transcript is inadmissible because in the first action, D had a different motive in cross-examining W than X has in this criminal trial.

(B) The transcript is inadmissible because X was not a party to the civil action.

(C)   The transcript is admissible because X is D's predecessor in interest and is bound by D's actions.

(D)   The transcript is admissible against X because it is admissible against D.

Civil action by P against D arising out of a hit-and-run accident. D claims that though she drives the same kind of car that was involved in the accident, she had nothing to do with the accident. D claims that X was the responsible party, and she subpoenas X to appear at trial. However, X refuses to testify (even when ordered to do so by the court), raising an invalid claim of privilege. Consequently, D wishes to call W to testify that a week after the accident, he was introduced to X for the first time, and that X told W that he had just been involved in an accident and "took off before the cops arrived."

118.   Which of the following statements is most accurate?

(A)   The evidence concerning X's statement to W is hearsay but admissible as a declaration against interest.

(B)   The evidence concerning X's statement is admissible as an admission.

(C)   The evidence concerning X's statement is admissible as an excited utterance.

(D)   The evidence concerning X's statement is inadmissible because X is not unavailable.

Prosecution of D for possession of cocaine. D claims he did not know that the substance found in his apartment was cocaine. To prove D knew it was cocaine, the prosecution calls W to testify that he saw X hand the substance to D while saying, "here is the coke you ordered."

119.   Which of the following statements is correct?

(A)   X's statement is inadmissible hearsay.

(B)   X's statement is hearsay but admissible as a present sense impression.

(C)   X's statement is admissible as an admission of D.

(D)   X's statement is not hearsay.

Products liability action by P against D, a new car dealer from whom she bought a car, alleging that a construction defect in the steering mechanism caused the accident that led to P's injury. At trial, to prove the defect, P testifies that after the accident, she showed her car to X, D's service manager. P states that X told her that the car's steering mechanism was not assembled correctly.

120.   Which of the following statements is correct?

(A)   If the judge finds that X was speaking about a matter within the scope of her employment, X's statement is admissible as an admission of D.

(B) If the judge finds that there is evidence sufficient to support a finding that X was speaking about a matter within the scope of her employment, X's statement is admissible as an admission of D.

(C) Even if the statement appears to qualify as an adoptive admission, it is inadmissible for lack of personal knowledge.

(D) The statement is inadmissible hearsay.

Prosecution of D for a double murder. To prove her innocence, D calls W to testify that shortly after D's arrest, W attended a press conference given by X, D's friend who was also her lawyer, and that at the press conference, X stated, "I was with D in another state on the day these horrible crimes took place, and D would not, could not, and did not commit these crimes."

121. Which of the following objections to this testimony is most appropriate?

    (A) Irrelevant.

    (B) Lack of personal knowledge.

    (C) Hearsay.

    (D) Unfair prejudice substantially outweighs probative value.

Prosecution of D for importing and selling bootleg copies of the software program "Mirrors XP," and with conspiracy to commit that act. To prove D's guilt, the prosecution calls W, who testifies that a few weeks before the police arrested D, X, and Y for the crime, she overheard a conversation between X and Y in which X stated, "D's bringing in a shipment of MXP on TAL flight 612, and we'll be meeting him at O'Hare."

122. Which of the following statements is correct?

    (A) If the judge finds that there is evidence sufficient to support a finding both that there was a conspiracy and that X was involved in it, the evidence is admissible under the coconspirator rule.

    (B) If the judge finds that there was a conspiracy and that X was involved in it, the evidence is admissible under the coconspirator rule.

    (C) Because the existence of a conspiracy is a fact the jury must ultimately decide, the judge need not make any preliminary determination of that fact. However, the evidence will not be admissible unless the judge finds that X was involved in any conspiracy the jury might decide existed.

    (D) X's statement is admissible as a simple party admission under FRE 801(d)(2)(A).

Prosecution of D for murder. D calls W, D's closest friend, to testify that D was not at the scene at the time the murder was committed. The prosecution objects to this testimony on grounds of lack of personal knowledge, claiming that W was not at the scene and had no other basis of knowledge about the facts.

123. Which of the following statements is correct?

   (A) The court should sustain the objection if it finds that W lacked personal knowledge.

   (B) The court should sustain the objection if it finds that there is not evidence sufficient to support a finding that W had personal knowledge.

   (C) The court should sustain the objection because even if W had personal knowledge, her testimony is manifestly self-serving and thus unreliable.

   (D) The court should overrule the objection.

Prosecution of D for the murder of V. D calls W to testify that just before he died, V said, "X did this to me." D claims the statement is admissible as a dying declaration.

124. In determining whether V's statement was made while believing his death was imminent, the trial court may consider

   (A) the circumstances surrounding the statement.

   (B) the statement itself.

   (C) other evidence, including inadmissible evidence, unless that evidence has been found to be privileged.

   (D) all of the above.

Prosecution of D for burglary of a mansion on Hilltop Drive. The stolen goods were recovered from a self-storage facility in River City. Shortly after the crime was committed, X told a friend, "I did that big house up on Hilltop last night, if you know what I mean. I stashed the stuff out in River City." At trial, D calls X to testify about this statement, but X refuses to answer on grounds of self-incrimination, even though he has already been granted immunity from prosecution for reasons unrelated to this problem. The court orders X to answer, but X still refuses to do so. D offers substantial evidence linking X to the crime.

125. Which of the following statements is most likely correct?

   (A) X's statement is admissible as an admission.

   (B) X's statement is against his interest but does not fall within the exception for declarations against interest.

   (C) X's statement is admissible as a declaration against interest.

   (D) X's statement is inadmissible unless it comes in through the friend's testimony rather than X's.

Breach of contract action by P against D. P claims that D failed to deliver CDs that P ordered. To prove D did not deliver the CDs, P wishes to testify that after a telephone conversation with D, P told her secretary, "D is not planning to deliver those CDs on time."

126.   Which of the following statements is correct?

   (A)   P's testimony is hearsay but admissible as an admission.

   (B)   P's testimony is hearsay but admissible under the state of mind exception.

   (C)   P's testimony is not hearsay because it constitutes words of independent legal significance (D's repudiation of the contract).

   (D)   P's testimony is inadmissible hearsay.

Civil action by P against D Corp. following a collision between P's car and a D Corp. delivery truck driven by X. P has also named X as a defendant. P claims X drove negligently, and that D Corp. should be held liable under the doctrine of respondeat superior. Prior to the trial in this case, X was prosecuted for reckless driving. At the trial of that case, the prosecution called W, a hitchhiker X picked up a few minutes before the accident. On direct examination, W testified that X was not paying much attention to the road and was swerving from one side of the road to the other. W died before the trial of P's civil action against D Corp. At the civil trial, X and D Corp. deny that X was driving recklessly at the time of the accident. P offers in evidence the transcript of W's testimony from the criminal trial.

127.   Which of the following statements is most likely correct?

   (A)   The transcript of W's testimony is not hearsay because it was not offered to prove the truth of the matter asserted.

   (B)   The transcript of W's testimony is not hearsay because it was not made out of court.

   (C)   The transcript of W's testimony is hearsay but admissible under the former testimony exception.

   (D)   The transcript of W's testimony is inadmissible hearsay.

Prosecution of D for possession of cocaine. At trial, the prosecution calls a number of witnesses, including D's roommate X. D admits that the cocaine was found in her apartment, but claims it belonged to X. To prove that fact, D calls W, who arrived at the scene a few minutes after D was placed under arrest. If permitted, W will testify that when D was being led to the police car, D turned to X, said "Those drugs were yours," and that X just smiled back.

128.   Which of the following statements is correct?

   (A)   D's allegation and X's response are admissible as an admission of X.

   (B)   D's allegation is hearsay but admissible as an excited utterance, and X's smiling response is admissible non-hearsay.

   (C)   D's allegation is inadmissible hearsay. X's smiling response is then irrelevant.

   (D)   D's allegation and X's smiling response are admissible as a declaration against interest by X.

Breach of contract action by P, a construction contractor, against D, a lumber wholesaler. P claims that D failed to make a timely delivery of a load of lumber, causing P to suffer significant anticipated consequential damages. D claims it delivered the lumber on time. P calls W, its custodian of records. P's attorney shows W a document, which W identifies as a record of the kind prepared by its job foreperson any time building materials are delivered to a construction site. W testifies that P kept the document in the company files, as was customary. The document appears to concern the questioned shipment, and bears a delivery date two weeks after the shipment was due. Evidence shows that the person who dated the document was unaware of any potential dispute between P and D. P offers the document into evidence.

129.   Which of the following statements is correct?

(A)   The document is hearsay and admissible as a business record.

(B)   The document is hearsay and admissible under the exception for past recollection recorded.

(C)   The document is hearsay and does not satisfy the business records exception because W did not have personal knowledge of the accuracy of its contents.

(D)   The document is not hearsay. It was used solely to refresh the recollection of the witness.

Prosecution of D and X, business partners, for participating in a fraudulent real estate scheme. Earlier, X had been sued by P, an investor who lost a great deal of money. At that civil trial, P testified about the scheme and identified X as the one who enticed her into investing her life savings. P died before the criminal trial. At the criminal trial, the prosecution wishes to call W, a newspaper reporter who was in the courtroom during P's testimony at the civil trial, to testify about P's trial testimony.

130.   W's testimony concerning P's civil trial testimony is

(A)   hearsay, and inadmissible against both D and X because it does not satisfy the former testimony exception because of the "similar motive" requirement of the former testimony exception.

(B)   hearsay, and inadmissible against both D and X because it is not offered in the form of the trial transcript.

(C)   hearsay, and admissible against X, but not against D.

(D)   hearsay, and admissible against both D and X.

Prosecution of D for arson. D denies committing the crime. At trial, D calls PO, a police officer who interviewed V, the owner of the burned building. D shows PO a document, which PO identifies as the report she prepared after the interview. The report describes the physical condition of the building and states that PO showed V a group of photographs, and that V identified an individual as the one she saw running from the building just before the fire broke out. That individual was not D. D represents that she will call V to testify later in the trial. D now offers PO's report into evidence.

131.   Which of the following statements is most likely correct?

(A)   The report is hearsay and inadmissible under the public records exception because it contains matters observed pursuant to duty imposed by law as well as factual findings resulting from an investigation. V's statement is thus also inadmissible.

(B)   The report is hearsay and admissible under the public records exception. V's statement is admissible non-hearsay if V testifies and is subject to cross-examination concerning the statement.

(C)   The report is hearsay and the description of the building is admissible under the public records exception. The part of the report describing V's identification of the perpetrator is inadmissible, however, because PO lacks personal knowledge of who committed the crime.

(D)   The report is non-hearsay because it is not offered to prove the truth of the matter asserted.

Prosecution of D for murder. At trial, the prosecution offers against D the out of court statement of a person not called as a witness. The court finds that the evidence is hearsay that does not fit within the regular exceptions to the hearsay rule, but that it satisfies the residual exception (FRE 807). D claims that the evidence should not be admitted because it would violate her confrontation rights under the Sixth Amendment.

132.   Which of the following statements is most likely correct?

(A)   Because the evidence satisfies the residual hearsay exception, it is admissible despite the confrontation clause.

(B)   Because the declarant never testified at the trial, D never had a chance to confront her and her statement must be excluded.

(C)   Even if the evidence satisfies the requirements of the residual exception, the court must still make an independent inquiry about the reliability of the statement, and may base its finding in part on whether the statement is corroborated by other evidence.

(D)   Even if the evidence satisfies the requirements of the residual exception, the court must still make an independent inquiry about the reliability of the statement, and may not base its finding on whether the statement is corroborated by other evidence.

Personal injury action by P against D arising from a collision between P's blue car and D's red car. P calls W, who testifies that she saw the accident and that D's red car ran a red light and struck P's blue car. On cross-examination, D asks W if it isn't true that a few moments after the collision, X came upon the scene and screamed, "Oh, no! That blue car just ran the light and struck the red car!"

133. Which of the following statements is correct?

(A) If P objects to D's question as impermissibly leading, the court will sustain the objection.

(B) X's statement is admissible as a prior inconsistent statement to impeach W's credibility.

(C) X's statement is admissible as an excited utterance.

(D) X's statement might be admissible as an excited utterance only if the court finds that there is evidence sufficient to support a finding that X had personal knowledge of the accident.

Breach of contract action by P against D. P claims that D failed to deliver the CDs that P ordered. To prove that D did in fact deliver the CDs, D calls W, her secretary, to testify that just before delivery was due, D said, "I'm planning to meet all orders."

134. Which of the following statements is correct?

(A) D's statement is admissible as an admission.

(B) D's statement is hearsay but admissible under the state of mind exception.

(C) D's statement is hearsay and fits within the state of mind exception, but because it is not clear that D was referring to this particular order from P, the court should exclude it as potentially irrelevant.

(D) D's statement is hearsay but admissible because its probative value substantially outweighs any danger of unfair prejudice.

Negligence action by third-grader P against classmate D arising from a playground collision. To prove that she suffered an arm injury, P calls her father to testify that when he took P to the hospital, he told the admitting nurse, "my daughter's arm really hurts and she can't move it."

135. Which of the following statements is correct?

(A) P's father's statement to the nurse is hearsay but admissible as a statement made for purposes of medical diagnosis or treatment.

(B) P's father's statement to the nurse is hearsay but admissible as an excited utterance.

(C) P's father's statement is not hearsay because it is not offered to prove the truth of the matter asserted.

(D) P's father's statement is inadmissible hearsay.

136.   As additional evidence that she suffered an arm injury from the collision, P calls W, the hospital's records clerk. W authenticates P's hospital record and testifies that the record was prepared by hospital personnel based on information they knew first-hand or which was provided by people with knowledge, that it was kept in the ordinary course of business, and that hospital procedure requires such records to be kept. P offers into evidence a portion of the record in which the attending physician wrote, "P says felt significant arm pain after having a collision with another person." Which of the following statements is most likely correct?

(A)   P's statement to the doctor is hearsay but admissible as a statement made for purposes of medical diagnosis or treatment. However, the statement is inadmissible because the document that contains it is hearsay for which no exception likely applies.

(B)   P's statement to the doctor is hearsay but admissible as a statement made for purposes of medical diagnosis or treatment. The hospital record containing the statement is likely admissible under the business records exception.

(C)   P's statement to the doctor is hearsay but admissible as a statement made for purposes of medical diagnosis or treatment. Because the doctor's statement about what P said is not offered to prove the truth of the matter asserted, it is not hearsay. Thus, this portion of the hospital record is admissible.

(D)   P's statement to the doctor is inadmissible hearsay and must be excluded because it is self-serving.

Prosecution of D for assault and battery on V. The prosecution calls W, who testifies that she was present in the bar where the altercation took place, and that just after the fight started, she heard X, another patron who was sitting close to V, scream, "Oh, my Lord, D just attacked that poor person from behind!" D claims the evidence constitutes inadmissible hearsay and that even if it satisfies the hearsay rule, its admission would violate her confrontation rights.

137.   Which of the following statements is most likely correct?

(A)   X's statement is hearsay but admissible as an excited utterance. The court may admit it despite the confrontation clause without further inquiry into its reliability.

(B)   X's statement is hearsay but admissible as an excited utterance. The court may admit it despite the confrontation clause if it finds that the statement bears sufficient independent indicia of reliability.

(C)   X's statement is not hearsay and its admission does not violate the confrontation clause.

(D)   X's statement is hearsay but admissible as an excited utterance. The confrontation clause will only be satisfied if X is produced or is found to be unavailable.

Breach of contract action by P, an ad agency, against D, a corporation that hired the agency. P alleges that D approved P's proposed print ad at a board meeting and was thus required to pay P's fee, but that D never paid. To prove that D did not approve P's ad, D calls W, the board secretary, who identifies a copy of the board minutes from the meeting in question. W testifies that he wrote these minutes, that he keeps all board minutes in a special file at the corporate office, and that the minutes were approved at a subsequent meeting. D offers in evidence a portion of the minutes containing the following statement: "After looking at the ad, Chairperson P said, 'What a piece of junk!' "

138. This portion of the minutes is most likely

    (A) inadmissible hearsay.

    (B) inadmissible because it is irrelevant.

    (C) inadmissible because it is too unreliable.

    (D) admissible.

Product liability action by P against D, a drug manufacturer. P claims he took D's drug for many years and suffered liver damage as a result. To prove the extent of his harm, P calls W, his physician. W identifies a document as a report she prepared in connection with an application P had made for health insurance. W testifies that the report was prepared in the ordinary course of her medical practice, that it was her usual practice to prepare such reports regarding her patients, and that she kept the report in her office. The report states that P has suffered "significant decline in liver function over the past several years." The report was prepared before P learned that D's drug might have caused her liver ailment. P offers the document into evidence.

139. Which of the following statements is most likely correct?

    (A) The report is hearsay but admissible as an authorized admission.

    (B) The report is hearsay but admissible as a business record.

    (C) The report is hearsay but admissible as a statement made for purposes of medical diagnosis or treatment.

    (D) The report is inadmissible hearsay.

Prosecution of D for burglary. The prosecution calls W, a police officer who investigated the crime. After testifying to certain facts, W states that she cannot remember anything else. The prosecutor shows W a document, which W identifies as the report she wrote in connection with her investigation. W testifies that she wrote the report in the ordinary course of her work, and that it was the normal procedure to prepare such a report. The report contains the statement, "Officer X states that D waived her Miranda rights and admitted that at the relevant time, she was in the neighborhood where the burglary was committed." The prosecution offers this statement into evidence.

140. Which of the following statements is most likely correct?

    (A) D's statement is admissible as an admission, and the rest of the statement is admissible as a business record.

(B)   D's statement is admissible as an admission, and the rest of the statement may be read to the jury under the past recollection recorded doctrine.

(C)   D's statement is admissible as an admission, and the rest of the statement is admissible as a declaration against interest.

(D)   The entire statement is inadmissible hearsay.

Personal injury action by P against D after an automobile accident between P's red car and D's blue car. P claims D ran the red light. D denies this. To prove D ran the red light, P calls W, a claims adjuster for P's insurance company who was assigned to handle the case. P asks W if she remembers what she learned in her investigation, and W is only able to give a few details. P then asks W if she interviewed any witnesses, and W testifies that she did, but that she cannot remember anything about the interviews. P shows W a document which W identifies as a note she wrote to herself at home one evening during her investigation. She states that she wrote it as a reminder of a talk she had with a witness to the accident, and that when she wrote the note, the conversation was fresh in her memory. She found the note at home recently. The note states that a witness said D ran the red light.

141.   Which of the following statements is correct?

(A)   The note is hearsay but satisfies the past recollection recorded exception. It may be read to the jury but not received as an exhibit.

(B)   The note is hearsay but satisfies the past recollection recorded exception. It may be admitted as an exhibit.

(C)   The note is hearsay but admissible as a business record.

(D)   The note is inadmissible hearsay.

Prosecution of D for murder. Eyewitnesses state that they saw two men commit the crime. To prove she had nothing to do with the crime, D calls W to testify that just after the murder, she overheard X, a friend of D, tell a police officer, "Two of us killed that guy. But D wasn't the other one involved. We dumped the body in the lake just outside of River City." At the time X made the statement, the body had not yet been found. After talking to X, the police located the body where X said it would be. X died in an auto accident before the trial. The prosecution lodges a hearsay objection to this statement.

142.   Analyze whether the court should admit the statement.

ANSWER:

Negligence action by P against D Corporation arising from the collision of P's green car and D's delivery truck. D denies negligence. To prove the accident was caused by P's negligence rather than any fault on the part of the truck driver, D calls its custodian of records who identifies an "accident report" which appears to have been written by the employee who drove the delivery truck. The custodian states that within 24 hours of any accident, employees with knowledge of the facts are required to make a report on this form and give it to their supervisors for inclusion in the company's files. D offers the report into evidence. The report states, "I was driving in my lane just below the speed limit when a green car veered into my lane, just ahead of me. I tried to avoid colliding with it, but was unable to do so." P objects on hearsay grounds.

143. How should the court rule, and why?

ANSWER:

Breach of contract action by P against D, an electronic parts wholesaler. P claims she placed an order with D and included a check with the order, but that D neither shipped the ordered parts nor returned the check. D denies ever receiving an order from P on or around the date P claims to have sent it. To prove that it did not receive an order from P, D calls its custodian of records, who identifies an "order log" kept by its order department. The log shows all orders received from one week before until one week after P claims to have placed the order. P's name appears nowhere on the report. P objects on hearsay grounds.

144. How should the court rule, and why?

ANSWER:

After a car driven by X struck and killed V while V was crossing the street in a crosswalk, P, the administrator of V's estate, sued X for wrongful death. At trial, P called W, who testified that he saw X run a red light and strike V in the crosswalk. The jury returned a verdict for P. Within the limitations period, the state decided to prosecute X and D, the owner of the car, for criminal negligence. The state's theory against D is that D knew X to be a reckless driver and that D should not have loaned X the car. Before this trial could take place, W died. The prosecution therefore wishes to offer in evidence the transcript of the testimony W gave in the earlier trial. X and D object.

145. How should the court rule, and why?

ANSWER:

Negligence action by P against D arising from an auto collision. To prove D caused the accident by driving recklessly, P calls W to testify that she was at home speaking to X, who was using her cell phone while driving to an appointment, and that at one point, W heard the sound of a horn, and X immediately said, "a blue Exterminator is weaving in and out of lanes like it's a sports car." Other evidence establishes that D was driving a blue Exterminator, that the accident happened on the same road X was traveling at the time, and that the collision occurred less than a minute after X made this statement.

146.   Which of the following statements is correct?

   (A)   X's statement is hearsay but admissible as a present sense impression.

   (B)   X's statement is inadmissible hearsay because there was nobody present to verify the accuracy of X's statement.

   (C)   X's statement is inadmissible because it constitutes an improper lay opinion.

   (D)   X's statement is admissible as an excited utterance.

Prosecution of D for assault and battery. D claims self-defense. During its case-in-chief, to prove D was the aggressor in the fight, the prosecution calls W, who testifies that she has lived in the same community as D for many years, that she is familiar with D's community reputation for violence or peacefulness, and that D's reputation is that she is a very violent person. D objects.

147.   Which of the following statements is correct?

   (A)   The court should sustain D's objection because the evidence is hearsay for which no exception applies.

   (B)   The court should sustain the objection because this is impermissible character evidence.

   (C)   The court should overrule the objection because D's character is in issue.

   (D)   The court should overrule the objection if the probative value of the evidence substantially outweighs the danger of unfair prejudice.

Prosecution of D for molestation of V, a child. D claims she was not the one who committed the crime. To prove that D molested V, the prosecution offers evidence that several years earlier, D molested another child. D objects.

148.   Which of the following statements is correct?

   (A)   The evidence is inadmissible character evidence.

   (B)   The evidence is admissible unless the court finds that that probative value of the evidence is substantially outweighed by the danger of unfair prejudice.

   (C)   The evidence is admissible to prove *modus operandi* to molest children, and thus prove D's identity as the perpetrator.

   (D)   The evidence is admissible regardless of the balance of probative value and unfair prejudice.

Civil action by P against D for battery during a professional basketball game. D had been cheering for the visiting team when P asked her to "cut it out." P claims D then punched P. D claims she never touched P. To prove her defense, D calls W to testify that she was with D at another

---

* The questions in this section do not address the use of character evidence to impeach a witness's credibility. For questions concerning that subject, see Topic 10.

59

game when D cheered for the visiting team, that a home team fan asked D to stop, and that D just shrugged it off. P objects.

149.   Which of the following statements is correct?

(A)   The evidence is admissible character evidence.

(B)   The evidence is admissible habit evidence.

(C)   The evidence is inadmissible because it is offered in the form of specific instances of conduct rather than reputation or opinion.

(D)   The evidence is inadmissible because D may not use character evidence to support her defense in this situation.

Libel action by P against D after D, the owner of a newspaper, published an article accusing P of committing a string of burglaries in the city. D claims the story was true. To prove P committed the burglaries, D offers evidence that P had been convicted of several burglaries in another city within the past few years. P objects.

150.   Which of the following statements is correct?

(A)   The evidence is admissible because character is in issue.

(B)   The evidence is admissible because it tends to show D's good faith.

(C)   The evidence is inadmissible because it is offered in the from of specific instances of conduct rather than reputation or opinion.

(D)   The evidence is inadmissible because D may not use character evidence to support her defense in this situation.

Negligence action by P against D. P claims that D failed to yield the right of way at an intersection and smashed into P. To prove that D failed to yield, P calls W to testify that a number of D's friends told her that D frequently drives through that intersection and almost always fails to yield. D objects.

151.   Which of the following statements is correct?

(A)   W's testimony is inadmissible because character is not admissible in this situation.

(B)   W's testimony is inadmissible because behavior will only constitute a habit if it is repeated invariably.

(C)   W's testimony is inadmissible hearsay.

(D)   W's testimony is admissible habit evidence.

Prosecution of D for the murder of V. To prove she acted in self-defense, D calls W, who has known D for many years, to testify that in her opinion, D is a peaceful person. The prosecution objects.

152. Which of the following statements is correct?

    (A) The court should sustain the objection because D may not offer character evidence to prove action in conformity on a specific occasion.

    (B) The court should sustain the objection because, although character evidence is admissible in this situation, D may only prove character by offering evidence of her community reputation.

    (C) The court should sustain the objection because the witness is biased.

    (D) The court should overrule the objection.

Prosecution of D for the murder of V while both were watching their sons compete in a high school football game. To prove self-defense, D offers the testimony of W that D is a peaceful person. The prosecution does not object. On cross-examination, the prosecutor asks W, "Did you know that D was involved in a barroom brawl just last year?" D objects.

153. How should the court rule?

    (A) The court should overrule the objection.

    (B) The court should sustain the objection because specific instances of conduct may not be used in this situation.

    (C) The court should sustain the objection because the question is impermissibly leading.

    (D) The court should sustain the objection because the circumstances of the barroom brawl were different than the barroom brawl that led to V's death.

Prosecution of D for assault and battery on V. D calls W, who testifies that she has lived in the same community as D for more than twenty years, and that D has a reputation as a peaceful person. The prosecution wishes to ask W whether she heard that D had once started a fight in a yogurt store. The prosecutor admits that although stories about D's involvement in the fight were all over town, it was actually someone else who was involved. D objects.

154. How should the court rule?

    (A) The court should sustain the objection because D was not involved.

    (B) The court should sustain the objection because the question should have been framed as "did you know?" rather than "have you heard?"

    (C) The court should sustain the objection because the question concerns a specific instance of conduct.

    (D) The court should overrule the objection unless the court determines that the probative value of the evidence is substantially outweighed by the danger of unfair prejudice.

Prosecution of D for the murder of V. To prove self-defense, D calls W to testify that V had a reputation in the community as a very violent person. The prosecution objects.

155. How should the court rule, and why?

ANSWER:

Prosecution of D for the murder of V. D claims V attacked her, and that D acted in self-defense. To prove self-defense, D calls W1 to testify that she saw V attack D. To rebut D's self-defense claim, the prosecution calls W2 to testify that she knew V for many years and that in her opinion, V was a non-violent person. D objects.

156. How should the court rule, and why?

ANSWER:

Prosecution of D, a trustee, for embezzling funds from the trust. D admits that the trust was depleted, but claims someone else was stealing the funds. To rebut D's defense, the prosecution wishes to present evidence that after the charged act, D embezzled more funds from the same trust. D objects.

157. How should the court rule?

    (A) The court should overrule the objection because the evidence is admissible to prove a plan, and thus D's identity as the perpetrator.

    (B) The court should overrule the objection because the evidence is admissible to impeach D by contradiction.

    (C) The court should sustain the objection because the uncharged act took place after the charged event.

    (D) The court should sustain the objection because this is inadmissible character evidence.

Prosecution of D for embezzling money from her employer. D declines to testify in her own behalf. To prove she did not embezzle, D calls W1 and W2, each of whom testify that that they have known D for many years, and that in their opinion, D is an honest person. To rebut the testimony of W1 and W2, the prosecution calls W3 to testify that she has also known D for many years, and that in her opinion, D is dishonest. D objects.

158. How should the court rule, and why?

ANSWER:

Prosecution of D for assault and battery on V. To prove V was the first aggressor, D calls W1 to testify that V has a reputation in the community as a violent person. In rebuttal, the prosecution wishes to call W2 to testify that D has a community reputation as a violent person. D objects.

159. How should the court rule?

(A) The court should sustain the objection because the prosecution may not offer evidence of D's bad character unless and until D offers evidence of her good character.

(B) The court should sustain the objection because D's community reputation is inadmissible hearsay.

(C) The court should sustain the objection because the prosecution may not call its own character witness to rebut D's witness, but must rely on cross-examination.

(D) The court should overrule the objection.

Prosecution of D for robbing a store. The robber entered before closing, put on a salesperson's uniform, and pretended to work there. After the store closed and everyone else left, the robber shed the uniform and stole all the DVD players. D denies involvement. To prove D's guilt, the prosecution offers evidence that a month earlier, D stole all the DVD players from a different store using the same method. D denies committing the prior robbery, and objects.

160. How should the court rule?

(A) The court should sustain the objection unless D was charged criminally for that robbery.

(B) The court should sustain the objection unless the prosecution convinces the court by a preponderance of the evidence that D committed the prior robbery.

(C) The court should sustain the objection unless the prosecution offers evidence sufficient to support a finding that D committed the prior robbery.

(D) The court should sustain the objection even if D admits committing the prior robbery.

Prosecution of D, a home care nurse, for the murder of V by poison. D testifies, denying involvement. D also calls two character witnesses to vouch for her non-violent character. The prosecution establishes that D makes a living caring for patients placed in his home, and that D cares for only one or two patients at a time. The prosecution calls several witnesses to testify that on three prior occasions, home care patients in D's care died of poisoning. D objects.

161. How should the court rule?

    (A)   The court should overrule D's objection because this evidence is admissible to rebut the evidence offered by D's character witnesses.

    (B)   The court should overrule D's objection because this evidence is admissible to prove D's guilt by means of the "doctrine of chances."

    (C)   The court should overrule D's objection because this evidence is admissible to impeach D.

    (D)   The court should sustain D's objection unless the prosecution proves D's guilt of each of the three prior offenses.

Prosecution of D for rape of V, who had agreed to a date with D. D admits having sexual intercourse with V, but claims V consented. To prove consent, D offers evidence that V had consensual sex with several of the people she dated in the past two years. The prosecution objects.

162. How should the court rule?

    (A)   The court should sustain the objection because the evidence was not offered in the form of opinion or reputation.

    (B)   The court should sustain the objection because D may not use character evidence to support his defense in this situation.

    (C)   The court should overrule the objection because the evidence is admissible as non-character to prove a pattern of behavior by V, which tends to suggest her consent on the charged occasion.

    (D)   The court should overrule the objection because the evidence must be admitted in order to protect the defendant's constitutional right to present a defense.

Prosecution of D for knowingly passing a counterfeit $100 bill. D admits passing the bill, but testifies that she did not know it was counterfeit. In rebuttal, the prosecution calls W, a convenience store clerk, to testify that the day before the charged act, D tried to buy a six pack of beer using the same $100 bill, and that W told D she could not accept the bill because it was "phoney." D objects.

163. How should the court rule, and why?

ANSWER:

Personal injury action by P against D arising from an automobile collision. P alleges that D wasn't paying attention and allowed the car to drift across the center line, striking P's car. D denies losing attention, and claims it was P's car that drifted across the center line. To prove she was paying attention, D calls W, a long-time friend who often rides with D to work, to testify that in her opinion, D is a careful driver who always pays attention. D objects.

164. How should the court rule?

(A) The court should overrule the objection because this is admissible habit evidence.

(B) The court should overrule the objection because by testifying that she did not lose attention, D has placed her character in issue.

(C) The court should overrule the objection because this is admissible evidence of D's good character for careful driving.

(D) The court should sustain the objection.

Prosecution of D1 and D2 for the murder of four restaurant patrons. D1 and D2 deny involvement in the crime. The prosecution wishes to call W to testify that she knows D1 and D2 as well as the victims, that all were illegal drug dealers, and that not long before the killings, the victims had tried to "muscle in" on territory controlled by D1 and D2. D objects.

165. How should the court rule?

(A) The court should overrule the objection because the evidence is admissible to show a tendency toward violent behavior.

(B) The court should overrule the objection because the evidence is admissible to show a motive to kill the victims.

(C) The court should sustain the objection because the evidence constitutes inadmissible hearsay.

(D) The court should sustain the objection because the probative value of the evidence is substantially outweighed by the danger of unfair prejudice.

Prosecution of D for murder. D claims she did not commit the crime, and calls W to testify that a long-time friend of D told her that D was as "gentle as a lamb." The prosecution objects.

166. How should the court rule?

(A) The court should overrule the objection because the evidence is hearsay but admissible to prove that D did not commit the crime.

(B) The court should overrule the objection because the evidence is admissible to show lack of a pattern of violent conduct.

(C) The court should sustain the objection because the evidence constitutes inadmissible hearsay.

(D) The court should sustain the objection because the evidence is inherently unreliable.

Prosecution of D for the murder of V. The prosecution alleges that D and V, two strangers, had a quarrel in a bar, that D left the bar momentarily, retrieved a shotgun from her car, returned to the bar, and shot V to death. D admits having an argument with V, but claims she never returned to the bar after she left. The prosecution calls W to testify that twice in the past five years, D has physically attacked strangers with whom she has had serious arguments. D does not deny that these prior events occurred, but objects to admission of the evidence.

167. How should the court rule?

(A) The court should overrule the objection because this is admissible habit evidence.

(B) The court should overrule the objection because this evidence is admissible to show a pattern of conduct or a common scheme or plan, and from that, D's intent.

(C) The court should overrule the objection because this evidence is admissible to show a pattern of conduct, or a common scheme or plan, and from that, to prove D shot V.

(D) The court should sustain the objection.

Fraud action by P against D, a car dealership. P claims that the car D sold to her only got 11 miles per gallon, even though D's salesperson told P that it would get "in the mid-twenties." D denies its salesperson made any such representation. To prove the representation was made, P wishes to offer the testimony of five other customers that the salesperson made the same representation to them about the same model of car. D does not deny that the other representations were made, but objects to admission of the evidence.

168. How should the court rule?

(A) The court should overrule the objection because the evidence is admissible pattern evidence to show that the representation was made.

(B) The court should overrule the objection because the evidence is admissible habit evidence.

(C) The court should sustain the objection because the evidence is inadmissible character evidence.

(D) The court should sustain the objection because the evidence, though relevant non-character evidence, is inadmissible because this is a civil action.

Negligence action by P against D, owners of a department store, after P was injured in a fall from an escalator. P claims D improperly maintained the escalator, causing it to jerk and throw P down. D admits that P was injured, but denies that the escalator jerked while P was riding it. At trial, P wishes to offer the testimony of several people that they were thrown down by the same escalator in the year prior to P's fall. D objects.

169. What information would you need in order to determine how the court should rule, and why? If the court admits the evidence, is D entitled to a limiting instruction?

ANSWER:

Negligence action by P against D, the owner of a football stadium, for injuries P suffered after a slip-and-fall accident on the steep stairs leading to her assigned seat. P claims the stairs are too steep and that the absence of handrails compounds the danger. To prove that the condition was safe, D wishes to offer the testimony of its stadium manager that in the two years prior to P's fall, it received no reports of other injuries in that location. P objects.

170.   What information would you need in order to determine how the court should rule, and why?

ANSWER:

TOPIC 9:   **QUESTIONS**

**EVIDENCE OF SUBSEQUENT REMEDIAL
MEASURES, COMPROMISE, HUMANITARIAN
ASSISTANCE, CRIMINAL PLEAS, AND LIABILITY
INSURANCE**

Personal injury action by P against D arising from P's fall on the floor in D's supermarket. P fell on a liquid spill that was not visible to her as she walked down the aisle, and claims D was negligent for not cleaning it up before the accident. D denies negligence. To prove D did not act reasonably, P wishes to offer evidence that a week after the accident, D's employees began patrolling for spills twice as often as before the accident. D objects.

171.   Which of the following statements is correct?

   (A)   The evidence is inadmissible hearsay.

   (B)   The evidence is inadmissible because it is irrelevant.

   (C)   The evidence is relevant but inadmissible.

   (D)   The evidence is relevant and admissible.

Personal injury action by P against D arising from P's fall on the floor in D's supermarket. P fell on a liquid spill that was not visible to her as she walked down the aisle, and claims D was negligent for not cleaning it up before the accident. W, D's manager, testifies that she had her employees patrol the aisles frequently, and that "we've had no reason to change the way we do things around the store." In rebuttal, P wishes to offer evidence that a week after the accident, W ordered store employees to patrol for spills twice as often as before the accident. D objects.

172.   Which of the following statements is correct?

   (A)   The evidence is inadmissible hearsay.

   (B)   The evidence is inadmissible because it is irrelevant.

   (C)   The evidence is relevant but inadmissible.

   (D)   The evidence is admissible to impeach W.

Negligence action by P against D, a supermarket owner, following P's slip and fall in the produce section. P claims D allowed slippery matter to collect on the floor, leading to his fall. P fell nearly an hour after D's employees last cleaned the floor. W, D's manager, testifies that she was not aware of anything slippery on the produce section floor at the time of P's fall. In rebuttal,

P wishes to offer evidence that shortly after P's accident, D started requiring its employees to clean the produce section floor every thirty minutes instead of once an hour. D objects.

173. Which of the following statements is correct?

   (A) The evidence is admissible to prove that until D changed the policy, D did not have the floor cleaned often enough.

   (B) The evidence is admissible to prove that the floor was slippery at the time of the accident.

   (C) The evidence is admissible to impeach W by contradiction and to prove the feasibility of more frequent cleaning.

   (D) The evidence is inadmissible.

Product liability action by P against D, a window manufacturer, after one of P's windows shattered in a strong wind, causing P's injuries. P claims D made the window with a type of glass that was not appropriate to the expected or foreseeable conditions to which it would be subjected. At trial, an expert witness testifies for D that the window glass used was "the strongest, most wind-resistant type available for windows of this kind." In rebuttal, P wishes to offer evidence that shortly after P's accident, D began using a stronger, more wind-resistant type of glass. D objects.

174. Which of the following statements is correct?

   (A) The evidence is admissible because the subsequent remedial measures rule does not apply to this kind of case.

   (B) The evidence is admissible to prove D's awareness of the weakness of the glass used.

   (C) The evidence is admissible to impeach the expert and prove that it was feasible to use a more wind-resistant glass.

   (D) The evidence is inadmissible.

175. Assume that instead of testifying that the glass used was the strongest available, the expert had testified that the glass used was the most "cost-effective" glass for this particular project. Describe D's best argument for excluding the evidence if P claims it is being offered to prove feasibility of precautionary measures.

ANSWER:

Negligence action by P against D City following an accident in which P's car was badly damaged when it hit a huge pothole in the middle of the small street on which P was driving. D City claims that the street on which the accident took place was a small private lane over which it had no authority. At trial, P wishes to call W to testify that a day after the accident, a D City road crew repaired the street, covering the pothole.

176. Which of the following statements is most accurate?

(A) The evidence is relevant but inadmissible for reasons of policy.

(B) The evidence is irrelevant and therefore inadmissible.

(C) The evidence is relevant and admissible as an act of independent legal significance.

(D) The evidence is relevant and admissible to demonstrate that D City had control over the street.

Personal injury action by P against D following an automobile collision. P claims she suffered $25,000 in damages. D wishes to testify that a week before trial, P approached her and said, "You were negligent, but I was distracted by something on the side of the road and was looking away at the time of the crash. I'll dismiss the action if you'll pay $5000."

177. Which of the following statements is most accurate?

(A) P's statement about being distracted is admissible as a party admission. The rest is inadmissible.

(B) P's entire statement is admissible as a party admission.

(C) P's entire statement is admissible as a declaration against interest.

(D) P's entire statement is inadmissible.

Breach of contract action by P against D. To prove D breached by failing to deliver a load of child's trading cards, P testifies that a week after P threatened to sue, D called P and said, "I simply blew it and forgot to ship the cards. Now, unfortunately, I'm sold out. Will you settle for a load of baseball cards instead?

178. What if any part of D's statement is admissible?

(A) The entire statement is admissible as an admission of D.

(B) Only the part of the statement in which D admitted failing to deliver the cards is admissible.

(C) Only the part of the statement in which D offered to ship P the baseball cards is admissible.

(D) The entire statement is inadmissible.

Negligence action by P against D arising from an automobile accident. P was the sole occupant of her car, and D was the driver of a car in which W was riding. Both P and W were injured in the accident, and sued D for their injuries. Prior to trial, D and W settled, and at trial, W testifies for D that P's car crossed the center line and crashed into D's car. On cross-examination of W, P wishes to inquire about the settlement between D and W. D objects.

179.   How should the court rule?

(A)   The court should exclude the evidence.

(B)   The court should admit the evidence only to prove D's negligence.

(C)   The court should admit the evidence only to impeach W by showing bias.

(D)   The court should admit the evidence both to prove D's negligence and to impeach W by showing bias.

Negligence action by P against D after the car D was driving struck P in a crosswalk. P seeks $1,000,000 compensation for personal injuries, pain and suffering, and lost earnings. Before trial, D's attorney approaches P's attorney and states, "My client does not deny negligence, but believes your client did not suffer the damages she alleges. We offer to pay $125,000 if you will dismiss the case." P's attorney turns down the offer after consulting with her client. At trial, P wishes to offer into evidence the part of D's attorney's statement that admitted negligence. D objects.

180.   How should the court rule?

(A)   The court should sustain the objection because the statement is inadmissible hearsay.

(B)   The court should sustain the objection because of the compromise rule.

(C)   The court should overrule the objection because liability was not contested.

(D)   The court should overrule the objection because the probative value of the evidence substantially outweighs any unfair prejudice that might result from its admission.

Civil action by P against D for battery. P wishes to offer evidence that D was criminally charged with assault and battery arising from the same incident, and that D had pleaded guilty and paid a small fine. D objects.

181.   Which of the following statements is correct?

(A)   The evidence is inadmissible because its probative value is substantially out-weighed by the danger of unfair prejudice.

(B)   The evidence is inadmissible character evidence.

(C)   The evidence is inadmissible because there are many reasons other than guilt why P might have pleaded guilty.

(D)   The evidence is admissible.

Prosecution of D for murder. Previously, D had pleaded guilty, but the court permitted her to withdraw her plea and enter a plea of not guilty. At trial, the prosecution wishes to offer evidence of D's earlier guilty plea. D objects.

182. How should the court rule?

(A) The court should sustain the objection.

(B) The court should overrule the objection but allow the evidence only to impeach D's credibility if she testifies that she did not commit the crime.

(C) The court should overrule the objection but allow the evidence only to prove D's guilt.

(D) The court should overrule the objection and allow the evidence for any relevant purpose.

Prosecution of D for murder. D agrees to plead guilty, and a hearing is held at which the plea is to be entered. During the hearing, the court asks D whether the charges are accurate, and D answers, "Yes, Your Honor. I am guilty of killing the victim." The court accepts D's guilty plea and sets a date for sentencing. Before the sentencing hearing, D has a change of heart and the court allows her to withdraw her guilty plea and enter a plea of not guilty. At trial, the prosecution wishes to offer into evidence D's statement at the earlier hearing. D objects both on hearsay grounds and on the basis of FRE 410.

183. How should the court rule, and why?

ANSWER:

Prosecution of D for importation of a large shipment of illegal drugs. D was arrested a few days after the crime was committed. On the way to the police station, after having been given his *Miranda* warnings, D said to one of the officers, "If you try to get me probation, I'll tell you who else was involved." At trial, the prosecution wishes to offer D's statement. D objects both on hearsay grounds and on the basis of FRE 410.

184. How should the court rule, and why?

ANSWER:

Negligence action by P against D arising from the collision of their cars on a busy highway. P alleges that D merged into P's lane without looking, colliding with P's car. D denies improperly merging. At trial, P wishes to offer evidence that the police issued D a traffic citation for illegal lane change, and that D pleaded guilty and paid the $75 fine by mail. D objects on the ground that the evidence is irrelevant because many people plead guilty to traffic violations to avoid the inconvenience of going to trial, not because they are guilty.

185. How should the court rule, and why?

ANSWER:

Civil action for battery by P against D. P was attacked from behind as he was leaving a football game. D denies being the attacker. At trial, P wishes to testify that immediately after P was knocked to the ground, D offered to take P to the hospital. D objects.

    186.   Which of the following statements is correct?

        (A)   D's statement is admissible as a party admission.

        (B)   D's statement is inadmissible because of the compromise rule (FRE 408).

        (C)   D's statement is a party admission but is inadmissible.

        (D)   D's statement is inadmissible because it is irrelevant.

Negligence action by P against D after P was struck by a car while she was crossing the street. D denies driving the car that struck P. To prove D's involvement, P wishes to testify that immediately after P was struck by the car, D walked up to P, said, "I didn't see you in the street," and offered to pay P's medical bills. D objects.

    187.   Which of the following statements is correct?

        (A)   D's entire statement is admissible as a party admission.

        (B)   D's entire statement is inadmissible because it constitutes an effort to compromise.

        (C)   D's entire statement is inadmissible under the rule barring evidence of payment and offers to pay medical and similar expenses.

        (D)   Only the statement, "I didn't see you in the street" is admissible.

Negligence action by P against D after the two surfers collided while trying to catch the same wave. P was injured and his board was broken in half. D denies negligence. To prove D's fault, P wishes to testify that a week after the collision, D gave P a new surfboard. D objects.

    188.   Which of the following statements is correct?

        (A)   Evidence of D's conduct is inadmissible because it is irrelevant.

        (B)   Evidence of D's conduct is inadmissible because of the compromise rule.

        (C)   Evidence of D's conduct is inadmissible under FRE 409.

        (D)   Evidence of D's conduct is admissible.

Negligence action by P against D arising from an automobile collision. D denies negligence. To prove D's negligence, P wishes to present evidence that D has liability insurance. D objects on grounds of relevance and FRE 411.

189.   How should the court rule, and why?

ANSWER:

Medical malpractice action by P against D, a surgeon. P alleges that D botched a surgical procedure, leaving P with a permanent physical impairment. D denies negligence. At trial, D calls an expert witness, who testifies that D performed the surgery in the appropriate way, and made no errors of medical judgment. To impeach D's expert, P wishes to present evidence that D and the expert both carry malpractice liability insurance with the same company. D objects.

190.   How should the court rule, and why?

ANSWER:

Negligence action by P against D arising from a boating accident that left P injured. D was piloting the boat when it capsized, causing P's injury. D denies negligence. P's lawyer learns that D carries liability insurance with a particular carrier. During jury selection, P's lawyer wishes to ask jurors whether any of them are employed by that company. D objects on the ground that this would violate FRE 411.

191.   How should the court rule, and why?

ANSWER:

Prosecution of D for perjury. D testifies that she did not lie under oath. D calls W, a long-time friend, to testify that in her opinion, D is a peaceful, non-violent person.

192. This evidence is

   (A) admissible only to prove D did not commit the crime.

   (B) admissible only to support D's credibility.

   (C) admissible both to prove D did not commit the crime and to support D's credibility.

   (D) inadmissible.

Prosecution of D for robbery of a liquor store. D testifies that she was not involved. On cross-examination, the prosecutor wishes to ask D if it isn't true that she is a drug addict with a $500 a day habit.

193. This question is

   (A) proper to impeach D's character for truthfulness.

   (B) proper to impeach D's recollection of the events.

   (C) proper to show a motive to commit the crime.

   (D) improper because it goes beyond the scope of the direct examination.

Civil action by P against D arising from a roller skating collision. P claims D ran into her on the sidewalk. D calls W, an eyewitness, who testifies that D was skating on her driveway, not the sidewalk, and that it was P who caused the collision when she lost control and headed up the driveway.

194. P wishes to ask W if it isn't true that shortly after the accident, W told X, a bystander, that D "was just learning to skate and should have stayed off the sidewalk." This question is

   (A) permissible both to impeach W and to show that D was on the sidewalk.

   (B) permissible only to impeach W.

   (C) permissible only to show that D was on the sidewalk.

   (D) impermissible.

195. Assume P is permitted to ask W about her prior statement., and that W denies making it. P then wishes to call X to testify to W's statement made shortly after the accident. X's testimony is

    (A) admissible only to impeach W.

    (B) inadmissible because W was not notified of the time and place of the alleged statement, nor of the persons present when it was made.

    (C) inadmissible because it constitutes extrinsic evidence of the alleged statement.

    (D) admissible both to impeach W and to show that D was on the sidewalk.

196. Assume, again, that W denies making the statement to X. P then wishes to call Z to testify that X told her (Z) that W told X that D was just learning to skate and should not have been on the sidewalk. Z's testimony is

    (A) admissible both to impeach W and to show that D was on the sidewalk, as long as W is given an opportunity to explain or deny making the statement.

    (B) admissible only to impeach W, and only if W is given an opportunity to explain or deny making the statement.

    (C) admissible to impeach W regardless of whether W is given an opportunity to explain or deny making the statement.

    (D) inadmissible.

197. P wishes to ask W if it isn't true that in a deposition taken several months after the accident, W testified that D "was just learning to skate and should not have been on the sidewalk." This question is

    (A) permissible both to impeach W and to show that D was on the sidewalk.

    (B) permissible only to impeach W.

    (C) permissible only to show that D was on the sidewalk.

    (D) impermissible.

Prosecution of D for murder. The prosecution calls W, who testifies that she was jogging past the corner of X and Y Streets in her blue jogging outfit when she saw D pull a knife and stab the victim. On cross-examination, D wishes to ask W if it isn't true that W was wearing her green outfit, not her blue outfit.

198. This question is

    (A) a permissible attempt to impeach W by contradiction.

    (B) a permissible attempt to impeach W by showing her inability to perceive accurately.

    (C) an impermissible attempt to impeach W by contradiction.

    (D)   an impermissible attempt to impeach W's character for truthfulness.

Prosecution of D for murder. D calls W, who testifies that she and D were in another country together when the crime was committed. On cross-examination, the prosecutor asks W if it isn't true that a year earlier, she tried to get into a gambling establishment with a false identification showing her to be over 21 years of age when she was in fact only 20.

    199.   This question is

        (A)   an impermissible attempt to impeach W's character for truthfulness.

        (B)   an impermissible attempt to impeach by contradiction on a collateral issue.

        (C)   impermissible because it is beyond the scope of the direct examination.

        (D)   permissible.

Negligence action by P against D. P calls W1, who testifies that she saw D's car swerving all over the road just moments before it struck P's car. D wishes to call W2 to testify that she has lived in the same community as W1 for many years, and that W1 has a reputation as a dishonest person.

    200.   W2's testimony is

        (A)   admissible to impeach W1.

        (B)   inadmissible because W1's reputation for truthfulness has not first been supported.

        (C)   inadmissible because this is a civil action.

        (D)   inadmissible because it injects irrelevant issues into the case.

Prosecution of D for murder. D testifies that she and her friend were home all night the evening the murder took place across town. On cross-examination, the prosecutor asks D if it isn't true that she was convicted of murder five years earlier. D objects.

    201.   Which of the following statements is most accurate?

        (A)   The court must sustain the objection.

        (B)   The court must overrule the objection.

        (C)   The court must sustain the objection unless it finds that the probative value of the evidence on the issue of D's credibility outweighs the danger of unfair prejudice.

        (D)   The court must overrule the objection unless it finds that the probative value of the evidence on the issue of D's credibility is substantially outweighed by the danger of unfair prejudice.

Prosecution of D for burglary. The prosecution calls W1, who testifies that D admitted committing the crime. D calls W2, W1's former boyfriend, to testify that W1 has been under the care of a psychiatrist for many years because she often loses touch with reality, "remembering" events that never occurred.

202.   Discuss D's strongest argument for admission of this testimony to impeach W1.

ANSWER:

Prosecution of D for a murder that took place at 7:00 p.m. in a pool hall. The prosecution calls W1, who testifies that she was walking along the sidewalk in front of the pool hall at 7:00 that evening wearing her blue raincoat when D ran out of the building. D calls W2, W1's spouse, to testify that W1 does not own a blue raincoat.

203.   W2's testimony is

(A)   admissible to impeach W1 by contradiction.

(B)   admissible to impeach W1's character for truthfulness.

(C)   inadmissible because it is irrelevant.

(D)   inadmissible because it constitutes extrinsic evidence.

Prosecution of D for murder. D calls W, who claims she and D were home all night the evening the murder took place across town. On cross-examination, the prosecutor asks W if it isn't true that she (W) was convicted of murder five years earlier. D objects.

204.   Which of the following statements is most accurate?

(A)   The court must sustain the objection.

(B)   The court must overrule the objection.

(C)   The court must sustain the objection unless it finds that the probative value of the evidence on the issue of W's credibility outweighs the danger of unfair prejudice.

(D)   The court must overrule the objection unless it finds that the probative value of the evidence on the issue of W's credibility is substantially outweighed by the dangers enumerated in FRE 403.

Prosecution of D for robbery. The prosecution calls W1, an alleged accomplice of D, who testifies that D committed the crime. D wishes to call W2, a police officer, to testify that W1 agreed to testify against D in order to avoid prosecution for the crime.

205.   Which of the following statements is correct?

(A) The evidence is admissible.

(B) This is an impermissible attempt to impeach W1 by extrinsic evidence.

(C) This is an impermissible attempt to impeach W1's character for truthfulness.

(D) This is an impermissible attempt to introduce compromise evidence.

Personal injury action by P against D arising out of a slip-and-fall in D's supermarket. P calls W, who testifies that P was walking her cart slowly around the store when she suddenly fell on a clear liquid that was difficult to see. On cross-examination, D wishes to ask W about a two-year-old misdemeanor Medicare fraud conviction. P objects.

206. The court

(A) should sustain the objection if the probative value of the evidence is substantially outweighed by the danger of unfair prejudice.

(B) should overrule the objection unless the probative value of the evidence is greater than the danger of unfair prejudice.

(C) must overrule the objection regardless of the danger of prejudice.

(D) must sustain the objection.

Personal injury action by P against D following an automobile collision. P testifies that she had the green light. D claims that it was P who ran the red light. In rebuttal, P wishes to call W to testify that at a recent party, P said she, not D, had the green light.

207. W's testimony is

(A) inadmissible hearsay.

(B) inadmissible because a party may not support the credibility of a witness unless the witness has been impeached.

(C) inadmissible because P, not W, must testify about the statement.

(D) admissible.

Prosecution of D for auto theft. The prosecution alleges that on the evening of February 6 at 11:00, D broke into the show room of a luxury car dealer in River City and stole a $75,000 luxury sports sedan. D's defense is an alibi. He claims that on the evening the crime was committed, he was in Cleveland attending a poodle show. As part of its case in chief, the prosecution calls W, the security guard for the car dealer. W testifies that at 10:45 on the night of February 6, he was taking a short break at Mel's Diner, across the street from the car lot, and that he saw D sitting in a booth sipping a Diet Coke. On cross-examination, D's attorney asks W if he recalls telling his brother X on February 7 that he had spent the entire previous evening at the movie theater, and that he'd gone home right after the show.

208. Which of the following statements is correct?

      (A) The question is a proper attempt to impeach W with a prior inconsistent statement.

      (B) The question is a proper attempt to establish the whereabouts of W on the evening of February 6.

      (C) Both (A) and (B) are correct.

      (D) Neither (A) nor (B) is correct.

209. Assume W denies making the prior statement. To impeach W's credibility, D calls X (W's brother), to testify that on February 7, W told him that he'd had the previous evening off, that he'd spent the entire evening at the movies, and that he'd gone home right after the show. Which of the following statements is most accurate?

      (A) This is an impermissible attempt to impeach W because once W denies having said such a thing, D is stuck with his answer.

      (B) This is an impermissible attempt to impeach W because the question of his whereabouts is collateral, and D is therefore stuck with the answer which W gave on cross-examination.

      (C) This is a permissible attempt to impeach W with a prior inconsistent statement.

      (D) This is a permissible attempt to impeach W by demonstrating his bad character for truthfulness.

210. Assume that during his cross-examination of W, D seeks to show that W made up his story about being in Mel's Diner on a break because he wanted to hide the fact that he went to the movies instead of going to work that evening. Allegedly, W made up the story on February 13, when his boss confronted him about where he'd been on the night of February 6. After the defense rests, the prosecution recalls W and seeks to elicit from W his testimony that very late on the evening of February 6, he told his children that he'd just seen an interesting man sipping a Diet Coke in a booth at Mel's Diner. Which of the following statements is correct?

      (A) The question is a permissible attempt to establish W's credibility.

      (B) The question is a permissible attempt to establish the whereabouts of W on the evening of February 6.

      (C) Both (A) and (B) are correct.

      (D) Neither (A) nor (B) is correct.

211. D takes the stand, and on direct examination testifies that he was at the poodle show in Cleveland on February 6. On cross-examination, the prosecution asks D if it isn't true that he hates poodles. Which of the following statements is most accurate?

      (A) The question is improper because it calls for irrelevant evidence.

(B) The question constitutes an improper attempt to impeach D by showing his bad character.

(C) The question is a proper attempt to impeach D by showing the implausibility of his alibi.

(D) The question is a proper attempt to impeach D by showing his bias.

Prosecution of D for battery on V. D testifies that V attacked D, forcing D to defend herself. To impeach D, the prosecution wishes to offer evidence that D was convicted of felony battery two years earlier.

212. The conviction evidence is

(A) inadmissible because the crime was the same as that for which D is currently on trial.

(B) admissible unless its probative value for impeachment purposes is substantially outweighed by the danger of unfair prejudice to D.

(C) admissible if its probative value for impeachment purposes outweighs the danger of unfair prejudice to D.

(D) admissible regardless of the balance of probative value and unfair prejudice.

Prosecution of D for attempted murder of V, her husband. D claims she acted in self-defense when V attacked her. D calls W, who testifies that V was the first aggressor. On cross-examination, the prosecution asks W if it isn't true that W and D were then, and are still now, having an affair.

213. This question is

(A) proper to impeach W by showing a motive to testify for D.

(B) proper to prove that D was the first aggressor.

(C) proper both to impeach W by showing a motive to testify for D and to prove that D was the first aggressor.

(D) improper.

Negligence action by P against D arising from a car crash. The only dispute is over who had the green light. P calls W1, who testifies that she was coming out of a movie theater after watching "Bar Wars" when she saw D's car run the red light and strike P's car. D calls W2 to testify that she was with W1 that night, and that the two had been attending a showing of "Beetleman," not "Bar Wars," when they saw the accident. "Beetleman" was playing at the same multiplex theater.

214. W2's testimony is

(A)   an improper attempt to impeach by contradiction.

(B)   improper because D did not give W1 an attempt to explain her testimony before calling W2.

(C)   a permissible attempt to impeach W1's memory.

(D)   permissible impeachment by contradiction.

Prosecution of D for the murder of V. D claims he acted in self-defense when V attacked him. D calls W, who testifies that she was at the scene of the killing when X screamed, "Watch out, D, V is coming at you with a knife!" The prosecution wishes to offer evidence that X was convicted of misdemeanor forgery five years earlier.

215.   The conviction evidence is

(A)   inadmissible because X did not testify at the trial.

(B)   admissible unless its probative value for impeachment purposes is substantially outweighed by the danger of unfair prejudice to D.

(C)   admissible if its probative value for impeachment purposes outweighs the danger of unfair prejudice to D.

(D)   admissible regardless of the balance of probative value and prejudice.

Prosecution of D for stealing a child's trading cards while the child was playing with them. D testifies that she paid the child for the cards. The prosecutor declines to conduct any cross-examination of D. D then calls W to testify that she has known D for years, and that in her opinion, D is an honest person.

216.   W's testimony is

(A)   admissible.

(B)   inadmissible character evidence.

(C)   inadmissible because honesty is not a pertinent trait of character.

(D)   inadmissible hearsay.

Prosecution of D for burglary. D testifies that she was in another state when the crime was committed. To impeach D, the prosecution gives appropriate notice that it wishes to offer evidence of D's fifteen-year-old conviction for misdemeanor perjury, and supplies evidence about the circumstances supporting the probative value of the conviction.

217.   The evidence is

(A)   admissible.

(B) admissible if the court finds that the probative value of the conviction outweighs the danger of unfair prejudice.

(C) admissible if the court finds that the probative value of the conviction, supported by specific facts and circumstances, substantially outweighs the danger of unfair prejudice.

(D) inadmissible.

A grand jury investigating the murder of V hears the testimony of W, who denies any involvement and claims to have been with D in another state when the crime was committed. Based on the testimony of other witnesses, the grand jury indicts D for murder. W is D's girlfriend. Prior to the trial, the prosecutor learns that after giving her grand jury testimony, W admitted to a friend that she and D were in town at their apartment on the day the murder was committed, and that D left the apartment around the time the killing occurred nearby. Even though the prosecutor is aware that W will continue to support her boyfriend by supplying the same alibi she gave before the grand jury, the prosecutor calls W at trial. W testifies that she and D were in another state on the relevant day. W then seeks to introduce, for purposes of impeachment, W's statement to the friend. D objects.

218. How should the court rule?

(A) The court should overrule the objection because a party may impeach her own witness.

(B) The court should overrule the objection because the jury is entitled to observe W's demeanor when she supplies the alibi.

(C) The court should sustain the objection because a party who calls a witness vouches for the witness'ss story, and may not impeach her.

(D) The court should sustain the objection because a party may not call a witness for the sole purpose of impeaching her.

Wrongful death action by P, the administrator of the estate of X, against D, arising from an automobile accident that resulted in the death of X about a week later. X was driving a red car, and D was driving a blue car. D denies negligence. At trial, P calls W1, who testifies that immediately after the crash, Z, a bystander, screamed, "That blue car just rammed that red car!" D now calls W2 to testify that just a few minutes later, Z said that it was the red car that rammed the blue car. The estate objects, and D responds that the evidence is being offered to impeach Z with a prior inconsistent statement.

219. How should the court rule, and why?

ANSWER:

Action to quiet title to a disputed piece of land that borders the property of both P and D. To prove it owns the disputed property, P calls W, a professional surveyor, who testifies to a location of the boundary that would give P all of the disputed land. On cross-examination, D asks, "isn't it true that your religion teaches that people with blue eyes are evil?" P objects to this question.

220. How should the court rule, and why?

ANSWER:

221. Assume P is a church, and that W, the surveyor, is a member of the congregation. On cross-examination, D asks W, "is it not true that you are a member of the P church?" D objects. How should the court rule, and why?

ANSWER:

Negligence action by P against D arising from an automobile accident. At trial, P calls W1, who testifies that she saw the accident occur, ran up to P's car, and noticed that P was crying and kept repeating, "why did that car hit me?" Unfortunately, P does not remember the accident, and does not testify at trial. D denies striking P's car, and in fact testifies that P's car backed into his car. D now calls W2, who, if permitted, will testify that she knows P's community reputation for truthfulness, and that P is generally known as a "liar extraordinaire." P objects to W2's testimony.

222. How should the court rule, and why?

ANSWER:

Prosecution of D for bank robbery. D claims he wasn't involved. At trial, the prosecution calls W1, who testifies that she was in the bank when D entered carrying a shotgun and ordered everyone to lie down on the floor. W1 testifies that D demanded that all the tellers empty their cash drawers and place the money in sacks which D gave them. On cross-examination, D's attorney asks W1 what the weather was like on the day of the robbery. W1 answers that it was a rainy day. D's attorney asks W1 if it isn't a fact that it was warm and sunny on the day of the robbery. W1 insists that it was raining. D now wishes to call W2, a meteorologist, to testify that the day of the robbery was warm and sunny. The prosecutor objects.

223. If the court applies common law rules, how should the court rule, and why?

ANSWER:

Breach of contract action by P against D. P claims D failed to deliver the goods called for in the contract. D asserts the doctrine of impossibility, based on the claim that severe storms caused flooding which destroyed all the goods in D's warehouse. To prove impossibility, P offers in evidence what appears to be a newspaper published in the town in which D's business is located, and which is dated a few days before D was supposed to ship P's order. An article in the paper reports the loss of all the goods in D's warehouse due to storm-related flooding. D objects on grounds of lack of authentication.

224.   How should the court rule?

    (A)   The court should sustain the objection if it finds that P has failed to show by a preponderance of the evidence that this is the newspaper P claims it to be.

    (B)   The court should sustain the objection because the newspaper is not the best evidence of whether flooding caused the destruction of the goods in D's warehouse.

    (C)   The court should sustain the objection if it finds that there is insufficient evidence to support a finding that this is the newspaper P claims it to be.

    (D)   The court should overrule the objection.

Negligence action by P against D's Heating and Cooling for injuries suffered when D allegedly failed to fix P's heater during a sub-zero cold snap. P, who is elderly and housebound, alleges that she phoned D as soon as the heater failed, that D promised to respond "within two hours," that P waited in vain for an entire night, and that D never appeared. While waiting for D, P alleges that she suffered cold-related injuries to her fingers and toes. P testifies that she placed her call to the number for D listed in the phone book, and that a voice answered, "heating service." D denies ever receiving the call, and moves to strike P's testimony from the record.

225.   How should the court rule?

    (A)   The court should deny D's motion because there is sufficient evidence to support a finding that the call was actually placed to D.

    (B)   The court should deny the motion if it finds that the call was not placed to D.

    (C)   The court should grant the motion because the party answering the phone did not identify itself as D's Heating and Cooling.

    (D)   The court should deny the motion because P has already testified, and it is too late to keep the evidence from the jury.

Prosecution of D for assault with a deadly weapon, a baseball bat. At trial, the prosecution wishes to authenticate a particular baseball bat as the one used by D. Assume the bat has no marks that would distinguish it from other bats of its type.

226.   What is the best way for the prosecution to authenticate the bat?
ANSWER:

Negligence action by P against D arising from an intersection collision controlled by traffic signals. P was driving east on one street, and D was driving north on the cross-street. Both parties claim the other ran the light at the intersection, leading to the collision. At trial, P wishes to use a photograph to show the positions of the cars about fifteen minutes after the collision. The photograph was taken by a passerby, who gave it to P. The passerby is not called to testify. P seeks to authenticate the photograph by testifying that it accurately depicts the scene as it appeared immediately after the collision. D objects, claiming lack of authentication.

227.   How should the court rule?

   (A)   The court should sustain the objection because P has not called the photographer to testify.

   (B)   The court should sustain the objection because the cars might have been moved between the time of the collision and the time the photograph was taken (fifteen minutes later).

   (C)   The court should sustain the objection because the photograph is not the best evidence of what happened at the time of the accident.

   (D)   The court should overrule the objection.

Negligence action by P against D arising from an automobile accident. P claims that a week after the accident, she received a handwritten letter from D accepting responsibility. D claims the letter is a forgery.

228.   Discuss two ways P may authenticate the letter.
ANSWER:

Medical malpractice action by P against D, a surgeon. P claims D failed to treat a leg injury properly, and that as a result of improper treatment, her leg had to be amputated. At trial, P wishes to testify that her leg required amputation due to complications that occurred during D's treatment. D objects on best evidence rule grounds, asserting that P's medical records must be used to prove the cause of the condition leading to amputation.

229.   How should the court rule?

    (A)   The court should sustain the objection because the medical records are the best evidence of P's medical condition.

    (B)   The court should sustain the objection unless P offers to produce the records to support her testimony.

    (C)   The court should sustain the objection unless P demonstrates that her medical records are not available for reasons beyond P's control.

    (D)   The court should overrule the objection.

Second trial of a murder case after the first trial ended with a hung jury. At the first trial, X testified for the prosecution. X died before the second trial. The prosecution wishes to call W, a family member of the victim who was in the courtroom during X's testimony, to recount X's testimony in the first trial. Defendant makes a best evidence rule objection to W's testimony.

230.   How should the court rule?

    (A)   The court should sustain the objection because the reporter's transcript is the best evidence of X's testimony.

    (B)   The court should sustain the objection unless the prosecution offers to produce the transcript to support W's testimony.

    (C)   The court should sustain the objection unless the prosecution demonstrates that the transcript of the first trial was destroyed through no fault of the prosecution.

    (D)   The court should overrule the objection.

Personal injury action by P against D arising from an inline skating collision. To prove P broke her leg in the collision, P calls Dr. W, who testifies that she concluded that P broke her leg by reviewing an X-ray of P's leg taken an hour after the accident. D objects on best evidence rule grounds.

231.   How should the court rule?

(A) The court should sustain the objection.

(B) The court should overrule the objection because an X-ray is not covered by the best evidence rule.

(C) The court should overrule the objection because the jury is not capable of interpreting an X-ray, making it a waste of time to produce it.

(D) The court should overrule the objection because Dr. W is testifying about her own impressions of the X-ray, not the contents of the X-ray itself.

Breach of contract action by P against D. P claims that D breached the written contract by failing to deliver 200 crates of apples by the specified date. At trial, D wishes to testify that the contract only called for delivery of 100 crates. P makes a best evidence rule objection.

232. How should the court rule?

(A) The court should sustain the objection.

(B) The court should overrule the objection because a contract is an agreement brought about by the meeting of two minds, not a writing. The writing is only a memorandum of the agreement, not the contract itself.

(C) The court should overrule the objection because D is not testifying about the contents of the writing, but about her understanding of the agreement. Thus, the best evidence rule does not apply.

(D) The court should overrule the objection because the central issue in the case concerns the terms of the agreement, and the jury is entitled to hear D's interpretation of the terms.

During the trial of a case, it is important for a party to prove that a certain parked automobile had a parking ticket on its windshield at a certain time. To prove this fact, a witness is called to testify that she saw a parking ticket on the car's windshield at that time.

233. Discuss the best evidence rule implications of this testimony.

ANSWER:

To prove that Elvis Presley is dead, a party calls a witness to testify that she visited Graceland in Memphis, Tennessee, and that she saw a tombstone on which were etched the lines "Elvis Aaron Presley," "January 8, 1935," and "August 16, 1977."

234. Discuss the best evidence rule implications of this testimony. If you have studied the hearsay rule, discuss the hearsay implications of this testimony as well.

ANSWER:

Negligence action by P against D arising from a unicycle collision. To prove D's negligence, P wishes to offer in evidence a photocopy of a letter from D accepting responsibility for the accident. D admits writing the letter but claims P altered it to appear as though D accepted responsibility when in fact she did not. Thus, D claims the photocopy violates the best evidence rule.

235. How should the court rule?

   (A) The court should overrule the objection because the photocopy is a duplicate and a duplicate is admissible to the same extent as an original.

   (B) The court should sustain the objection because a photocopy is not a duplicate.

   (C) The court should sustain the objection because even though the photocopy qualifies as a duplicate, it would be unfair to allow P to offer the duplicate.

   (D) The court should overrule the objection because the jury should be permitted to view the photocopy and make its own decision about whether it was tampered with.

Assume each of the following facts is relevant to the determination of a factual dispute at issue in a case.

236.   Which would probably <u>not</u> be a proper subject of judicial notice?

    (A)   That palm trees grow better in warm climates than in cold climates.

    (B)   That deuterium is an isotope of hydrogen in which the nucleus of the atom contains both a proton and a neutron.

    (C)   That a certain road was not plowed for twenty-four hours after a particular snow storm.

    (D)   That stores in the state in which the case is being tried are not allowed to sell packaged liquor on Sundays.

Negligence action by P against D after the Expunger SUV D was driving struck P in a crosswalk, injuring P. D admits striking P, but denies negligence, claiming that he was momentarily blinded by an extremely bright sun shining directly into his eyes just before the accident. P asks the court to take judicial notice that the sun was obscured by heavy clouds for the entire day. To support judicial notice, P presents the court with an official National Weather Service log showing that on the day in question, the entire area was shrouded by heavy clouds. After hearing argument, the court agrees to take judicial notice.

237.   Which of the following statements is correct?

    (A)   After the court takes judicial notice, D may offer a witness to testify that the day was sunny.

    (B)   During closing argument, D may encourage the jury to find that she was momentarily blinded by bright sunshine at the time of the accident.

    (C)   The court may instruct the jury to accept as conclusive that the sun was obscured by heavy clouds for the entire day.

    (D)   The court must instruct the jury to accept as conclusive that the sun was obscured by heavy clouds for the entire day.

Civil rights action by P, a prison inmate, against D, the warden, for requiring him to subject himself to a test for AIDS. D argues that the intrusion on P is justified because of the danger posed by the disease. At trial, however, D presents no evidence of the danger caused by the disease. Instead, she asks the court to take judicial notice of the danger.

238.   Which of the following statements is most likely true?

   (A)   It would be proper for the court to take judicial notice.

   (B)   Because these facts are central to D's defense, it would be improper for the court to take judicial notice. D should be required to offer evidence.

   (C)   Because D waited until the trial had begun before requesting the court to take judicial notice, it would be improper for the court to take notice.

   (D)   Because proof of these facts would require the consideration of inadmissible hearsay, it would be improper for the court to take judicial notice.

Prosecution of D for child molestation. One element of the crime is that the victim be under the age of 18. V, the alleged victim is a prosecution witness, but the prosecutor neglects to ask V his age or to submit other evidence of V's age at the time of the alleged crime. At the close of all evidence, D moves for an acquittal on the ground that the prosecution has not offered any evidence that V was under 18 years of age at the time of the alleged crime. The prosecutor responds by showing the court a certified copy of V's birth certificate, and asks the court to take judicial notice of V's age. The birth certificate contains a birth date that would have made V seven years old at the time of the alleged crime, which was only six months prior to trial.

239.   Which of the following statements is correct?

   (A)   Because this is a criminal case, the court may not take judicial notice of any fact that would operate against the defendant.

   (B)   Because this is a criminal case, the court may not take judicial notice of any fact that constitutes an element of the crime.

   (C)   The court may take judicial notice of the fact but must instruct the jury that it is not required to accept the fact as conclusively established.

   (D)   The court may take judicial notice of the fact and may instruct the jury that it must consider the fact to be conclusively established.

Negligence and strict liability action by P against D, a pharmaceutical company, for serious injury allegedly caused by a drug D manufactured and which was prescribed to P. D moves to dismiss the strict liability count on the ground P must prove negligence to prevail. The state has not previously decided the precise question raised by D's motion: whether a pharmaceutical company may be held strictly liable for a design defect in its drug that causes personal injury. During argument on the motion, D asks the court to take "judicial notice" of the fact that strict liability would discourage the development of new and useful drugs.

240.   May the court take notice of this fact? Why or why not?
ANSWER:

Negligence action by P against D arising from an automobile accident. P has the burden of persuasion as to the essential elements of the *prima facie* case, which include duty, breach, causation, proximate cause, and damages. Assume that on the question of D's negligence, P calls a witness who testifies that she saw D's car cross the center line and strike P's car head-on.

241. Which of the following statements best indicates what should happen if D fails to present any evidence contesting this item of evidence?

(A) The court should allow the jury to decide whether P has presented sufficient evidence to persuade the jury by a preponderance of the evidence that D acted negligently.

(B) The court should instruct the jury that D was negligent.

(C) The court should instruct the jury that D now has the burden of persuasion on the negligence question, and allow the jury to decide whether P has convinced the jury by a preponderance of the evidence that D was not negligent.

(D) The court should direct a verdict for P and award judgment.

242. Assume P fails to offer any evidence as to D's negligence, and only calls witnesses to testify that P suffered serious injuries in the collision. If D moves for a directed verdict at the close of P's case, what should the court do?

(A) The court should deny the motion because the jury is entitled to decide whether to render a verdict for P.

(B) The court should deny the motion and order D to present her case.

(C) The court should withhold a ruling on the motion until D has presented her case.

(D) The court should grant the motion.

243. Assume P produces no evidence of D's negligence. In opposition to D's motion for directed verdict, P admits that she can produce no witnesses who have first-hand knowledge of the accident. P argues, however, that if given an opportunity, she can, through cross-examination of D's witnesses, either get them to admit that D was negligent or demonstrate to the jury that the demeanor of D's witnesses shows that they are lying. Should the court grant or deny D's motion for directed verdict under these circumstances?

ANSWER:

Paternity action by P against D. D claims that he was not the father of the child. Assume that the following rebuttable presumption applies: *A child born within ten months of the last date on which a male and female were cohabiting is rebuttably presumed to have been fathered by the male.* This is the only presumption that applies in the case. The action is being tried in a jurisdiction that adheres to the majority ("bursting bubble") theory of presumptions. At trial, P testifies that she and D cohabited continuously for five years and only stopped living together one month before the baby was born. D, in turn, calls an expert witness who testifies that she performed blood tests on D and on the child, and determined that there is only a tiny probability that D could have fathered the child. At the close of all evidence, P's attorney asks the court to instruct the jury that if it finds that the child was born within ten months of the last date on which P and D were cohabiting, it must find that D was the father.

244.   The court should

   (A)   find that P has produced sufficient evidence to meet her burden of production on the foundational facts, and give P's requested instruction.

   (B)   find that all of the foundational facts are true, and instruct the jury that D is the father.

   (C)   find that D's expert has produced sufficient evidence to support the conclusion that D could not have been the father of the child, and not give P's requested instruction.

   (D)   find that the expert is correct that D could not have been the father of the child, and not give P's requested instruction.

Action by P against D to quiet title to a piece of land. Both P and D claim ownership. Assume that the following rebuttable presumption applies to the case: *A deed purporting to create an interest in real property is presumed to be authentic if it is at least 30 years old, is in such condition as to create no suspicion as to its authenticity, was kept in a place where such a writing would likely be found, and has been acted upon as authentic by persons having an interest in the matter.* At trial, P offers the deed in evidence after testifying that it is 40 years old, was never altered, was kept in her safe deposit box, and that it has always been treated as authentic. The deed purports to convey to P a fee simple interest in the property. D then calls W, P's sister, who testifies that for many years, P has kept the purported deed in the glove compartment of his car, and has never kept the document in a safe deposit box. At the close of all evidence, P's attorney asks the court to instruct the jury that it must find that the deed is authentic if it finds that it is at least 30 years old, is in such condition as to create no suspicion as to its authenticity, was kept in a place where such a writing would likely be found, and has been acted upon as authentic by persons having an interest in the matter.

245.   The court should

   (A)   find that P has produced sufficient evidence to meet her burden of production on all of the foundational facts, and give P's requested instruction.

   (B)   find that all of the foundational facts are true, and give P's requested instruction.

(C) find that D has produced sufficient evidence to support the conclusion that the deed was not kept in the safe deposit box, and not give P's requested instruction.

(D) find that the deed was not kept in the safe deposit box, and not give P's requested instruction.

Prosecution of D for possession of a firearm in violation of a statute forbidding convicted felons from possessing firearms. At trial, the prosecution presents evidence that D is a convicted felon, and that D was arrested when a firearm was found under the front seat of a car in which she was riding as a passenger. D stipulates that she is a convicted felon, but declines to take the stand in her own defense or call any witnesses. The jurisdiction in which the case is being tried maintains the following rebuttable presumption: *All occupants of a vehicle are presumed to be in possession of any firearm contained in the vehicle.*

246. Which of the following jury instructions would it be appropriate for the court to issue?

(A) If you find that D was an occupant of the vehicle at the time the firearm was found in the vehicle, you must find that D was in possession of the firearm.

(B) If you find that D was an occupant of the vehicle at the time the firearm was found in the vehicle, you may, but need not, find that D was in possession of the firearm.

(C) If you find that D was an occupant of the vehicle at the time the firearm was found in the vehicle, you must find that D was in possession of the firearm unless D has persuaded you otherwise.

(D) No jury instruction would be appropriate in this situation.

Paternity action by P, the mother of a child, against D, whom P alleges to be the child's father. The jurisdiction in which the case is being tried has the following statute: *The child of a wife cohabiting with her husband, who is not impotent or sterile, is conclusively presumed to be a child of the marriage.* P presents evidence that P and D are married, that they were cohabiting, and that D is not impotent. In his defense, D wishes to present evidence of a blood test that establishes that he could not have fathered the child.

247. Which of the following statements is correct?

(A) The court should allow D to present the blood test evidence but should instruct the jury that it should weigh the value of the presumption against D's evidence.

(B) The court should allow D to present the evidence but should instruct the jury that D has the burden of persuading the jury that he is not the father.

(C) The court not allow D to present the evidence, and should instruct the jury that D is the father.

(D) The court should not allow D to present the evidence, and should instruct the jury that if it finds that P and D were married and cohabiting, and that D is not sterile, it must find that D is the father of the child.

Prosecution of D for the murder of V. At trial, the prosecution calls D's attorney as a witness, and asks the attorney if it isn't true that during an interview in the attorney's office, D admitted to her that she killed V and asked for help to "beat this charge." Assume D did make this statement to the attorney. The attorney objects on grounds of the attorney-client privilege.

248. How should the court rule?

(A) The court should overrule the objection because, if the prosecutor knows about D's statement to her attorney, D must have waived the privilege.

(B) The court should overrule the objection because D sought her attorney's help to cover up the crime.

(C) The court should overrule the objection as to D's asking for help to "beat this charge," but sustain the objection as to D's statement that she killed V.

(D) The court should sustain the objection.

249. Assume D's husband and the attorney's secretary were present in the attorney's office when D made the statement to the attorney. How should the court rule on D's attorney's objection?

(A) The court should overrule the objection because the husband's presence waives the attorney-client privilege.

(B) The court should overrule the objection because the secretary's presence waives the attorney-client privilege.

(C) The court should overrule the objection unless D can show that her husband's assistance is needed for her defense.

(D) The court should sustain the objection.

Negligence action by P against D, a grocery store owner, following a slip-and-fall in the produce section of D's store. P claims she slipped on a puddle of liquid, and that D either should have prevented the liquid from spilling on the floor or cleaned it up sooner. Before trial, the former secretary for D's attorney, angry at being fired, contacted P's attorney and told her that she sat in on a conversation in which D and the attorney discussed paying off store employees who saw the accident to get them to deny that there was any liquid on the floor and to state that P tripped because she was running through the produce section. The secretary told P's attorney that the meeting was taped, and gave P's attorney her notes of this meeting, which summarize the conversation, but without detail. P subpoenas the tape of the meeting. D objects on grounds of privilege. P responds that the conversation was not privileged due to the crime-fraud exception, and asks the court to conduct an *in camera* inspection of the tape.

250. Discuss the procedure the court should follow in deciding on the admissibility of the secretary's testimony.

ANSWER:

Negligence action by P against D arising from a scooter collision. P claims she suffered severe back injuries in the accident. Prior to trial, P's attorney referred P to Dr. X to obtain an opinion about the prospects for P's long-term recovery. X examined P and sent a report directly to P's attorney. D wishes to take Dr. X's deposition in order to ask about her examination and report. P objects on grounds of privilege.

251. How should the court rule?

(A) The court should sustain P's objection because examination and report are subject to the attorney-client privilege.

(B) The court should sustain P's objection because the examination and report are subject to the physician-patient privilege.

(C) The court should sustain P's objection because the examination and report are subject to both the attorney-client privilege and the physician-patient privilege.

(D) The court should overrule P's objection.

Federal prosecution of D for the murder of V. V's killer lay in wait outside V's house one rainy night, and shot V when V returned. That same night, D went out alone. When D returned an hour later, W and a friend, who had been watching television together, noticed that D's clothes were wet and his shoes muddy. W is D's wife. At the time of the trial, W's friend is in another country. The prosecutor wishes to have W testify to what she saw that night. W is willing to testify, but D objects.

252. How should the court rule?

(A) The court should sustain the objection based on the privilege for confidential communications between spouses.

(B) The court should sustain the objection based on the privilege against adverse spousal testimony.

(C) The court should sustain the objection based on both privileges.

(D) The court should overrule the objection.

253. Assume W was alone in the house when D returned home, and that in addition to the other facts, D whispered to W, "I don't think V is going to bother you anymore."

After V's murder but before the trial, D and W obtained a divorce. The prosecution wishes to have W testify to what she saw when D came home as well as to what D told her. D objects on grounds of the privilege for confidential communications between spouses and the adverse spousal testimony privilege. How should the court rule?

(A)   The court should sustain the objection as to what D told W, but should allow W to testify to what she saw.

(B)   The court should sustain the objection as to what W saw, but allow her to testify to what D told her.

(C)   The court should sustain the objection as to both aspects of W's proposed testimony.

(D)   The court should overrule the objection in its entirety.

Negligence action by P against D arising from an automobile accident. D learns that at trial, P plans to call W, who will state that she was at the scene at the time of the accident and that she saw D's car run a red light and strike P's car. D also learns that W has been under the care of PSW, a psychiatric social worker, for several years. Hoping to develop evidence that W is an unreliable witness, D takes the deposition of PSW and asks about the nature of the treatment. At W's request, PSW objects to any questions concerning her treatment of W. D makes a motion to compel PSW to answer the questions.

254.   Which of the following statements is correct?

(A)   The court should overrule the objection because this is only discovery and not trial, and the rules of evidence do not apply. The court should order PSW to answer the questions.

(B)   The court should overrule the objection because neither W nor PSW is a party to the action, and they may not assert any privilege. The court should order PSW to answer the questions.

(C)   The court should overrule the objection because there is no privilege in federal court between a patient and her psychiatric social worker. The court should order PSW to answer the questions.

(D)   The court should sustain the objection.

255.   Explain why few states recognize a privilege for confidential communications between parent and child. (Assume that the privilege, if recognized, would apply only to minor children.)

ANSWER:

Action in federal court by P, a clothing manufacturer, against D Corp., a competitor. P alleges that D Corp. unlawfully interfered with P's contractual relationship with Store, a large department store chain, leading the chain to drop P's clothing line and start selling D Corp.'s line. D Corp. denies any wrongdoing. Prior to trial, P takes the deposition of W, a sales representative for D Corp. who is now in charge of the Store account. P asks W to relate any communications she had with D Corp.'s attorney concerning the contract with Store. D objects on grounds of attorney-client privilege. Assume W's boss told W that any communications she had with the attorney were to be treated as confidential.

256.   Which of the following statements is correct?

(A)   If W is not in a high enough position within D Corp. to act on any legal advice given by the attorney, communications between W and the attorney are not privileged.

(B)   If W's communications with the attorney took place in order to secure legal advice for D Corp., upper echelon management did not possess all the information needed to obtain proper legal advice, and the communications concerned matters within the scope of W's job, they are subject to the attorney-client privilege.

(C)   Because a corporation does not enjoy any attorney-client privilege, W's communications with the attorney are not privileged.

(D)   Because W worked for D Corp., W's communications with the attorney are subject to the attorney-client privilege.

Legal malpractice action by P against Attorney. Attorney formerly represented P in a breach of contract case. P lost that case, and now claims it was because of incompetent representation by Attorney. Attorney claims she represented P competently, and that early in the litigation process, she advised P to take certain action to maximize her chances of prevailing, but that P refused to follow her advice. At trial, Attorney wishes to testify about the advice she gave P and P's responses. P objects on grounds of attorney-client privilege.

257.   How should the court rule?

(A)   The court should sustain the objection because P is the holder of the privilege, and P has manifested her intention to maintain the privilege.

(B)   The court should sustain the objection because the attorney-client privilege continues as long as there is a client in existence.

(C)   The court should overrule the objection because there is no privilege for communications relevant to an alleged breach of duty by the attorney or client arising from their relationship.

(D)   The court should sustain the objection as to statements made by P to Attorney, but overrule the objection as to the advice Attorney gave to P.

Assume each of the opinions listed below is relevant to a case.

258.   Which of the following opinions is a court *least likely* to allow a lay witness to give?

   (A)   The house smelled of gas just before the explosion.

   (B)   The car that passed us as we were trying to cross in the crosswalk was going at least 50 miles per hour.

   (C)   The damage to the basement was caused by the water that seeped into the basement.

   (D)   The driver appeared to be intoxicated when he stepped out of the car moments after the crash.

Prosecution of D for burglary. To prove innocence, D calls W, a six-year-old child, who will testify that D was home watching television at the time the crime was committed. To establish W's basis for knowing D's whereabouts, D's lawyer asks W to state her relationship to D. If permitted, W will testify that D is her mother.

259.   Of the following objections to W's testimony, which is the most appropriate (even if it might not succeed)?

   (A)   Improper opinion.

   (B)   Lack of personal knowledge.

   (C)   Hearsay.

   (D)   The child is incompetent to testify.

Negligence action by P against D arising from an automobile accident. P claims the accident was caused by D's careless driving.

260.   Of the following, which statement by an eyewitness is the court *most likely* to permit?

   (A)   D was driving carelessly.

   (B)   D was driving negligently.

   (C)   D was driving erratically.

   (D)   D was driving recklessly.

Negligence action by P against D arising from an automobile accident. D alleges she suffered permanent injuries to her legs as a result of the way her car crumpled.

261.   Which of the following statements would a court be *least likely* to permit P's expert, an orthopedic surgeon, to make?

(A)   P's legs were fractured by the sudden, extreme, inward movement of the steering column and instrument panel.

(B)   A force slightly less than that exerted by the crash would not have fractured P's legs.

(C)   A more strongly designed passenger cage would not have collapsed from the force exerted in the accident, and thus would not have fractured P's legs.

(D)   Even after the fractures in P's legs have healed, P is likely to suffer permanent impairment of motion.

Prosecution of D for arson. To prove the fire was set intentionally, the prosecution calls W, a police arson investigator who has served in that capacity for ten years after spending several years as a beat officer. W never attended college and had no special schooling in arson investigation, but learned investigative techniques from a senior investigator with whom she worked for two years. From techniques learned through this experience, W spoke with eyewitnesses who saw the fire at various stages, and concluded from that information as well as her own investigation of the fire scene that the fire was set intentionally.

262.   Which of the following objections to W's testimony is the court likely to sustain, if either?

(A)   W is not a qualified expert.

(B)   W's testimony about the cause of the fire should be excluded as inadmissible hearsay.

(C)   The court is likely to sustain both of these objections.

(D)   The court is likely to overrule both of these objections.

263.   The prosecution wishes to have W testify not just to her conclusion that the fire was caused by arson, but also to the basis for that conclusion. Such testimony would include repeating what the eyewitnesses told her about the fire. If D requests the court to issue a limiting instruction concerning the testimony about the bystander statements, which of the following would be most appropriate?

(A)   You may consider the bystander statements only for the purpose of showing that the fire proceeded as described by the witnesses, and not to explain the basis of W's testimony.

(B)   You may consider the bystander statements only for the purpose of explaining the basis for W's testimony, and not as proof that the fire proceeded as described by W.

(C)   You may consider the bystander statements only for the purpose of demonstrating the bystanders' belief about how the fire proceeded, and not as proof of how the fire actually proceeded.

(D)   No limiting instruction is appropriate in this situation.

Prosecution of D for murder. D claims insanity. To support the insanity defense, D wishes to call W, a psychiatrist who examined D.

264.   Which of the following opinions would the court be *least likely* to permit the expert to state?

(A)   At the time of the killing, D suffered from paranoid schizophrenia.

(B)   At the time of the killing, D suffered from a severe mental disease that made it impossible for her to appreciate the nature and quality or the wrongfulness of her acts.

(C)   At the time of the killing, D was mentally ill.

(D)   At the time of the killing, D suffered from psychosis.

Negligence action by P against D arising from a motorcycle collision. P claims serious emotional injuries as a result of the accident. D denies that P suffered any such injuries. To prove her injuries, P wishes to call W, a psychiatrist.

265.   From which of the following sources may W learn the facts or data that form the basis of her opinion?

(A)   Personal observations and testing of P.

(B)   Tests performed by a clinical psychologist.

(C)   A hypothetical question posed to W before or during W's testimony.

(D)   All of the above are permissible sources of information.

Product liability action by P action against D, manufacturer of an implantable medical device designed to regulate pancreas function. A surgeon implanted the device in P, and P later developed pancreatic cancer. P claims the device was the cause of the cancer. To prove causation, P calls W, a Ph.D. in biochemistry who works for a major university. If permitted, W will testify that based on certain animal studies she conducted on D's device, she has concluded that the device can cause pancreatic cancer. D objects to W's proposed testimony on the ground that it is not valid science.

266.   If the action is tried in a state court that follows the *Frye* test, which of the following best states the principle the court should use in ruling on the admissibility of W's testimony?

(A)   W's testimony will only be admissible if the court finds that it is based on a theory or method that is generally accepted in the relevant scientific community.

(B)   W's testimony will only be admissible if the court finds that there is evidence sufficient to support a conclusion that it is based on a reliable scientific theory or method and that the application of the theory or method is relevant to the case.

(C)   W's testimony will only be admissible if the court finds that it is based on a reliable scientific theory or method and that the application of the theory or method is relevant to the case.

(D)   W's testimony will only be admissible if it is based on a theory or method that has been subjected to publication and peer review.

267.   If the action is tried in federal court, which of the following best states the principle the court should use in ruling on the admissibility of W's testimony?

(A)   W's testimony will only be admissible if the court finds that it is based on a theory or method that is generally accepted in the relevant scientific community.

(B)   W's testimony will only be admissible if the court finds that there is evidence sufficient to support a conclusion that it is based on a reliable scientific theory or method and that the application of the theory or method is relevant to the case.

(C)   W's testimony will only be admissible if the court finds that it is based on a reliable scientific theory or method and that the application of the theory or method is relevant to the case.

(D)   W's testimony will only be admissible if it is based on a theory or method that has been subjected to publication and peer review.

268.   Assume the trial court applies the *Daubert* standard and holds that the testimony of W is inadmissible. D prevails, and P appeals. Based on the standard of review applicable to this situation, discuss the likelihood of P obtaining a reversal.

ANSWER:

PRACTICE FINAL EXAM

PRACTICE FINAL EXAM

Instructions: This exam consists of two parts. The first part contains 40 multiple choice questions. You should allow no more than 80 minutes to complete these questions. The second part consists of 8 short answer questions. Try to answer these questions in no more than 40 minutes.

Part I
Multiple Choice Questions

Prosecution of D for robbing a yogurt shop. D claims that the police arrested the wrong person. To prove that he was not at the shop at the time of the robbery, D calls W, a police officer, and shows W a document that W identifies as a report she made of an interview conducted at D's home on an unrelated matter, and notes that it records a date and time of the interview that correspond to the time of the yogurt shop robbery. W further testifies that she is required to make and file reports of all citizen interviews.

269. Which of the following statements is most accurate?

(A) The document may be read into the record under the doctrine of refreshing recollection.

(B) The document is hearsay but is admissible under the doctrine of past recollection recorded.

(C) The document is hearsay but is admissible as a public record.

(D) The document is inadmissible.

Libel action by P against D, the publisher of a newspaper. P claims that D published an article calling P a "notorious gangster," which P claims is completely false. At trial, P wishes to testify about the allegedly libelous statements in the article.

270. Which of the following statements is most accurate?

(A) Though P's testimony is not hearsay, it is inadmissible because it violates the best evidence rule.

(B) P's testimony violates the best evidence rule and constitutes inadmissible hearsay.

(C) P's testimony does not violate the best evidence rule but constitutes inadmissible hearsay.

(D) P's testimony is admissible.

Prosecution of D for armed robbery of a bank. The prosecution alleges that D and several colleagues, all wearing red, white, and blue berets, entered the bank carrying shotguns, forced the tellers to perform a specific dance, then took all the $5, $10, and $20 bills from the cash drawers. D denies participating in the robbery. The prosecution wishes to offer evidence that three years before this event, D robbed another bank in the same way. D denies involvement in the earlier robbery as well.

271. Which of the following statements is most accurate?

(A) The trial judge must determine whether there is sufficient evidence from which the jury could conclude that D took part in the first robbery. If the court believes sufficient evidence exists, the judge must allow the jury to hear about that event.

(B) The trial judge must determine whether there is sufficient evidence from which the jury could conclude that D took part in the first robbery. Even if such evidence exists, the judge must still determine its relevance to the crime for which D is charged and whether the probative value of the evidence is substantially outweighed by the danger of unfair prejudice.

(C) The trial judge must determine whether D took part in the first robbery, but even if it makes that finding, the judge must still determine its relevance to the crime for which D is charged and whether the probative value of the evidence is substantially outweighed by the danger of unfair prejudice.

(D) Because the first robbery is not sufficiently similar to the act for which D has been charged, the evidence is inadmissible.

Prosecution of D for bank robbery. At trial, the prosecution calls W, who testifies that an hour after the robbery, she was riding on a bus and saw D, whom she knew. If permitted, W will then testify that she walked up to D, said "That was quite a bank job you pulled off today," and that D laughed. D makes a hearsay objection to W's testimony concerning her out-of-court statement to D and D's response.

272. Which of the following constitutes the prosecution's strongest argument in favor of admissibility?

(A) W's statement is hearsay but admissible as an excited utterance.

(B) W's statement is hearsay but admissible as a present sense impression.

(C) Standing alone, W's statement is inadmissible hearsay. However, D's response makes both statements admissible as a declaration against interest.

(D) Standing alone, W's statement is inadmissible hearsay. However, by his response, D adopted W's statement, making it admissible as an adoptive admission.

Prosecution of D1 and D2 for stealing V's wallet as V was waiting to cross a busy street. The prosecution alleges that defendants accomplished their crime by having D1 stand in front of V at a busy downtown intersection, while D2 stood behind V. When the "Walk" signal went on, D1 allegedly started to cross, and then stopped suddenly, causing V to bump into D1. While V was distracted by this event, D2 allegedly reached into V's back pocket and removed his wallet. This is a common scheme used by pickpockets. D1 and D2 were found in possession of V's wallet, but claim they picked it up on the street and were planning to return it. At trial, the prosecution wishes to offer evidence that when they were arrested, D1 and D2 were found to possess two other wallets that had been reported stolen by their owners several weeks earlier. D1 and D2 claim they were planning to return these wallets also, and object to admission of this evidence.

273. Which of the following statements is most likely correct?

(A) The evidence is admissible to show intent.

(B) The evidence is admissible to establish the identity of the pickpockets by means of showing *modus operandi*.

(C) The evidence is admissible to establish a habit of stealing wallets which was likely repeated in this instance.

(D) The evidence is inadmissible.

Personal injury action by P against D arising out of a skateboard accident. P alleges that the accident caused him permanent, painful impairment of his right leg. At trial, D calls Dr. W, the physician who treated P for the injuries she sustained in the accident. Dr. W proves to be antagonistic to D's questions, so the court permits D to proceed with leading questions. D asks Dr. W whether it isn't true that when P first consulted her, P said his right leg "isn't hurting too badly." P objects.

274. Which of the following statements is most likely true?

(A) P's statement is not hearsay and is not subject to any privilege.

(B) P's statement is inadmissible hearsay and is subject to the physician-patient privilege.

(C) P's statement is not hearsay but is subject to the physician-patient privilege.

(D) P's statement is admissible hearsay and is not subject to any privilege.

Prosecution of D for assault with a deadly weapon on V. At trial, the prosecution calls several witnesses who testify that D and V were standing next to each other at a bar when suddenly and without provocation, D punched V in the stomach. D then testifies that he only punched V after seeing that V was about to bash him with a large moose head which V had dislodged from the wall. D then wishes to call W to testify that in the lobby of the courthouse during jury selection, D told W that V had attacked D with a moose head.

275. Which of the following constitutes the court's most likely ruling?

(A) W's testimony is only admissible to establish that D acted in self-defense.

(B) W's testimony is only admissible to establish D's credibility by virtue of prior conduct evidencing a character for truthfulness.

(C) W's testimony is admissible both to establish that D acted in self-defense and to establish D's credibility.

(D) W's testimony is inadmissible.

Prosecution of D for murder. D claims she was in another country when the crime was committed. At trial, the prosecution wishes to offer into evidence a transcript of a meeting between D and her lawyer. D objects that the transcript is subject to the attorney-client privilege. The prosecution responds that the privilege does not apply because of the crime-fraud exception. Assume the transcript of the conversation was obtained legally.

276. Which of the following statements is most accurate?

(A) Without any showing by the prosecution, the court may conduct an *in camera* hearing to determine the admissibility of the transcript. At the hearing, the court will not be bound by the rules of evidence.

(B) Without any showing by the prosecution, the court may conduct an *in camera* hearing to determine the admissibility of the transcript. At the hearing, the court may consider any evidence, admissible or not, except evidence which has been claimed to be privileged.

(C) If the prosecution produces evidence sufficient to support a reasonable belief that an *in camera* review may yield evidence showing that the crime or fraud exception applies, the court may conduct an *in camera* hearing to determine the admissibility of the transcript. At that hearing, the court may consider any evidence it wishes.

(D) If the prosecution produces evidence sufficient to support a reasonable belief that an *in camera* review may yield evidence showing that the crime or fraud exception applies, the court may conduct an *in camera* hearing to determine the admissibility of the transcript. At that hearing, the court may consider any evidence except material that has been found privileged.

Prosecution of D for setting a brushfire that destroyed hundreds of canyon homes. D claims it was X, rather than he, who set the fires. At trial, D calls W to testify that a week before the fires started, X, a close friend of W, told W to take all her valuables out of her canyon home.

277. Which of the following statements is most accurate?

(A) X's statement would be admissible as an admission under the Federal Rules.

(B) X's statement would be admissible non-hearsay under the Federal Rules.

(C)   X's statement would be admissible non-hearsay under a declarant-based definition of hearsay.

(D)   X's statement would be admissible non-hearsay under both the Federal Rules and a declarant-based definition of hearsay.

Prosecution of D for theft of a series of valuable bicycles that were chained together in a parking lot. D claims she had nothing to do with the theft. At trial, the prosecution wishes to call W, D's husband, to ask W whether D told him on the night of the crime that she had participated in it.

278.   Which of the following statements is most accurate?

(A)   If D objects to W's testimony on privilege grounds, W may not testify even if she is willing to do so.

(B)   Even if D does not object on privilege grounds, D can raise a successful hearsay objection to W's testimony.

(C)   If W does not claim his privilege, D cannot prevent W from testifying.

(D)   Because no privilege is applicable to these facts, W must answer the question even if he does not wish to do so, and even if D objects.

Prosecution of D for the murder of V. D admits killing V, but claims that she acted in self-defense when V attacked her. To prove that V attacked D, D wishes to offer evidence that V had a community reputation as a violent person. D was unaware of this fact at the time she killed V.

279.   Which of the following statements is most accurate?

(A)   Because D was unaware of the story about V at the time she killed V, the evidence is irrelevant.

(B)   Even though D was unaware of the story about V at the time she killed V, the evidence is relevant and admissible to show that V was the first aggressor in the fight.

(C)   The evidence is relevant but is an improper attempt to impeach V.

(D)   The evidence is relevant but is an improper attempt to use character evidence to prove V's out of court conduct.

Wrongful death action by P against D Corp. arising out of a collision between a D Corp. truck and P's car. Several people including P's deceased were killed in the crash. P alleges that the driver of the D Corp. truck was drunk at the time of the accident. At trial, P calls W to testify that the day after the collision, X, an officer of D Corp., called the spouse of P's deceased and said, "I speak for the company when I tell you how sorry we are about this accident. We plan to review our procedures for enforcing our policy against alcohol consumption by truck drivers." D Corp. makes a hearsay objection to this testimony.

280. Which of the following statements is most accurate?

(A) If the trial court finds that X was authorized to speak for the company, the statement is admissible as an authorized admission.

(B) Because X is not a party and no hearsay exception applies, X's statement is inadmissible hearsay.

(C) When deciding whether to admit the statement, the court may not take the statement itself into account in determining if X had authority to speak for D Corp.

(D) If the court finds that a reasonable jury could decide that X had authority to speak for D Corp., the court should admit the statement.

Prosecution of D for the murder of V. At trial, the prosecution calls W, and wishes to have her testify that she was with V just before he died, and that V winced in pain, pulled W close to his face, and whispered, "I know this is the end. D did this to me." D objects to this statement on grounds its admission would violate her 6th Amendment right to confront the witnesses against her.

281. Which of the following statements is most accurate?

(A) If the court determines that the statement satisfies the dying declarations exception and that the circumstances of its making demonstrate its reliability, the court should admit the statement.

(B) If the court determines that the statement satisfies the dying declarations exception and that its reliability is corroborated by other evidence, the court should admit the statement.

(C) If the court determines that the statement satisfies the dying declarations exception, the court should admit the statement.

(D) Because the defendant never had an opportunity to confront V, the court should not admit the statement.

Negligence action by P against D arising from a car accident. At trial, P calls W, a police officer, who testifies that she arrived at the scene moments after the accident and saw X, a bystander, sitting on the curb sobbing uncontrollably. When she walked up to X, X immediately screamed, "That red car just ran right through the light and cut that blue car in half!" D makes a hearsay objection, and P responds that the evidence is admissible under the excited utterance exception. D then offers to prove by W2, another witness to the accident, that just before X made the statement to the police officer (but still after the accident), X was chatting with W2 about the weather.

282. Which of the following statements is most accurate?

(A)   The court must sustain D's objection because X's statement concerning the accident does not satisfy the excited utterance exception.

(B)   The court will admit both of X's statements and instruct the jury that if it finds that X's statement concerning the accident was made under the stress of excitement caused by the accident, it should consider the statement, but if it finds that X's statement was not made under such stress, it must disregard the statement.

(C)   The court will determine whether X's statement concerning the accident was made under the stress of excitement caused by the accident. If it finds that it was, the court will admit that statement and exclude the earlier statement concerning the weather, which is irrelevant.

(D)   The court will determine whether X's statement concerning the accident was made under the stress of excitement caused by the accident. If it finds that it was, the court will admit the statement as an excited utterance, but will also admit the earlier statement concerning the weather.

Prosecution of D for running a house of prostitution. At trial, the prosecution calls W, a police officer who took part in the raid on D's establishment. The prosecution wishes to have W testify that moments after the raid began, the phone rang three times, and on each occasion, the caller asked to make an appointment with a particular woman at a particular time that evening.

283.   Which of the following statements is most accurate?

(A)   The callers' statements are more likely to be classified as hearsay under the assertion-based definition of hearsay than under the declarant-based definition.

(B)   The callers' statements are more likely to be classified as hearsay under the declarant-based definition of hearsay than under the assertion-based definition.

(C)   The callers' statements are hearsay under either definition.

(D)   Because the police officer is on the stand and subject to cross-examination, the callers' statements are not hearsay under either definition.

Negligence action by P against D arising out of an automobile collision. As part of her case in chief, P calls D to the stand. During the direct examination of D, P's attorney asks, "Isn't it true that at the time of the accident, you were going 65 miles per hour?"

284.   Which of the following statements about this question is accurate?

(A)   The question is leading but proper.

(B)   The question is an improper leading question.

(C)   The question is not leading and is proper.

(D)   The question is not leading but assumes a fact not in evidence.

Prosecution of D for the murder of V. D claims he killed V in self-defense after V viciously attacked D with a knife. At trial, D calls W to testify that she is well-acquainted with V's community reputation, and that V had a reputation as a very violent person.

285.   Which of the following statements is most accurate?

(A)   The evidence is inadmissible because it is irrelevant.

(B)   The evidence constitutes inadmissible hearsay.

(C)   The evidence is inadmissible because D is not permitted to offer character evidence in this situation.

(D)   The evidence is admissible.

Prosecution of D for burglary. D fears that if he chooses to testify at trial, the prosecution will seek to impeach his credibility by cross-examining him about a prior burglary conviction. Before trial, D makes a motion *in limine* to prevent the prosecution's use of the prior conviction. The court denies the motion. D does not take the stand at trial and is convicted. D has now appealed on the basis that the court should have granted his motion *in limine*.

286.   Which of the following constitutes the prosecution's strongest response to D's claim?

(A)   The trial court was correct to deny D's motion because it had no discretion to exclude this relevant evidence.

(B)   The determination of whether to admit this evidence rests solely with the sound discretion of the trial court, and that court's decision may not be overturned on review.

(C)   Because D did not take the stand at trial, D may not raise this issue on appeal.

(D)   Because it would be a denial of due process to refuse to allow the prosecution to offer this impeaching evidence, the trial court's ruling was clearly correct and should not be overturned on appeal.

Prosecution of D for embezzlement from V, D's employer. At trial, D testifies that she never took any money from V. On cross-examination, the prosecutor wishes to ask D if it isn't true that three years ago, D was convicted of misdemeanor perjury.

287.   Which of the following statements is most accurate?

(A)   This evidence is admissible only to impeach D's credibility.

(B)   This evidence is admissible both to impeach D's credibility and to establish that D is the kind of person who would embezzle.

(C)   This evidence is admissible only to impeach D and only if the probative value of the evidence outweighs the danger of unfair prejudice to D.

(D)   This evidence is inadmissible.

Fraud action by P against D, a used car seller, arising from the sale of a car. P claims D advertised the car as new when in fact its odometer had been set back to zero from 5,000 miles. Prior to trial, P took the deposition of W, D's sales manager. During the deposition, which was taken under oath, W admitted that the seller sometimes set back odometers on cars before they were sold. At trial, *D* calls W, who testifies that he "preps" all cars for D and that no odometers were ever set back while W worked for D. On cross-examination, P asks W whether he remembers having his deposition taken and stating that odometers sometimes were set back. W admits to having had his deposition taken but denies making the statement. P wishes to read into evidence that portion of W's deposition transcript containing W's statement that odometers sometimes were set back.

288.   Which of the following statements is most accurate?

(A)   The portion of the transcript is admissible only to impeach W's credibility.

(B)   The portion of the transcript is admissible both to impeach W's credibility and to prove that the odometer was set back.

(C)   The portion of the transcript is inadmissible for either purpose because W is not unavailable.

(D)   The portion of the transcript is inadmissible for either purpose unless D's lawyer cross-examined W at the deposition.

Prosecution of D for car theft. At trial, the prosecution calls W, the custodian of records for D's employer. W is shown a document which W identifies as D's personnel record. That record contains the statement, "Following investigation, it has been determined that D has been stealing office supplies from our storeroom. Personnel has notified D of this finding and informed D that any further infractions will result in immediate termination." W testifies that written personnel records are kept of each employee, and that items in each record are written by individuals with personal knowledge of the matters recorded.

289.   Which of the following statements is most accurate?

(A)   The document is admissible as a business record.

(B)   The document is inadmissible because it is irrelevant.

(C)   The document is hearsay and fails to satisfy the business records exception.

(D)   The document satisfies the business records exception and is relevant, but is inadmissible.

Prosecution of D for burglarizing V's home. At trial, the prosecution calls V to testify about the items he found missing after the break-in. V can remember some of the items, but not all. The prosecutor then shows V a document listing all missing items, asks V to read it, takes it back, and asks V if he now remembers what else what missing. V says he does. The prosecutor then wants V to list the other missing items.

290.   Which of the following statements is most accurate?

   (A)   Because V has not laid the proper foundation for past recollection recorded, V
          should not be permitted to list the other missing items.

   (B)   Because the document is offered against a defendant in a criminal case, it is
          inadmissible.

   (C)   Because the document has not been shown to have been prepared in the ordinary
          course of business, it is inadmissible.

   (D)   V will be allowed to list the other missing items.

D drove a car that struck and killed V as V was crossing a street. P, the administrator of V's
estate, sued D for wrongful death. At trial, P called W, who testified that he was standing on
a street corner near where the accident took place and saw D run a red light and strike V in
a crosswalk. The jury returned a verdict for P. Within the limitations period, the state decides
to prosecute D for involuntary manslaughter. At trial, W raises a wholly improper "privacy"
claim and refuses to testify even when ordered by the trial court. The prosecution therefore wishes
to offer in evidence the transcript of W's testimony in the earlier trial.

291.   Which of the following statements is most likely correct?

   (A)   Because the prosecution cannot succeed without W's testimony, the transcript is
          admissible.

   (B)   Because the transcript is admissible hearsay and its use does not violate the
          confrontation clause, the transcript is admissible.

   (C)   Because W is available to testify, the transcript is inadmissible.

   (D)   Because the civil trial came first, D's confrontation rights would be violated if
          the transcript were used. Therefore, the transcript is inadmissible.

Proceeding for injunctive relief brought by the state of Muckaska against Messon Oil Co. to
compel Messon to complete the cleanup of Muckaska beaches which were badly soiled when
a Messon Oil tanker ran aground and spilled millions of gallons of crude into a pristine bay.
To prove that Messon does not intend to resume cleanup operations after the winter season,
Muckaska offers evidence that at the end of the warm season, Messon's public relations officer
held a press conference in which she stated, "Messon believes that the job is finished! We think
the entire bay is prettier and cleaner than ever!"

292.   Which of the following constitutes Muckaska's strongest argument for admissibility
        of this statement?

   (A)   The statement is hearsay but admissible as a declaration against interest.

   (B)   The statement is hearsay but admissible as an excited utterance.

(C) The statement is not hearsay because it is not offered to prove the truth of the matter asserted.

(D) The statement is admissible as an authorized admission.

Prosecution of D for murder. At trial, D testifies that she was in another country when the crime took place. D also calls W1 to testify that she was with D at that time. On rebuttal, the prosecution wishes to call W2 to testify that W1 has been D's lover for five years.

293. Which of the following statements is most accurate?

(A) W2's testimony is admissible to impeach W1 by showing that she has a bad character for truthfulness.

(B) W2's testimony is admissible to impeach W1 by showing that W1 has a reason to testify in D's favor.

(C) W2's testimony is admissible to impeach W1 by contradiction.

(D) W2's testimony is inadmissible.

Slander action by P, the owner of an art gallery, against D. P alleges D gave a public speech in which she asserted that P was a "well-known art forger." At trial, D testifies that she was not the person who made the speech. Also during the trial, P calls W, who testifies that he was in the audience during the speech but because he was not wearing his glasses, he could not see the speaker clearly. However, W testifies that he made a tape recording of the speech on a very high-quality machine and brought it to court with him. P wishes to play for the jury that portion of the tape recording in which the speaker calls P a "well-known art forger."

294. Which of the following statements is most accurate?

(A) If the court finds that the jury, comparing the voice on the tape with D's, could conclude that the voice is D's, the court should allow the jury to hear the tape.

(B) If the court finds that the voice on the tape is D's, the court should allow the jury to hear the tape.

(C) Even if the tape has been authenticated, the court must not allow the jury to hear the tape because it constitutes inadmissible hearsay.

(D) Because P did not call an expert to identify the voice on the tape as D's, the court must not allow the jury to hear the tape.

Prosecution of four police officers for using excessive force when arresting V. A witness recorded the incident on videotape. The tape, played for the jury, clearly shows the officers inflicting more than forty blows on V with night sticks, and kicking V as well. At trial, the officers each take the stand in their own defense, and none deny that the blows were inflicted on V. Despite what appears to be overwhelming evidence of guilt, the jury acquits the officers of the criminal charges.

295. Which of the following statements is accurate?

    (A) The prosecution may ask the court to set aside the verdicts of acquittal and order a new trial on the basis that the verdicts are against the overwhelming weight of the evidence.

    (B) The prosecution is entitled to a hearing at which it will present affidavits of jurors that demonstrate that the jury ignored crucial evidence.

    (C) The prosecution is entitled to a hearing at which it will present affidavits of jurors that demonstrate that the jury ignored the court's jury instructions.

    (D) The prosecution has no recourse.

Negligence action by P against D after P's bicycle and D's bicycle collided. At trial, P testifies that D was riding with "no hands" and lost control of his bike when he hit some sand on the road. D testifies that both of his hands were on the handlebars. P wishes to call W to testify that he has gone on bicycle rides with D at least 20 times, and that on each occasion D rode for at least part of the time with "no hands."

296. Which of the following constitutes P's strongest argument in favor of the admissibility of W's testimony?

    (A) The evidence is admissible to show that D is a careless bicycle rider.

    (B) The evidence is admissible to show that D habitually rides with "no hands."

    (C) The evidence is admissible impeachment by contradiction.

    (D) The evidence is admissible to establish D's intent to ride with "no hands."

Prosecution of D for child molestation. At trial, the prosecution calls W, the 10-year-old alleged victim. After establishing W's competency to testify, the prosecution asks W about the alleged assault. W states that he cannot remember what happened. The prosecution then asks W, "Now, you went to an apartment with D, didn't you?"

297. Which of the following statements concerning this question is most accurate?

    (A) The question is leading but proper.

    (B) The question is not leading and is proper.

    (C) The question is leading and improper.

    (D) The question is argumentative, compound, and improper.

Prosecution of D for bank robbery committed by use of a sophisticated and little-known safe-cracking technique. The prosecution wishes to offer evidence that twice before, D robbed other banks using the same technique. D claims that he was in another state when the charged crime took place.

298. Which of the following statements is most accurate?

   (A) The evidence is irrelevant and therefore inadmissible.

   (B) The evidence is irrelevant because its probative value is substantially outweighed by the danger of unfair prejudice to D.

   (C) The evidence is relevant because the fact that D committed bank robberies on other occasions using this unusual technique makes it somewhat more likely that he was the one who committed the robbery for which he is being tried. Therefore, the evidence is admissible.

   (D) The evidence is relevant for the reasons explained in answer (C), but the court may exclude the evidence if it finds that the probative value is substantially outweighed by the danger of unfair prejudice.

Negligence action by P against D Construction Co. (D) arising out of a collision between P's car and a truck driven by W, an employee of D. At trial, the jury found for P and the court entered judgment accordingly. However, D appealed and the appellate court reversed because of errors unrelated to evidence issues and remanded for a new trial. Unfortunately for P, W died before the second trial could be held. At the first trial, P had called W as an adverse witness, and W admitted that she ran a red light, causing the collision. At the second trial, P calls X, a friend who was in the courtroom during the entire first trial. If permitted, X will testify that W gave this testimony at the first trial.

299. Which of the following statements is most accurate?

   (A) Because the transcript, and not X's testimony, is the best evidence of W's testimony at the first trial, X's testimony is inadmissible.

   (B) Because W was called as an adverse witness and D would have no motive to conduct a searching cross-examination, the transcript is inadmissible.

   (C) Because W's testimony is so central to the case that it would be unfair to D to allow it to be entered into evidence, the transcript is inadmissible.

   (D) The transcript is admissible.

Paternity action by P against D. D claims that he was not the father of the child. Assume that the following rebuttable presumption applies: *A child born within ten months of the last date on which a male and female were cohabiting is rebuttably presumed to have been fathered by the male.* Assume that this is the only presumption that applies in the case. Assume further that this action is being tried in a jurisdiction that adheres to the minority (Morgan/McCormick) theory of presumptions. At trial, P testifies that she and D cohabited continuously for five years and only stopped living together one month before the baby was born. D, in turn, calls an expert witness who testifies that she performed blood tests on D and on the child, and determined that D could not have fathered the child. At the close of all evidence, P's attorney asks the court to instruct the jury that if it finds that the child was born within ten months of the last date on which P and D were cohabiting, it must find that D was the father unless D persuades the jury that he was not.

300.   Which of the following statements is most accurate?

(A)   If the court finds that P has produced sufficient evidence to meet her burden of production on the foundational facts, the court should issue the instruction.

(B)   If the court finds that all of the foundational facts are true, the court should issue the instruction.

(C)   If the court finds that D's expert has produced sufficient evidence on which the jury could find that D could not have been the father of the child, the court should not issue the instruction.

(D)   If the court decides that the expert is correct that D could not have been the father of the child, the court should not issue the instruction.

Prosecution of D for murder. D admits killing the victim but claims she was insane at the time she did so.

301   Which of the following may serve as the basis of an expert psychiatrist's testimony concerning the psychiatric condition of a criminal defendant?

(A)   The witness's pre-testimony psychiatric treatment of defendant.

(B)   The defendant's "raw scores" on a battery of psychological tests performed by another expert who testified about those tests prior to this witness's testimony.

(C)   A hypothetical question posed by counsel before the psychiatrist took the stand and which is based on facts supported by testimony in the case.

(D)   All of the above are permissible bases of the psychiatrist's testimony.

Prosecution of D for child molestation. At trial, the prosecution calls W, the 5-year-old alleged victim. Prior to taking testimony about the event, the judge takes W into her chambers, along with the attorneys, D, and the court reporter. The judge then asks W whether he understands what it means to tell the "truth." W says he does. After probing this issue in more detail, the judge asks W whether he understands that he must tell the truth when they go back into the courtroom. W says he does. The group then returns to the courtroom, where the prosecution questions W concerning the facts of the case.

302.   Which of the following statements concerning the proceedings in the judge's chambers is most accurate?

(A)   Because FRE 602 does away with all tests of witness competency, the judge acted improperly in questioning W before taking his testimony.

(B)   Because the child's competency to testify has not been determined beyond a reasonable doubt, the court has committed error by permitting him to testify to the facts of the case.

(C)   Because a 5-year-old is unable to truly understand the concept of "truth" and the obligation to tell the truth when under oath, the court has committed error by permitting W to testify to the facts of the case.

(D)   The court acted properly.

Negligence action by P against D, the owner of the amusement park Sidneyland. P claims that the "Bar Tours" ride was not properly maintained, causing her to be injured when it lurched forward suddenly, pitching her out of the vehicle. D claims that there was nothing wrong with the ride, and that P must have stood up while the vehicle was moving. P denies doing so. At trial, P wishes to call W to testify that he went on the ride a week before the accident, that he was sitting in his seat in the proper manner, and that the vehicle lurched forward suddenly, nearly throwing him out. The ride is indoors, and had not been altered between the two events.

303.   Which of the following statements concerning W's testimony is most accurate?

(A)   The evidence is admissible to show a similar event under similar circumstances, making it more likely that the accident happened as P claims.

(B)   The evidence is admissible to show that D tends to be careless in maintaining the "Bar Tours" ride, making it more likely that the accident happened as P claims.

(C)   The evidence is admissible to show that D habitually fails to maintain the "Bar Tours" ride.

(D)   The evidence is inadmissible.

Medical malpractice action by P against D after D performed unsuccessful brain surgery on P. At trial, P calls Dr. W to prove that D failed to use proper surgical techniques. P's attorney establishes Dr. W's experience, but D's attorney objects to Dr. W's testifying as an expert, claiming that she has not been shown to be an expert on the matters involved in this case. The court hears arguments concerning D's objection and then sustains the objection, refusing to allow Dr. W to testify on P's behalf. P has no other experts waiting in the wings to testify.

304.   Which of the following represents P's best course of action?

(A)   P's attorney should ask to have the jury excused and then should make a record of what Dr. W would have said if she had been permitted to testify.

(B)   P's attorney has already placed on the record his response to D's objection. This preserves the point for appeal.

(C)   P's attorney should ask that the court allow Dr. W to testify after reminding the jury that it must disregard his testimony if it finds him unqualified as an expert in the matters involved in this case.

(D)   P's attorney should threaten to gather up her marbles and go home unless the court changes its mind.

Libel action by P against D. P alleges that D wrote a letter to a newspaper stating that P was a "major drug kingpin." D denies writing any such letter. At trial, P offers the letter in evidence. The letter bears D's name on the signature line. In addition, P offers a letter containing a signature which D admits to be his.

305. Which of the following statements is most accurate?

(A) Because P has not called a handwriting expert to compare the signatures and offer an opinion, no reasonable jury could find that the signature was D's, and the court should exclude the letter.

(B) Because P has not called a handwriting expert to compare the signatures and offer an opinion, P has not offered enough evidence for the court to find that the signature on the letter is genuine, and the court should exclude the letter.

(C) Even without expert testimony, the court may determine that there is sufficient evidence from which the jury can decide that the letter is genuine, and the court can therefore admit the letter.

(D) Even without expert testimony, the court may decide that the signature is genuine and admit the letter.

P sues D, a private elementary school, for negligence following an accident in which P was struck by a car while trying to cross a street in front of the school. P does not base her claim on the theory of respondeat superior, but rather on the theory that D was itself negligent for retaining an unreliable employee. D admits that its crossing guard was absent on that occasion, but denies any negligence in hiring or retaining the guard. At trial, P wishes to offer evidence that the guard had been absent twice in the previous month.

306. Which of the following statements is most likely correct?

(A) If offered to prove the guard was absent on the day of the accident, the evidence is relevant and admissible.

(B) If offered to prove D had notice that the guard was unreliable, the evidence is irrelevant because the number of past absences is insufficient to establish a pattern. Therefore, the evidence is inadmissible.

(C) If offered to prove that the guard was unreliable, and that D had notice of this fact, the evidence is relevant and admissible.

(D) If offered to prove D had notice that the guard was unreliable, the evidence is relevant, but the court must exclude it because its low probative value is substantially outweighed by the danger of unfair prejudice.

Civil action by P against D arising out of a business dispute. At trial, P calls W, whose testimony helps to establish P's version of the facts. On cross-examination, D wishes to ask W if it isn't true that W has sued D's spouse in an unrelated matter. W denies that this is true. D now wishes to call X, the court clerk, to testify that W has indeed filed such an action.

307. Which of the following statements is most accurate?

   (A) X's testimony should not be permitted because the existence of a lawsuit between W and D's spouse is irrelevant to the present case.

   (B) X's testimony should not be permitted because it would constitute impermissible use of extrinsic evidence to impeach.

   (C) X's testimony should not be permitted because it would constitute improper use of specific instances of the conduct of a witness to impeach the witness's credibility.

   (D) X's testimony is admissible.

Wrongful death action by P, administrator of V's estate, against D. P alleges that V was walking on a sidewalk adjacent to a construction site when he was crushed by a steel crane which fell onto the sidewalk. D admits that V was struck by the crane, but claims that at the time, V was trespassing on the construction site. (The position of V's body following the accident leaves doubt as to where he had been walking.) To prove that V was on the sidewalk outside of the construction site, P calls W to testify that as he was lying on the ground just before he died, V told W, "I've had it! You aren't safe anymore on the sidewalks of the city." D makes a hearsay objection to this evidence.

308. Which of the following statements is most accurate?

   (A) Because the statement is relevant and is not offered to prove the truth of the matter asserted, it is admissible non-hearsay.

   (B) The statement is hearsay and does not satisfy the dying declarations exception because it does not concern the causes or circumstances of V's impending death.

   (C) The statement is hearsay, but if the court finds that V believed he was about to die when he made the statement and that the statement concerns the cause or circumstances of what V believed to be his impending death, it will be admissible under the dying declarations exception.

   (D) The statement is hearsay, but if the court finds that there is evidence sufficient to support a finding that V believed he was about to die when he made the statement, it will be admissible under the dying declarations exception.

END OF PART I
* * * * * * *

Prosecution of D for robbing V on a street corner. D claims that the police arrested the wrong person. At trial, the prosecution calls W, a police officer, who testifies that after the robbery, she interviewed X, a bystander, and that during the interview, X pointed to D (who was standing on the corner), and said, "He's the one who robbed V." The prosecution does not call X to testify at trial. D moves to strike the officer's testimony.

309. How should the court rule, and why?

ANSWER:

Medical malpractice action by P against D Utility Co. following the death of X, P's father, from cancer. P's theory is that D caused X's cancer by placing high voltage electrical lines too close to X's residence. D denies that the high voltage lines could have caused X's cancer. At trial, P wishes to call W, an M.D. engaged in cancer research who holds a faculty position at a major research hospital. If permitted, W will testify that the electromagnetic fields produced by high voltage lines are capable of causing cancer.

310. Assume W's view is held by only a small minority of cancer experts. D objects to P's testimony. How should the court analyze this problem?

ANSWER:

Prosecution of D for the crime defined in the statute as "aiding and abetting in the possession of narcotics with intent to sell." D admits that the narcotics were in his car when he was arrested, but claims the drugs belonged to a passenger and that he did not intend to participate in any illegal transactions, including distribution of the drugs. At trial, the prosecution calls W, a 30-year veteran of the police force with extensive experience in investigation of narcotics offenses. Prior to trial, the prosecutor informed W of each of the facts on which she intended to offer evidence to establish D's guilt. When W takes the stand, the prosecutor first establishes W's experience in investigating narcotics offenses, and then asks W whether he has an opinion concerning D's conduct in relation to the drugs. If permitted, W will answer that in his opinion, D "aided and abetted in the passenger's possession of narcotics with the intent to sell." D objects to W's proposed testimony.

311. How should the court rule, and why?

ANSWER:

Personal injury action by P against D following an incident in which D's car struck P as P crossed the street. P claims he was in a crosswalk when D struck him. D claims P ran out from between two parked cars in the middle of the block. At trial, P calls W, who testifies that she had just emerged from a movie theater on the corner after watching "Cohasset Park" when she saw D's car strike P as he crossed the street in a crosswalk. On cross-examination, D asks W if it isn't true that she could not possibly have been emerging from a showing of "Cohasset Park" because that movie did not open until a year later. P objects to the question on the ground that it constitutes improper impeachment.

312.   How should the court rule, and why?

ANSWER:

Prosecution of D for burglary of a home. The prosecution alleges that D climbed down the chimney of the home and made off with only the owners' expensive cowboy boots. D claims she was in another state when the crime took place. At trial, the prosecution calls W to testify that the city police chief told him that on two prior occasions, D entered homes through the chimney and stole only the owners' expensive cowboy boots. D objects to this testimony as offered.

313.   How should the court rule, and why? If the court should sustain the objection, is there a way the prosecution could present the evidence of D's other burglaries without violating the rules of evidence? Explain.

ANSWER:

Negligence action by P against D arising from an intersection collision between their automobiles. P claims D ran a red light, causing the accident. At trial, P wishes to testify that a police report of the accident records a bystander's statement, taken an hour after the accident, that D ran the red light. D objects based on both the hearsay rule and the best evidence rule.

314.   How should the court rule, and why?

ANSWER:

Prosecution of D for the burglary of several homes during a serious brush fire. At trial, D calls W, who testifies that she was with D in another state at the time the fire and burglaries took place. On cross-examination, the prosecution wishes to ask W if it isn't true that seven years prior to this trial, she was convicted of filing a false federal income tax return. D objects.

315.   How should the court rule, and why?

ANSWER:

Prosecution of D for killing the neighbor's cat. At trial, the prosecution calls W, D's spouse, and wishes to have W testify that on the night of the killing, D had cat hair all over him and that when they went to bed, D told W that he'd "just taken care of that howling animal." W is willing to testify about these matters. D objects to W's testimony both about the cat hair and about what D said.

316.   How should the court rule, and why?

ANSWER:

Prosecution of D for bank robbery. D denies involvement. A few days before trial, X, an eyewitness who would have identified D as the perpetrator, suddenly left the country for a foreign destination. X refuses to return and is beyond the court's subpoena power. The prosecution calls PO, a police officer, to testify that shortly after the robbery, X told PO that she saw D rob the bank. D objects on hearsay grounds. The prosecution responds that D threatened to kill X unless X left the country.

317.   How should the court rule on D's hearsay objection, and why?

ANSWER:

Prosecution of D for fraud. The prosecution alleges that D fraudulently induced V to invest in an illegal pyramid scheme. D claims she was the victim of V's inducement, and not the other way around. To prove this, D calls W1, who testifies that V has a community reputation for dishonesty in business dealings. The prosecution wishes to call W2 to testify that D has a community reputation for business dishonesty. D objects on the ground that the prosecution's evidence constitutes an impermissible use of character evidence.

318.   How should the court rule on D's character evidence objection, and why?

ANSWER:

END OF PART II
END OF PRACTICE FINAL EXAM

ANSWERS

1. **Answer (D) is correct.** When the court sustains an objection to evidence a party wishes to offer, the party must place on the record an indication of what the evidence would have been. Sometimes a reviewing court will need to know what the evidence would have been in order to determine whether the trial court erred. And almost always, a court will have to know what the evidence would have been in order to determine whether any error "affected a substantial right of a party" (FRE 103(a)). In this case, the evidence would have consisted of a witness's oral testimony, so the lawyer should make sure the record reflects the answer the witness would have given.

   Answer (A) is incorrect because moving on to the next question would not leave any record of what the evidence would have been. This would place a reviewing court in the position of guessing, something it is unlikely to do.

   Answer (B) is incorrect because it is not necessary to make a formal "exception" to the ruling. Also, this would not indicate what the evidence would have been.

   Answer (C) is incorrect because simply by continuing with the witness's examination, the party does not waive the right to appeal. Such a rule would make no sense because it would prevent the party from offering other admissible testimony from that witness.

2. **Answer (C) is correct.** FRE 103(a)(1) requires that objections to evidence be "timely" and that they state "the specific ground of objection, if the specific ground was not apparent from the context." The facts do not indicate that the context makes clear what the ground of the objection was. Assuming that is correct, FRE 103(d) offers D the only refuge. That rule (the "plain error" rule) allows an appellate court to take notice of "plain errors affecting substantial rights although they were not brought to the attention of the court." Even so, the record will have to show clearly what the court's error was. In addition, reversal is not appropriate unless that error "affected" "a substantial right of a party" (FRE 103(a)).

   Answer (A) is incorrect because an objection at the appropriate time is not sufficient to preserve error. As noted above, the objecting party should also state the ground of the objection.

   Answer (B) is incorrect because, as explained above, it is not enough that the trial court erred. The error must also have been prejudicial (affected a substantial right of the party).

   Answer (D) is incorrect because it does not take account of the "plain error" rule.

3. **Answer (B) is correct.** FRE 103(d) sets forth the "plain error" doctrine, which permits the appellate court to take notice of "plain errors affecting substantial rights although

they were not brought to the attention of the court." FRE 404(a) categorically forbids the prosecution from offering character evidence during its case-in-chief to prove circumstantially that the defendant acted in a particular way on a specific occasion. The record clearly reflects the error. If the error affected a substantial right of D, the appellate court will reverse.

Answer (A) is incorrect because it assumes automatic reversal once error is found. Unless the error affected a substantial right of a party, the appellate court will not reverse.

Answer (C) is incorrect because FRE 404(a) is categorical; there is no rule allowing the trial court to admit prosecution character evidence in this situation, even if the evidence has substantial probative value. Thus, the error is plain.

Answer (D) is incorrect because it fails to take account of the plain error doctrine.

4. **Answer (B) is correct.** Rulings based on FRE 403 involve the exercise of discretion. Though the appellate court might be in as good a position as the trial court to determine the probative value of the evidence if it is accurate, the trial court is in a much better position than the appellate court to assess the likely prejudicial effect of the evidence. The likely effect on this particular jury, for example, is something that the appellate court cannot determine as well as the trial court. Thus, because the standard of FRE 403 requires the exercise of discretion, the appellate court will apply an "abuse of discretion" standard of review to the alleged error.

Answer (A) is incorrect because the existence of trial court discretion does not mean the appellate court has no review authority. To say that review is deferential in this type of situation is not to say the appellate court lacks authority to review.

Answer (C) is incorrect because, as explained above, the proper standard of review in this situation is "abuse of discretion."

Answer (D) is incorrect because there is no indication that the trial court applied an incorrect standard. On the contrary, the court's ruling suggests that it understood and applied the applicable standard.

5. **Answer (C) is correct.** FRE 404(a) sets up a categorical rule that does not involve the exercise of discretion. It is clear from the rule that in a murder prosecution, the prosecution may not offer evidence of the character of a person in order to prove how the person behaved on a particular occasion. The facts also demonstrate categorically that none of the exceptions stated in the rule apply. Thus, the appellate court should review the trial court's action as an error of law, sometimes referred to as "*de novo*" review.

It should be noted that not all appellate courts recognize that some evidence rules are not discretionary. It is common, for example, to see statements in appellate opinions such as, "We review alleged errors in the admission and exclusion of evidence on an abuse of discretion standard."

Answer (A) is incorrect because, as explained above, this rule does not grant the trial court discretion. Even if it did, the appellate court would still possess the authority to review.

Answer (B) is incorrect because, as explained above, "abuse of discretion" is not the proper standard of review.

Answer (D) is incorrect because the trial court's application of the wrong standard does not automatically result in reversal. The appellate court must also determine whether the error affected a substantial right of D. If the ruling did not have that effect, the error will be deemed harmless.

6. **Answer (A) is correct.** The question is unobjectionable.

   Answer (B) is incorrect because the evidence sought by the question is relevant to whether W correctly heard D's statement.

   Answer (C) is incorrect because, although the question is leading, it is permissible (and in fact desirable) to lead a witness on cross-examination.

   Answer (D) is incorrect because the question does not assume any facts not in evidence.

7. **Answer (A) is correct.** The question is unobjectionable.

   Answer (B) is incorrect because the question does not assume W was standing on the corner of First and Main; it seeks that information.

   Answer (C) is incorrect because it is permissible to lead a witness on direct examination if the witness is having difficulty remembering the facts.

   Answer (D) is incorrect because even though the question was asked, W did not answer it. In addition, the questioning party has a right to ask a question in a different way if the purpose is to help develop the witness's testimony.

8. The court should overrule the objection. A question is within the scope of the direct examination if it concerns a subject that was explicitly raised on direct examination or if the matter is implied by something that was the subject of the direct examination. P's testimony on direct examination left the impression that any impairment to P's knee resulted from the skating accident. Under the circumstances, the court should allow D to raise doubt about that matter. It would not be fair to force D to wait until it is time to present her own case, when she might recall P as a witness or otherwise present evidence correcting the impression left by P's testimony.

9. The court should overrule the objection. In addition to questions that inquire about matters explicitly or impliedly raised during direct examination, a question is considered within the scope of the direct examination if it relates to the credibility of the witness. Here, the question goes to W's credibility. If W and D were former business partners who had a falling out shortly before the crime was committed, it is possible that W would be biased against D and would therefore testify against D. D's question seeks to reveal this possible source of bias or motive.

10. **Answer (C) is correct.** If a question calls for inadmissible testimony, the opponent should always try to object before the witness has an opportunity to answer. This will

prevent the jury from hearing the inadmissible evidence, which it might find difficult to ignore even if instructed to do so. Sometimes, however, the opponent is unable to object in time. In such a case, the opponent should move to strike the witness's testimony, state the ground of the motion, and also ask the court to instruct the jury to ignore the testimony.

Answer (A) is incorrect because an objection is not timely.

Answer (B) is incorrect because it fails to mention the request for a jury instruction to ignore the testimony.

Answer (D) is incorrect because, as explained above, there is something the opponent can do. In fact, if the opponent does not make a motion to strike, there is a real possibility that the record will not be preserved for appeal.

11. D should object on the ground that this is a *compound question*. A witness is supposed to be given only one question at a time, whether on direct examination or cross-examination.

     D should also object that the second part of the question *calls for a narrative*. Particularly on direct examination it is appropriate to ask the witness to relate some information, but questions are supposed to be reasonably confined. A witness should not be asked to tell a full, unstructured story. "What happened?" is very open-ended, and the problem usually can be solved by asking questions such as "What happened next?" or "What was the first thing you saw?"

12. D should object on the ground that the answer assumes a fact not in evidence: that D's car ran the red light. W was P's first witness, and there is no suggestion that D has stipulated that she ran the red light. Thus, the question assumes, without any testimony in the record to support it, that D ran the red light. The way to cure the problem is to ask what W saw, without suggesting that W might have seen a particular thing. It might take several questions to get to the testimony that W saw D run the red light, but this is the appropriate way to elicit that testimony.

13. The court should overrule D's objection. FRE 601 removes all common law grounds of incompetency by providing that "[e]very person is competent to be a witness except as otherwise provided in these rules." There is no provision regarding the age of the prospective witness. At common law, a party was usually required to prove that the prospective witness was capable of accurate observation, recollection, and narration, and that the person understood the obligation to tell the truth while testifying. That rule is not preserved by FRE 601, which generally leaves such matters to the fact-finder as questions of weight. If a prospective witness is so clearly useless that it would be a waste of time to take the person's testimony, the court has authority under FRE 403 to refuse to permit the person to testify.

14. **Answer (A) is correct.** FRE 601 provides that "in civil actions and proceedings, with respect to an element of a claim or defense as to which state law supplies the rule of decision, the competency of a witness shall be determined in accordance with state law." Because the claim in this case is governed by state law, that state's rules of witness competency apply, and the state's dead man statute would forbid P from testifying to statements made by the deceased prior to his death.

Answer (B) is incorrect because X's statement would almost certainly constitute a declaration against interest under FRE 804(b)(3). X is unavailable and the statement is so far contrary to X's pecuniary interest that a reasonable person in X's position would not have made the statement unless believing it to be true. Thus, hearsay is not a proper ground of objection.

Answers (C) and (D) are incorrect for the reasons just given.

15. The court should overrule the objection. FRE 603 provides that "[b]efore testifying, every witness shall be required to declare that the witness will testify truthfully, by oath or affirmation administered in a form calculated to awaken the witness's conscience and impress the witness's mind with the duty to do so." This rule does not prescribe a particular form of oath or affirmation, and stresses only that the statement be of the kind that calls upon the person's conscience to be truthful. While the word "truthfully" is contained in the rule, there is no requirement that that word be included in the oath or affirmation. This question is based on *United States v. Ward*, 989 F.2d 1015 (9th Cir. 1992), in which the court held that it was error for the trial court to refuse to allow the criminal defendant to testify when she wished to substitute the words "fully integrated Honesty" for the word "truth."

16. **Answer (B) is correct.** FRE 605 provides that "[t]he judge presiding at the trial may not testify in that trial as a witness. No objection need be made in order to preserve

the point." This is a simple rule that forbids the judge from testifying, and because it applies to all cases, **answer (D) is incorrect.** By providing that no objection need be made, the rule recognizes that an objection would be useless, and might in fact cause a lawless judge to turn even more against the aggrieved party. Thus, no objection is required, and **answer (C) is incorrect.**

This does not mean, however, that the error will be reversible. FRE 103(a) states that "[e]rror may not be predicated upon a ruling which admits or excludes evidence unless a substantial right of a party is affected. . . ." Although this was not technically a *ruling* admitting the evidence, the reversible error concept would still apply. In most instances, the judge's testifying would affect a substantial right of a party because the jury is very likely to be unduly swayed by the judge's testimony. But the requirement still applies. Thus, **answer (A) is incorrect**.

17.   **Answer (A) is correct.** It is a basic principle that all evidence should be taken in the presence of the parties, and that it is improper for the jurors to investigate the facts during deliberations. At the same time, the jurors are entitled to examine the exhibits and to treat the exhibits consistently with the way they were treated at trial. In this case, neither P nor any other witness took the bike apart in open court, and when the jurors did so, they broke new ground. It would be unfair to allow them to do this without giving the parties an opportunity to meet this new evidence.

The jury's conduct in this situation therefore probably amounted to the introduction of extraneous prejudicial information. In such a case, FRE 606(b) does not forbid juror testimony (or evidence of juror statements) about what happened in the jury room.

Even if FRE 606(b) would forbid juror testimony or evidence of juror statements to impeach the verdict, that is not the source of the information in the present case. Here, the bailiff observed the jurors engaging in the experiment. FRE 606(b) does not forbid the bailiff's testimony about her own observations.

Answer (B) is incorrect because jurors may handle exhibits. They may not do truly new things with the exhibits, as explained above, but they certainly may handle them.

Answer (C) is incorrect because, as noted above, FRE 606(b) probably does not apply here. Even if it does, the rule only restricts jurors from testifying or providing affidavits (and restricts the use of juror statements for that purpose).

Answer (D) is incorrect because there is no rule forbidding the parties from interviewing jurors about their verdict. The jurors may decline to discuss the matter, but there is no rule forbidding the inquiry.

18.   **Answer (C) is correct.** FRE 606(b) forbids juror testimony about "any matter or statement occurring during the course of the jury's deliberations or to the effect of anything upon that or any other juror's mind or emotions as influencing the juror to assent or to dissent from the verdict or indictment or concerning the juror's mental process in connection therewith, except that a juror may testify on the question whether *extraneous prejudicial information was improperly brought to bear upon any juror*."

(Emphasis added.) In *Tanner v. United States*, 483 U.S. 107 (1987), the Supreme Court gave the italicized language a very narrow interpretation, holding that evidence of drunkenness, drug use and drug dealing, and jurors falling asleep were not proper subjects of juror testimony to impeach the verdict. The Court left open juror testimony that would show such activities made the jurors truly *incompetent*, but the facts given were insufficient.

For the reasons given above, **answers (A) and (B) are incorrect. Answer (D) is incorrect** because the juror's behavior, though reprehensible, is merely a statement of her own feelings, and not the result of some outside influence. Though the juror's behavior really seems to have undermined some key precepts of our system, the Court's reasoning in *Tanner* probably would not allow testimony about a juror's racial bias.

Answer (C) is correct because a possible book deal clearly amounts to an outside influence brought to bear on the jurors. Jurors are being asked to render their verdict not based on the evidence, but based on a motivation to make money. Defendant may call the juror to testify about this matter.

19. **Answer (C) is correct.** In *Rock v. Arkansas*, 483 U.S. 44 (1987), the Supreme Court held that a state may not apply against a criminal defendant a per se rule that prohibits from testifying any individuals who have been hypnotized to enhance their recollection of the events. The Court did not hold that a criminal defendant always must be permitted to testify, but only that the trial court must make a case-by-case determination of whether the person's testimony would be so unreliable as to overcome the defendant's right to testify at her own trial.

Answers (A), (B), and (D) are incorrect for the reasons just stated.

20.   The evidence is relevant. The evidence is offered to show V's action. A possible chain of reasoning:

EVIDENCE: V committed numerous acts of violence in months before killing.

→ INFERENCE: V was a violent person.

GENERALIZATION: One who commits several acts of violence is more likely a violent person than is a person chosen at random.

→ INFERENCE: V started the fight with D.

GENERALIZATION: One who has a violent character is more likely to start a fight than is a person chosen at random.

→ INFERENCE: D acted in self-defense.

GENERALIZATION: A person who kills another who has attacked her is more likely to have killed in self-defense than is one who kills a person who has not attacked her.

It does not matter that D was unaware of V's prior violent acts because D does not claim she attacked V out of fear that V was about to attack her. Instead, she claims that V started the fight. The evidence tends to show V's possible violent character, which tends to support the claim that V attacked D.

(Note that the fact that the evidence is relevant in this case does not mean it is admissible. In fact, this evidence probably violates FRE 404(a), which severely restricts the use of character evidence to prove a person's conduct on a particular occasion.)

21.   The evidence is relevant. Relevant evidence is evidence having *any* tendency to make more or less likely the truth of any proposition of consequence to the action (FRE 401). This evidence is relevant because it shows D's possible involvement in the crime. A possible chain of reasoning:

EVIDENCE: D spoke with the killer.

→ INFERENCE: D knew the killer.

GENERALIZATION: A person who speaks with another person is more likely to know that other person than is a person chosen at random.

→ INFERENCE: D knew what the killer was about to do.

GENERALIZATION: One who knows another person is more likely to know about that person's impending acts than is one chosen at random.

→ CONCLUSION: D was involved in the killing.

GENERALIZATION: One who knows about another's future acts is more likely to be involved in those acts than is a person chosen at random.

22.   The evidence is relevant. It shows D's actions, even if D's beliefs are silly. A possible chain of reasoning:

EVIDENCE: D believed in astrology, and D's horoscope for the day of the crime warned D not to do anything risky.

→ INFERENCE: D read her horoscope that day.

GENERALIZATION: One who believes in astrology is more likely to read her horoscope daily than is one chosen at random.

→ INFERENCE: D believed her horoscope.

GENERALIZATION: One who believes in astrology is more likely to believe in the truth of a horoscope's prediction than is one chosen at random.

→ CONCLUSION: D stayed home that day.

GENERALIZATION: One who believes in astrology is more likely to act consistently with her horoscope than is one chosen at random.

The horoscope need not be a valid predictor of what would happen to D if she undertakes a "risky endeavor." All that matters is that D believed the horoscope was accurate, making it somewhat more likely than it would be without the evidence that D stayed home that day and thus did not commit the crime).

(Note that the evidence here probably violates the best evidence rule (FRE 1002) because it constitutes testimony about the contents of a writing. The best evidence rule requires that the writing itself be produced to prove its contents. None of the exceptions to that rule appear to apply here.)

23.   The evidence is not relevant. D claims that the officers reasonably believed that D would act violently. The only basis for such a conclusion revealed by the facts is that P had acted violently when confronted with the police on two prior occasions. If the officers were unaware of these acts of violence, the acts could not have formed the basis of a belief that force was necessary.

24.   The answer is unclear. Whether the evidence is relevant depends on the validity of the generalization that one's unconscious thoughts bear some relation to one's actual behavior. If relevant, the reasoning would be as follows:

EVIDENCE: A few days after the murder, D told a friend that he had just dreamed that he killed V.

    $\rightarrow$ INFERENCE: D believed that he killed V.

        GENERALIZATION: One who dreams of having done something is more likely actually to have believed he acted in that way than is a person who has not had such a dream.

          $\rightarrow$ CONCLUSION: D killed V.

            GENERALIZATION: One who believes he acted in a certain way is more likely actually to have acted in that way than is one who does not harbor that belief.

(Note: If faced with a relevance challenge in this case, an interesting question is whether the court should rely on its own knowledge about the nature of dreams, or should instead insist that the party offering the evidence (here, the prosecution) call an expert witness to testify that there is a relationship between unconscious thoughts and waking action. Some judges might not feel qualified to make that judgment without the assistance of expert opinion.)

25. **Answer (C) is correct.** The evidence is relevant because if D was a housekeeper for V, D had some connection with V that might have placed D in V's home. (In more technical language, this evidence gives rise to the inference that D had *opportunity* to commit the crime.) FRE 403, however, allows the court to exclude relevant evidence *if its probative value is substantially outweighed by the danger of unfair prejudice.* Prejudice here comes from the reason D had opportunity: her status as an inmate on work release. Hearing that D was an inmate might lead the jury to punish D for her prior crimes rather than for what she might have done on this occasion. Alternatively, the jury might consider the evidence of D's inmate status for the wrong reason: that one who has committed a crime is more likely to have committed the charged crime. As we will learn, this inference is forbidden by the rules of evidence. The issue is whether, in this instance, the danger of unfair prejudice is so great as to substantially outweigh the probative value of the evidence. That is a close question. A court might find that all the jury really needs to know is that D was a housekeeper, not that she held that job as part of a prison work-release program. Answer (C) states the issue that way.

Answer (A) is incorrect because the centrality of a factual issue to a case does not *per se* mean that no evidence offered to prove that fact can be too prejudicial. The balancing must be done on a case-by-case basis.

Answer (B) is incorrect because D's status as an inmate on work-release is relevant to rebut D's defense that she was on vacation in another state at the time of the crime. It is highly unlikely that an inmate on work-release would be allowed to take such distant vacations.

Answer (D) is incorrect because the evidence is relevant.

26.   **Answer (D) is correct.** The photographs are relevant because they make it somewhat more likely than it would be without the evidence that V was retreating when shot. The court may exclude the photographs if it finds that their probative value is substantially outweighed by the danger of unfair prejudice or other dangers mentioned in FRE 403. Among those is the "needless presentation of cumulative evidence." The evidence here is cumulative in the sense that it corroborates oral testimony. But the court is unlikely to find them "needlessly cumulative" because they add something to the oral story: they *show* the jury what the witness was talking about, making it easier to understand the oral testimony. The jurors might also be able to judge whether the witness accurately described the condition of the head. There is also the risk of unfair prejudice if the jury might react emotionally rather than logically to the evidence, and the court should weigh this danger as well. On balance, the court is likely to admit the evidence.

   Answer (A) is incorrect because cumulative evidence is relevant.

   Answer (B) is incorrect because, as explained above, the probative value of the photographs might be great depending on the circumstances. On the facts given, we cannot judge them to have minimal probative value.

   Answer (C) is incorrect because the judge should not be determining the reliability of the evidence. Reliability is a matter to be determined by the trier of fact. The judge should be deciding the probative value of the evidence *if the jury decides it is reliable.*

27.   **Answer (A) is correct.** In *Old Chief v. United States*, 519 U.S. 172 (1997), the Supreme Court adopted a very narrow exception to the general principal that a party may prove her case with any otherwise admissible evidence, and may not be forced to accept a stipulation. The exception applied where the issue on which the disputed evidence would have been offered — defendant's status as a felon within the meaning of a statute — was an issue that could not benefit from any "evidentiary richness." D either was or was not a felon within the meaning of that statute, and D essentially offered to stipulate that he was. In this situation, D's offer to stipulate to his speed prior to the crash does tend to establish that he was going considerably in excess of the speed limit, but it does not demonstrate the catastrophic effect of his actions as well as the photographs.

   Answer (B) is incorrect because, as explained above, the stipulation would not give P everything that the photographs would have shown.

   Answer (C) is incorrect because, as explained above, there are very limited situations in which the general principal does not apply.

   Answer (D) is incorrect because the opposite is true: Courts usually admit gory photographs because they generally hold that their probative value is not substantially outweighed by the danger of unfair prejudice.

28.   **Answer (A) is correct.** A person's wealth is relevant to the amount of punitive damages that should be awarded because the amount of money it takes to "punish" a person

depends in part on the person's wealth. A punitive damage award of $1000 might be significant to a poor defendant, but would likely mean little to a wealthy person.

Answer (B) is incorrect because it relies on a faulty generalization: that a wealthy person is likely to be careless because she will not be concerned about the financial impact of a tort judgment. That generalization is almost certainly wrong.

Answer (C) is incorrect because wealth will not be relevant to all substantive theories of recovery. For example, punitive damages are not awardable in negligence cases, and because all persons are judged according to the same standard (reasonable care under the circumstances), the wealth of a person is irrelevant to the question of reasonable care.

Answer (D) is incorrect because, as explained above, wealth is relevant to the possible award of punitive damages in an intentional tort case.

29. Under FRE 401, evidence is relevant if it advances or impedes to *any* degree the likelihood of a fact of consequence to the case being true. This is an extremely lenient standard. Here, D wishes to show that W, perhaps because of a faulty memory, was wrong about the movie for which she was buying tickets. D wants to raise the possibility that if W was wrong about this fact, she might also have a faulty memory as to the identity of the person she saw emerging from the bank. Of course, that her memory is faulty concerning a trivial detail (the name of the movie) does not say much about whether she might have a faulty memory about something more striking, but the relevance rule is extremely easy to satisfy. If the evidence is to be excluded, it will have to be based on another rule. (As it happens, this evidence is probably admissible.)

30. The "prosecutor's fallacy" as applied here incorrectly asserts that the probability of error is only one in 500,000, which is not what the statistical evidence suggests. The statistics, if accurate, only show that one in 500,000 white men could have produced this sample. They do not distinguish who, among the small number who could have produced the sample, did in fact produce it. The prosecutor has incorrectly correlated the fact that few people could produce the sample with the probability that it was D who produced it. Finally, the prosecutor's argument encourages the jury to ignore the other evidence in the case that might shed light on D's guilt or innocence, such as an alibi, or the existence of a motive in another person.

31. The "defense counsel's fallacy" as applied here incorrectly characterizes the nature of the statistical evidence. That evidence does not imply that there is only a one in ten chance D committed the crime. At most, it suggests that only one in ten white males who live in the metropolitan area could have left the blood sample found at the scene; it says nothing about who, among those people, was responsible. For example, some of those who could have produced the sample might have been away from the city at the time the crime was committed. As to those people, there is a zero percent chance of guilt. As with the prosecutor's argument, D's argument to the jury over-emphasizes the value of the statistical evidence and encourages the jury to ignore other evidence that might shed light on whether D committed the crime.

32. **Answer (B) is correct.** The preliminary question of fact here is whether the declarant was speaking under the stress of excitement caused by the startling event or condition (the accident). The statement will not be admissible unless the declarant was in that condition. But the statement is relevant even if the declarant wasn't speaking under stress caused by the condition. (The statement is relevant because it says something about how the accident happened.) That means that this is not a situation of "conditional relevancy" governed by FRE 104(b). Instead, FRE 104(a) applies, meaning that the judge must decide whether the fact is true. The standard the judge will use is "preponderance of the evidence."

     Answer (A) is incorrect because it assumes that this is a "conditional relevancy" problem. As explained above, it is not.

     Answer (C) is incorrect because there are some facts the court must decide under FRE 104(a). Indeed, most preliminary facts are for the judge under FRE 104(a); this is the default rule that applies unless the situation involves conditional relevancy. This one does not.

     Answer (D) is incorrect because it is not necessary to identify the declarant to know whether he or she was speaking under the stress of excitement caused by the accident. That fact may be inferred from circumstantial evidence (tone of voice, facial expression, and so forth).

33. **Answer (A) is correct.** This is a question for the court under FRE 104(a) because the confession is relevant whether the police read D her *Miranda* rights or did not do so. Thus, it is not a situation of "conditional relevancy." The Supreme Court has declined to impose any higher standard for the determination of preliminary facts relevant to a constitutional question than for other situations. Thus, the proper standard is preponderance of the evidence.

     Answers (B) and (C) are incorrect because they assume a higher standard of proof applies. It does not.

     Answer (D) is incorrect because it assumes this is a situation of "conditional relevancy," which it is not. The confession is relevant even if the police did not read D her *Miranda* rights. In addition, FRE 104(c) provides that "[h]earings on the admissibility of confessions shall in all cases be conducted out of the hearing of the jury." This suggests that under the Federal Rules, admissibility of confessions is always a question for the court under FRE 104(a).

34. **Answer (A) is correct**, but only because of a specific rule (FRE 104(c)) that provides that hearings on the admissibility of confessions must always be conducted out of the

presence of the jury. That means the court must make the finding, and from the previous question, we know that the standard of proof is preponderance of the evidence. (In some states, evidentiary questions that implicate constitutional matters are always decided by the court. **Answer (A) would be correct in those states as well.**)

Note that but for FRE 104(c), this result might be contrary to the language of FRE 104(b), which gives the jury a role in preliminary fact-finding when the situation is one of conditional relevancy. Here, if D's story is true, the confession is arguably irrelevant because it says nothing about D's actual guilt. Thus, there is no harm in letting the jury decide whether D was tortured because if it finds she was, it will ignore the confession, and if it finds that she was not tortured, the jury will consider the confession. As long as there is evidence sufficient to support a finding that there was no torture (a condition necessary to admissibility), the court should leave the matter to the jury. On the other hand, how likely is it that the jury will really ignore the evidence. See the next question.

Answer (B) is incorrect for the reasons stated above. This is true even though it seems correct based on the logic of FRE 104(b).

Answer (C) is incorrect because no questions of preliminary fact are *always* for the jury. Even if a situation involves conditional relevancy, the jury will only be empowered to decide the question of preliminary fact if the court finds that there is evidence sufficient to support a finding that the preliminary fact is true.

Answer (D) is incorrect because, while *admissibility* of evidence is always for the court, some preliminary facts necessary to the *consideration* of evidence are left to the jury. Those situations are ones that fall within FRE 104(b).

35. **Answer (D) is correct.** The answer depends on the jurisdiction. The issue here is whether this is a case of "conditional relevancy" governed by FRE 104(b). The preliminary fact at issue is whether, by his action, P adopted D's statement as true. If, by giving D an angry look and taking back the skateboard, P was adopting D's statement as true, it would tend to show that D knowingly rode a defective skateboard. But who should decide that question, ultimately? There are two approaches.

Some jurisdictions hold that because the evidence (here, D's statement about the skateboard's trucks) is relevant whether or not P adopted it as true, the court must decide adoption pursuant to FRE 104(a). If the matter were left to the jury, these courts reason, the jury might find that P did not adopt the statement but consider it anyway because it tends to show that the wheel trucks were defective. Because it is not admissible for that purpose if P did not adopt the statement as true, the jury would be considering evidence it should ignore. **In these courts the correct answer would be (B).** (Arguably, this is the better approach.)

Other jurisdictions point out that P's response to D's statement (the angry expression and taking back the skateboard) would not be relevant if D was not adopting the truth of D's statement. (It wouldn't advance or impede the finding of any other proposition of consequence to the action.) For that reason, these courts would hold that this is a case of conditional relevancy. **In these courts the correct answer would be (A).**

Answer (C) is incorrect because it fails to recognize that some questions of fact are for the court under FRE 104(a).

36. The underlying problem has to do with the roles of judge and jury and the importance of maintaining the rules of evidence. Jurors properly view their primary job to be determining the truth—figuring out what happened on the relevant occasion. When a person has such a role, she is likely to consider any evidence that is relevant. She is not likely to care much whether a rule of evidence would forbid consideration of certain relevant evidence; she will not understand the reasons for the rule. Courts, on the other hand, understand the importance of evidence rules.

    Based on these roles, the judge is the only party who can be trusted to maintain the rules of evidence. If a piece of evidence will be relevant even if some preliminary question of fact is not true, letting the jury decide that preliminary question of fact is risky because the jury is likely to consider the underlying evidence even if the fact is not true.

    When the underlying evidence will not be relevant unless the preliminary fact is true, there is no real danger that the jury will consider the evidence unless that fact is true. The definition of relevant evidence under FRE 401 is not a technical one. It relies on everyday logic, and does not require legal expertise. If evidence is not relevant, a jury is as likely as a judge to know that fact.

37. **Answer (B) is correct.** FRE 602 provides that a witness may not testify to a matter "unless evidence is introduced sufficient to support a finding that the witness has personal knowledge of the matter." This standard is the same as the standard found in FRE 104(b). That is, personal knowledge is treated as a question of conditional relevance. The court need not conclude that the witness had personal knowledge; it need only find that a rational jury could conclude that the witness had personal knowledge.

    Answer (A) is incorrect because it assumes the court must make the finding of personal knowledge.

    Answer (C) is incorrect because if the court concludes that there is *not* sufficient evidence to support a finding that W had personal knowledge, the court should not allow the jury to consider the testimony.

    Answer (D) is incorrect because a motion to strike and a request that the court issue an instruction to the jury to ignore the testimony is the proper vehicle for dealing with a situation in which the witness has already testified to the facts.

38. The conditional relevancy doctrine makes a certain type of assumption about how people think. It assumes that the existence of fact in a person's mind is an on/off question. On the facts of this problem, for example, the theory assumes that the jury

will decide conclusively whether W had personal knowledge or not, and that if it decides W lacked personal knowledge, the jury will simply ignore W's testimony. That is not how people think, however. People consider unknowns along a scale from true to false, including every point between. Realistically, that is, jurors are likely to be at least somewhat uncertain about the personal knowledge question. This means they will give W's testimony *some weight* even if they believe it's more likely than not that W lacked personal knowledge of the accident.

39.   **Answer (B) is correct.** We will assume that "whacked" means killed. The statement, "The Jets whacked V" is relevant because it makes it more likely than it would be without the evidence that the Jets whacked V. This, in turn, makes it less likely that D, who is not a member of the Jets, was involved. The statement is hearsay, however. The declarant (X) made the statement other than while testifying at the trial, it asserts that the Jets killed V, and it is offered to prove that the Jets killed V. Thus, it is relevant but hearsay.

Note: A type of statement that tends to confuse students learning the hearsay rule is one which asserts one thing but *appears* to be "offered to prove" another thing. Here, the statement presumably says the Jets killed V, and the problem states that the evidence is offered to prove D did not commit the crime. This confusion can be cleared up in one of two ways, and they amount to the same thing. (1) For purposes of the hearsay rule, assume that "offered to prove" refers only to the *first inference* from the evidence. In this case, the first inference from the evidence is that the Jets killed V. Because this is the same thing as the assertion contained in the statement (the thing X, the declarant, was trying to say), the evidence is hearsay. (2) Another way to look at it is to ask whether the statement at issue *must be true* in order for it to be relevant for the stated purpose. Here, ask whether it must be true that the Jets killed V in order to be relevant to whether D killed V. The answer, of course, is yes. Thus, X's statement is hearsay.

Answer (A) is incorrect because the purpose of offering evidence is to prove facts favorable to the party offering the evidence. Being self-serving is not, therefore, a proper objection. The evidence is not a waste of time because it bears on a crucial issue and might carry high probative value.

Answer (C) is incorrect because it assumes the evidence is not hearsay when offered to prove D's innocence. Also, there is no meaningful danger of unfair prejudice. It's not *unfairly* prejudicial to the prosecution's case.

Answer (D) is incorrect because the statement is hearsay.

40.   **Answer (C) is correct.** This is a very difficult question. First, the statement, "I killed V this way and the body can be found in this place" is relevant because it makes it somewhat more likely than it would be without the evidence that X is the killer. This, in turn, increases the probably that D was not the killer. The problem is that if offered to prove that X was the killer, the statement is hearsay. It was made by X other than while testifying at the trial or hearing, it asserts that X was the killer (and that the

crime was committed in a particular way and that the body could be found in a certain place), and it is offered to prove that X was the killer. Thus, if D offers the statement on this basis, it will be relevant but hearsay.

There is another basis on which the evidence might be used, however. Note that X gave great detail about the crime just after it took place, and thus most likely before it was publicized. The crime was committed in a distinctive way—a way nobody would be likely to guess. Under these circumstances, X's very *knowledge* of the facts might be relevant in itself. The evidence, then, would be used not to prove the facts X stated are true, but to show X's knowledge of those facts. (Other evidence will be offered to prove the facts.) For this purpose, the evidence is not hearsay. The reasoning would be approximately as follows:

EVIDENCE: X described the killing in detail, indicated where the body could be found, and took responsibility for the killing.

→INFERENCE: X knew these facts.

→INFERENCE: X was at the scene of V's killing at the time of the killing and disposal of the body.

→CONCLUSION: X was involved in the killing and disposal of the body.

Some courts have approved this theory. *See, e.g.*, Bridges v. State, 19 N.W.2d 862 (Wis. 1945); United States v. Muscato, 534 F. Supp. 969 (E.D.N.Y. 1982). Students should be cautious about the theory, however. Every statement of fact is also implicitly a statement that the declarant knows the fact or believes the fact to be true. The statement, "The red car hit the blue car" is both an assertion that this happened and circumstantial evidence that the declarant knew or believed that this is what happened. If an attorney were able to assert that the statement, "The red car hit the blue car" is being offered not to prove that this is what happened, but to prove that the declarant knew or believed it to be true, the hearsay rule would be eviscerated because this argument always could be made. It is only when there is something unique about the facts, when the declarant has no other likely source of the information other than to have been present at the relevant time, and when the declarant gives a detailed description, that the theory might be used appropriately.

Answers (A), (B), and (D) are incorrect for reasons that should be clear from the preceding discussion.

41. **Answer (A) is correct.** The statement, "There is a puddle of liquid on the floor" is hearsay if offered to prove the floor was slippery. It was made by W other than while testifying at the trial. It asserts that there was a puddle of liquid on the floor. The first inference in a chain of inference leading to the floor being slippery is that there was, in fact, a puddle of liquid on the floor. Thus, the statement is "offered to prove the truth of the matter asserted." Note that it doesn't matter that W is the declarant as well as the witness testifying about the out-of-court statement. A statement is hearsay even if the person testifying about it is the person who made the statement.

The statement is not hearsay, however, if offered to prove that D had been notified about the puddle. Notice is relevant in itself because a defendant in a negligence case is more likely to be classified as being negligent if she failed to act even when notified of the danger. In other words, notice helps to prove breach of duty. The statement is not hearsay for this purpose because it is not offered to prove that there was a puddle on the floor. The mere fact that the statement was made to D is relevant, as just explained. (Of course, to prevail, P will have to prove that the floor was slippery, which means proving there was a puddle of liquid on the floor. But W's statement will not be proof of that fact because it is hearsay when offered for that purpose.)

Answer (B) is incorrect because, as explained above, the statement is hearsay when offered to prove the floor was slippery even though W didn't say that it was. The first inference is that there was a puddle of liquid, and that inference must be true for the evidence to prove that the floor was slippery. In addition, as explained above, the statement is not hearsay if offered to prove D knew the floor was slippery.

Answers (C) and (D) are incorrect for the reasons explained above.

42. **Answer (B) is correct.** The assertion-based definition of hearsay, which is embodied in FRE 801(c), classifies as hearsay only those statements that assert the matter they are offered to prove. The statement, "You are the scum of the Earth" is not offered to prove that D is the "scum of the Earth." Instead, it is circumstantial evidence that V believed D was the burglar. Because it does not assert that D was the burglar (that is, one must infer that V believed this to be true), it is not hearsay. We would classify the statement as circumstantial evidence of V's state of mind, and not hearsay.

Under a declarant-based definition of hearsay, a statement is hearsay if its value depends on the credibility of the declarant. "Credibility" in this context, means the declarant's perceptions, sincerity, memory, and ambiguity (whether we correctly understand what the declarant was trying to say). In this situation, it is difficult to judge V's sincerity at the time she made the statement. Was V trying to frame D for the crime, for example? Because the declarant-based definition does not require that a statement assert the matter it is offered to prove in order to be classified as hearsay, any situation that leaves meaningful doubt about the declarant's credibility at the time the statement was made might be classified as hearsay.

Thus, the statement is more likely to be classified as hearsay under a declarant-based definition of hearsay than under an assertion-based definition of hearsay. Though we cannot be certain of the outcome, a hearsay objection would have a greater chance of being sustained under a declarant-based definition.

Note that the Federal Rules and virtually every state code use the language of an assertion-based definition of hearsay.

Answers (A) and (C) are incorrect for the reasons given. **Answer (D) is incorrect** because the problem provides sufficient information to answer the hearsay question.

43. The statement, "V is planning to kill you the next time she sees you" is hearsay if offered to prove that V attacked D. That is because the statement was made by V other than while testifying at the trial, it asserts that she was going to kill (attack) D, and it is offered to prove that she did so. The statement is also relevant to show D's fear, however. A valid self-defense claim can exist when one acts out of reasonable fear of imminent attack by the other person. If D heard X's statement, D might reasonably have feared V, and this would justify D's striking V. For that purpose (to prove D believed V was going to attack her), the statement is not hearsay.

44. **Answer (C) is correct.** Assume X's statement to D was, "P supports neo-Nazi organizations." That statement is relevant both to prove that P in fact supported such organizations and to show that D had a good-faith belief that P did so. If offered to prove that P really does support such organizations, the statement is hearsay because it was made by X other than while testifying at the trial and it would be offered to prove the truth of the matter asserted. If offered to prove D's good faith basis for publishing the story, however, the statement is not hearsay. That is because the statement need not be true for it to serve as the basis for good faith. D need only have believed it to be true.

Answers (A) and (B) are incorrect for the reasons just given.

Answer (D) is incorrect because the problem provides sufficient information to answer the hearsay question.

45. **Answer (B) is correct.** Though it might not appear so at first glance, reputation can be hearsay. Consider what "reputation" means: it is what people are saying about another person or group. It is, therefore, a sort of group statement. Because it is being made out of court, it is hearsay if offered to prove the truth of what it asserts. Thus, in this case, the community's statement would be, "V is violent." (Note that the statement is an assertion that V is violent. The statement is *not* that V has a reputation for violence.) That statement is relevant to prove that V attacked first because a person who is violent is more likely to be the first aggressor in a fight than is one who is not violent. However, if the statement is offered to prove that V attacked first, it is hearsay.

Suppose, however, that D claims she attacked V first because she reasonably feared that V would attack her imminently. This is also a self-defense claim, albeit based on a somewhat different view of the facts. If this is D's defense, however, the evidence of V's reputation for violence would be irrelevant because D did not know V's reputation at the time of the altercation. Thus, V's reputation could not have served as the basis of a reasonable fear of V.

The result is that the evidence is irrelevant if offered to prove D acted out of a reasonable fear of V, and relevant, but hearsay, if offered to prove that D was the first aggressor.

Answers (A), (C), and (D) are incorrect for the reasons given.

46. P's statement is hearsay. P's statement was made other than while testifying at the trial, it is an assertion that she accepted D's offer, and it is offered to prove that P did so. P's statement does not constitute words of independent legal significance because it is a *statement about* the acceptance of D's offer. It is not the acceptance itself. That occurred prior to the time P made the statement to W, and P is only reporting to W about that event.

47. **Answer (A) is correct.** As discussed in connection with a previous question, a declarant-based definition of hearsay would be likely to classify as hearsay a statement the value of which depends on the credibility of the declarant. Here, if the testator was being insincere, she might have wanted to create the impression that she was insane. One way to do that might be to say something that made no sense. (Other testimonial infirmities, such as problems with the declarant's perceptions, might also be present.) Under the declarant-based definition, therefore, the testator's statement might be classified as hearsay.

    The statement would not be hearsay under the assertion-based definition, however. The testator has given an order or made a request here; she has not made an assertion of fact. The statement is relevant not because of what it says, but because of what it *implies* about the testator's sanity. We would call this "circumstantial evidence of the declarant's state of mind" and classify it as non-hearsay.

    Answers (B), (C), and (D) are incorrect for the reasons given.

48. The testimony of a witness that D spoke the words would not be hearsay. Even though the witness will be repeating D's out-of-court utterance, the utterance would constitute words of independent legal significance (what some would call a "verbal act"). The utterance, in other words, is not offered as proof of some fact; the utterance is the fact itself that is being proved.

    The newspaper review would be hearsay, however. It is an assertion (by the writer of the article) that D uttered the words. This assertion is not being made while the writer of the article is testifying at the trial. It is being made in an out-of-court context (the newspaper review).

For the following questions, indicate whether each item is hearsay for the purpose for which it is offered, and explain your answer. Apply the Federal Rules of Evidence. If something would not be hearsay under the Federal Rules, call it non-hearsay. Also, do not assume that a declarant is a party unless the facts indicate such.

49. **Hearsay.** There are two statements here. P is saying, "I own the lot." That statement is not hearsay because it constitutes words of independent legal significance. (It is the *act* of open and notorious possession, an element of adverse possession.) X's statement is, "P is saying she owns the lot." That statement is hearsay because it is an out-of-court assertion that P is making the statement, offered to prove that P is making the statement.

50. **Not hearsay.** The community statement (reputation) is, "P is a brilliant corporate leader." That statement is not being offered to prove the truth, but just to show that P enjoyed a great reputation before D's alleged slander.

51. **Not hearsay.** The dispatcher's statement, "P is armed" is not being offered to prove that P was armed, but to show that D had reason to think P was armed. This would help form the basis of a claim that D acted reasonably in shooting P.

52. **Hearsay.** The statement here is not "Observe!" but X's act of jumping up and down and shaking the bridge. This was assertive conduct. X's purpose was to communicate that the bridge was safe; that was the reason X performed the act. This assertive act is offered to prove that the bridge was safe, and so it is hearsay.

53. **Not hearsay.** D's statement, offered by P, is an admission under FRE 801(d)(2)(A). All statements that fit into FRE 801(d) are classified as non-hearsay even if offered to prove the truth of the matter asserted. It really is that simple; a statement of a party offered against the party is not hearsay. In this example, the statement is against the party's interest, but it need not be. If D had said, "You cut me off, dude," and P for some reason wanted to offer that statement into evidence to prove the truth of the matter asserted, it would still qualify as an admission. (Keep this in mind; the term "admission" in the law of evidence does *not* mean that the declarant is admitting any sort of fault.)

54. **Not hearsay.** W's statement was the assertive conduct of pointing to D in response to the prosecutor's question. Thus, it is equivalent to the statement, "D killed V." However, W made the statement while testifying at the trial. Therefore, it is not hearsay.

55. **Not hearsay.** The people at the beach were not trying to *assert* that it was sunny. They were simply acting on the belief that it was sunny. (That is what makes their conduct relevant.) Because there is no assertion, the statement is not hearsay. This example fits into the category of "non-assertive conduct."

56. **Hearsay.** The forecaster's statement, understood in context, was an assertion that it was raining. Generally, orders or requests are not hearsay because they do not contain an intended assertion of fact. This one does. If offered to prove that it was raining, the statement is hearsay.

57. **Hearsay.** P's statement is not part of the contract, but is an assertion that there was a contract. The statement is hearsay to prove there was a contract. Note that this is not an admission because P is offering her own statement, not her opponent's statement.

58. **Not hearsay.** The physician's conduct is non-assertive. She was not trying to *say* she was afraid of contracting AIDS from X; she was merely acting consistently with such a belief. Thus, the conduct is relevant, but not hearsay.

59. **Hearsay.** D's statement that X is "my favorite person in the whole world" is an assertion that D likes X. The statement is offered to prove that fact, so it is hearsay.

60. **Not hearsay.** Though it is true that the only way W would know that X is her mother is that someone told her, W's testimony does not repeat the out-of-court statement. If W had testified, "Someone told me X is my mom," that would have been hearsay. (If there is any objection to W's testimony here, it might be that W lacks personal knowledge. But even that objection is fairly weak; in virtually any circumstance, the opponent would feel silly objecting.)

61. **Not hearsay.** To be a "statement" within the definition of that term in FRE 801(a), the conduct must be that of a person. The issue here is one of relevance and probative value, not hearsay.

62. **Hearsay.** Professor Wigmore was asserting that the time was 5:10. The statement is offered to prove that it was 5:10.

63. **Hearsay.** The owner's statement would only be relevant if by claiming to be the "king," he meant that he was a sales leader. If that is the case, the statement is hearsay.

64. **Hearsay.** Whoever commissioned the tombstone wished to assert that Elvis is dead. Therefore, the writing on the tombstone is an out-of-court statement. When offered to prove Elvis is dead, it is hearsay.

65. **Hearsay.** P's out-of-court statement was an assertion that the car that, as other evidence will show, was driven by D, hit P's car. It is hearsay when offered to prove that fact. Note that it doesn't matter that P is testifying about her own statement; it is still hearsay.

66. **Not hearsay.** W's prior statement impeaches W's credibility by showing that W spoke inconsistently about the same event. This makes W a less reliable witness than she would be without the inconsistency. Used in this way, the statement is not offered to prove the truth of the matter asserted; it is not offered to prove that P had the green light. Thus, it is not hearsay. (No doubt D will seek a limiting instruction under FRE 105, informing the jury that it may consider the evidence only to impeach W, and not to prove that P had the green light.)

67. **Not hearsay.** The automated message is not treated as a "statement" for purposes of the hearsay rule because no person was present and making an assertion at the time. As with the conduct of animals, admissibility of things done by mechanical devices is analyzed as a question of relevance and probative value, not one of hearsay.

68. **Not hearsay.** As the facts are stated, P does not appear to have been *asserting* her emotional distress; she was merely reacting to it. Without an assertion, there can be no hearsay.

69. **Not hearsay.** This utterance is the slander itself. It is not evidence of the slander. Thus, it constitutes words of independent legal significance. (Consider what would happen if the hearsay rule barred this evidence. How would plaintiff in a slander case ever

prove that defendant uttered the slander? The law of evidence would be "trumping" the tort law that establishes a cause of action for slander.)

70. **Not hearsay.** This is D's statement, offered by the prosecution. It is therefore an admission, classified as non-hearsay under FRE 801(d)(2)(A).

71. **Hearsay.** The bystander's act of pointing in response to W's question appears to have been an assertion that D was the responsible party. It was made other than while testifying at the trial, and it is offered to prove the truth of the matter asserted. It is therefore hearsay. Note that the bystander's pointing action apparently amounted to the identification of a person made after perceiving the person. Had the bystander testified at the trial, her conduct therefore might have qualified under FRE 801(d)(1)(C). But because the bystander was not a witness at trial, the rule's requirements are not satisfied and the conduct is hearsay.

72. **Hearsay.** The out-of-court statement was, essentially, "P was once convicted of embezzlement." D's defense is that it fired P because P had been convicted of a crime involving dishonesty, and embezzlement is such a crime. Therefore, the statement at issue is being offered to prove the truth of the matter asserted.

73. **Not hearsay.** The deceased's statement is relevant because it *suggests, circumstantially*, that she did not like P. If that is true, it is more likely that she left the deceased out of her will intentionally. Because she did not directly assert that she disliked P, the statement is not hearsay. (Note that if the deceased had said, "I don't like P," the statement would be hearsay. One might reasonably ask at this point whether the law of evidence makes any sense at all. Does admissibility here really depend on the exact words the decedent just happened to utter? Actually, and happily, the answer is no. As worded in the problem, the statement is not hearsay because it is circumstantial evidence of the declarant's state of mind. Thus, it is admissible. If the decedent had said, "I don't like P," the statement would be hearsay, but it would be admissible under FRE 803(3), an exception for statements of the declarant's then-existing state of mind. In both cases, then, the statement is admissible.)

74. **Not hearsay.** The other driver's act of moving forward is relevant because it makes it more likely that the driver was reacting to a green light. But the act is not hearsay because there is no indication that the driver was moving forward to *assert* that the light was green. There is a difference between acting to assert a fact, and acting *because* of that fact. The former is hearsay. Under modern evidence law, the latter (which we call non-assertive conduct) is not hearsay. (Note that at common law, non-assertive conduct was more likely to be excluded as hearsay because its value depends on the credibility of the actor.)

75. **Not hearsay.** P's statement to D was not an assertion that a contract existed, but constituted the acceptance of an offer, which is part of the act of making the contract. Thus, it constituted words of independent legal significance, and is not hearsay.

76. **Not hearsay.** A fish cannot be a declarant. The conduct of the fish is either relevant or not relevant, but it is not hearsay.

77. **Not hearsay.** This statement is being offered to show its effect on the listener (D). What matters is not whether the statement is true, but whether D believed it to be true. If D held that belief, there is a possible basis for her claim of provocation. Because the statement is relevant even if not true, it is not hearsay.

78. **Not hearsay.** The pilot's behavior is relevant because it suggests that she believed the plane to be airworthy. (If she did not believe the plane was safe, it is unlikely she should have gone aboard and flown off.) Because the pilot did not inspect and board the plane in order to *assert* that it was airworthy, her conduct is not hearsay. It falls into the category of non-assertive conduct. (Note that at common law, this conduct probably would have been classified as hearsay because its relevance and probative value depend in part on the credibility of the pilot. Perception might be a particularly important issue. If, for example, the pilot did not do a good job of inspecting the plane, her act of boarding would carry little weight as to the plane's safety.)

79. **Not hearsay.** This is an example of a statement offered to show the effect on the listener, and not to prove the truth of the matter asserted. If D's president believed the story about P was true, it is far more likely she acted in good faith in firing P than if she did not believe the story.

80. **Hearsay.** The declarant in this example is the friend. The friend asserted that it was "12:00 sharp." The statement is being offered to prove that it was in fact 12:00 at that time. Thus, the statement is hearsay. (Note that if the friend had been the witness, and had testified that the killing occurred at 12:00, her testimony that she knew it was 12:00 because she looked at her watch would not be hearsay. In that situation, there would be no declarant because the watch would not be a declarant.)

81. **Hearsay.** The declarant in this case is the writer of the newspaper article. The writer asserted that the temperature had hit a high of 112 degrees. That statement is hearsay because its value depends on its being true. (Some students might respond that the statement might be relevant even if it was not accurate. That is, D is not using the statement to prove that the temperature had hit 112 degrees, but only to show that it was "unbearably hot" that day. This is incorrect. The law treats the chain of inferences leading from the statement as beginning with the truth of the statement.)

82. **Not hearsay.** The statement is being offered as circumstantial evidence of the professor's state of mind. The statement suggests that the declarant is insane because a sane person is less likely to make such a claim than an insane person. Thus, the statement is not being offered to prove that the professor is in fact the "king of the Federal Rules."

83. **Hearsay.** The declarant is the husband. His assertion was that the rooster was crowing and that it was time to get up. For this statement to be relevant to whether it was about dawn, the statement must be true. Note that the rooster is not a declarant.

84. **Hearsay.** The death certificate is an assertion that a person is dead. The declarant is the person who filled out the certificate. Because it is offered to prove that X is dead, the death certificate is hearsay. (The death certificate does not constitute words of independent legal significance. It is true that there are legal consequences to the death certificate. But that document did not kill X; X would be dead whether or not a death certificate existed. The death certificate is only evidence that X is dead. Of course, in some circumstances, the law treats a death certificate as particularly persuasive, or even conclusive, evidence of the person's death. But even in those situations, the death certificate is evidence of the fact.)

85. **Hearsay.** It is important to identify the declarant in this situation. It is not A's president or B's president (though they uttered words). It is X. X has made an out-of-court statement that A's president and B's president uttered these words. For testimony concerning X's statement to be relevant, it must be true. Therefore, it is hearsay. (This is not a hearsay within hearsay case. The words spoken by A's president and B's president are words of independent legal significance, and thus not hearsay.)

86. **Not hearsay.** The execution of the deed is part of the act of conveying the property. The deed therefore constitutes words of independent legal significance. (It is like a written contract in that sense.) Therefore, it is not hearsay.

87. **Hearsay.** Usually, a question is not an assertion and is therefore not hearsay. In this case, however, the question does contain an assertion, which is that X has blond hair. Because it was made out of court, and is offered to prove that X is a blond, the statement is hearsay.

88. **Not hearsay.** Absent evidence to the contrary, it appears that P was not asserting that she was in pain; she was merely reacting to the pain. The conduct is therefore non-assertive conduct, which we classify as non-hearsay. (If P had said, "My leg hurts," there would be an assertion, and it would be hearsay if offered to prove P was in pain.)

89. **Not hearsay.** X's statement to D is not offered to prove that the notes were bogus, but to prove D's knowledge of that fact. This is therefore an example of a statement offered to prove its effect on the listener. (D will almost certainly ask for a limiting instruction under FRE 105 instructing the jury to consider the evidence only to show D's knowledge, and not to prove the notes were counterfeit.)

90. **Hearsay.** X's confession is an out-of-court statement offered to prove the truth of the matter asserted (that X is guilty). This statement, in turn, is relevant because it makes D's guilt less probable. The statement is therefore hearsay on the question of D's innocence even though X did not assert D's innocence.

91. **Hearsay.** D is the declarant. Her assertion that "The Shrimptons is my favorite television program" is relevant only if true. The reasoning is that if the show is D's favorite, it is more likely D was home at 8:00 that night than if the show was not D's favorite.

92. **Not hearsay.** D's statement is a party admission under FRE 801(d)(2)(A). Even though it is an out-of-court statement offered in evidence to prove the truth of the matter asserted, it is classified as non-hearsay under the Federal Rules.

93. **Not hearsay.** This is non-assertive conduct. P was not playing catch using that arm to assert that the arm was uninjured. The evidence is relevant, however, because it tends to make it more likely that P did not suffer an injury than if P was not engaging in this activity.

94. **Not hearsay.** X was not testifying as a witness when she made the statement. As a result, the statement is not being "offered" by any party. It is merely an unfortunate event that the people in the courtroom, including the jurors, have witnessed. The court should instruct the jury to ignore the event, or, if the danger of unfair prejudice is too great, declare a mistrial.

95. **Hearsay.** The teacher's assertion that Y did "excellent work" is only relevant to Y's knowledge if it is true. It is therefore hearsay.

96. **Not hearsay.** This statement would be classified as circumstantial evidence of the declarant's state of mind. A person who calls another person "stupid" is less likely to like the other person than is one who makes a more flattering statement about that individual. Because the statement that Y is stupid is not an assertion that X does not like Y, it is not hearsay.

97. **Not hearsay.** The officials were not placing X's body into the van to assert that X was dead. They were doing so *because* X was dead (or perhaps because they believed X was dead). This is therefore an example of non-assertive conduct, which we classify as non-hearsay.

98. **Not hearsay.** The manager's utterance constitutes words of independent legal significance. Making that statement to P is one of the acts of sexual harassment. (This is a better answer than classifying the utterance as non-hearsay because it is not offered to prove the truth of the matter asserted. The utterance is not a statement for purposes of the hearsay rule, so we never reach the question of whether it is offered to prove the truth of the matter asserted.)

99. **Hearsay.** This is a direct statement of X's state of mind. It must be true to be relevant on the question of whether X likes Y. The first inference from the statement is that X does hope Y will go out with her, and the next inference is that X likes Y.

100. **Hearsay.** Under the circumstances, the act of raising one thumb is an assertion that the prototype automobile was working well. If it was not, the act is probably irrelevant. Because this was assertive conduct, and because the assertive conduct is offered to prove the matter asserted, it is hearsay.

101. **Answer (D) is correct.** W's question to V is not an assertion, so is not hearsay. But V's pointing action probably amounts to a statement that the crime was committed at D's house. It is hearsay because it is being offered to prove that the crime happened at D's house, which, in turn, makes it more likely that D committed the crime. (There is no other relevant purpose for the evidence.) This is a homicide prosecution, V is unavailable, and the statement concerns the cause or circumstances of death. If the judge finds that V believed he was about to die, V's statement will be admissible as a dying declaration.

     Answer (A) is incorrect because it assumes no exception applies. **Answer (B) is incorrect** because it assumes V's pointing is not a statement. **Answer (C) is incorrect** because the concept of "adoption" deals with admissions, and V is not a party.

102. **Answer (B) is correct.** Either X was asserting the direction from which the shots were fired, or X's pointing is irrelevant. If X was asserting the direction from which the shots were fired, X would be making a hearsay statement because the only relevant purpose would be to prove the truth of the matter asserted. However, it would likely be admissible as a present sense impression under the circumstances. Because it would be irrelevant if not an assertion of the direction from which the shots came, and would be admissible if it was such an assertion, there is no danger in allowing the jury to decide whether it was an assertion (as long as there is evidence sufficient to support that conclusion).

     Answer (A) is incorrect because it assumes the judge should make all preliminary factual findings here. **Answer (C) is incorrect** because it assumes the statement could only be admissible as an excited utterance. That's possible if more facts could be shown, but the present sense impression exception seems more applicable here. **Answer (D) is incorrect** because it assumes no hearsay exception would apply.

103. **Answer (C) is correct.** X's statement is analytically hearsay because it asserts that P did the work, and P is offering it to prove that it did. But the statement would be an admission if X was authorized to speak for D, which is most likely the case.

     Answer (A) is incorrect because the making of the statement is not part of the contract itself, but just circumstantial evidence that a contract had been entered into. **Answer (B) is incorrect** because it assumes the statement isn't hearsay, but the first inference is that P did the work, from which one can infer that D hired P to do so. The first inference is one of the things asserted in the statement. **Answer (D) is incorrect** because there is little indication in the facts that D employed X to work with polling information.

104.   **Answer (D) is correct.** The judge makes preliminary findings under FRE 801(d)(2)(E) because the statement is still relevant even if the preliminary facts are not present. The statement which is at issue can be used as part of the foundation for its own admissibility. (This is what the Supreme Court held in *Bourjaily v. United States*, 483 U.S. 171 (1987).)

   Answer (A) is incorrect because it assumes the preliminary facts are for the jury. **Answer (B) is incorrect** because preliminary fact questions decided by the court are decided on a preponderance standard. **Answer (C) is incorrect** because the Supreme Court held in *Bourjaily* that the "bootstrapping" rule did not survive the adoption of the Federal Rules.

105.   In *Bourjaily*, the Supreme Court explicitly reserved this question. However, Congress amended FRE 801(d)(2) in 1997 to add the following sentence: "The contents of the statement shall be considered but are not alone sufficient to establish the declarant's authority under subdivision (C), the agency or employment relationship and scope thereof under subdivision (D), or the existence of the conspiracy and the participation therein of the declarant and the party against whom the statement is offered under subdivision (E)." The effect of that amendment is to render the statement alone insufficient to establish the existence of the conspiracy. The court would not be acting properly if it allows the case to go to the jury.

106.   **Answer (D) is correct.** The prosecution's strongest argument would be to employ the theory used in cases such as *Bridges v. State*, 19 N.W.2d 529 (Wis. 1945) and *United States v. Muscato*, 534 F.2d 959 (E.D.N.Y. 1982) that the statements are admissible as non-hearsay to show knowledge of a fact that will be proven with other evidence. V is unlikely to have been shown the van at any time other than when he was assaulted. The description is quite detailed and the interior of the van rather unusual (I hope). V testifies, so V can be cross-examined about the statement.

   Answer (A) is incorrect because mere trustworthiness does not render a hearsay statement admissible. **Answer (B) is incorrect** because the statement was not made while observing the van or immediately thereafter. **Answer (C) is incorrect** because V is not unavailable.

107.   **Answer (C) is correct.** FRE 602 makes the existence of personal knowledge a fact to be determined under the same standard set forth in FRE 104(b). Preliminary facts for admissibility of excited utterances are decided by the court under FRE 104(a) because the statement would be relevant whether or not the preliminary facts are true.

   Answers (A) and (B) are incorrect because they assume the wrong allocation of responsibility between judge and jury on personal knowledge. In addition, answer (B) assumes the incorrect standard to be applied to the finding. **Answer (D) is incorrect** because it assumes the wrong allocation of responsibility for excited utterances.

108.   **Answer (B) is correct.** This appears to be a direct statement of D's then-existing state of mind, which would be relevant to show that he acted in accordance with the

statement. Thus, it is an application of the *Hillmon* doctrine (derived from *Mutual Life Ins. Co. of New York v. Hillmon*, 145 U.S. 285 (1892)). The Federal Rules have adopted the *Hillmon* concept.

Answer (A) is probably incorrect because the statement appears to state directly his feelings or intentions ("I think I'll go."). **Answer (C) is incorrect** because the statement only relates to the declarant's future intentions. **Answer (D) is incorrect** because it assumes the statement is not relevant. Note: The statement is not admissible as an admission because D was offering his own statement; it was not being offered against D.

109. **Answer (D) is correct.** The prosecution's strongest argument is that the Federal Rules have adopted a broad interpretation of the *Hillmon* rule, which would allow a statement that implicates the conduct of a third person. The cases are split on this question.

    Answer (A) is incorrect because the statement is hearsay, and the only relevant purpose is to prove the truth of what it asserts. **Answer (B) is incorrect** because it was not made in furtherance of a conspiracy (X mumbled the words to himself). **Answer (C) is incorrect** because there is no indication X is unavailable. The prosecution knows where he is and can bring him in for the trial.

110. **Answer (B) is correct.** D's strongest argument against admissibility would attack the validity of too broad a reading of the *Hillmon* rule. That attack should be made on the basis that the policies behind the hearsay rule would be violated by admission.

    Answer (A) is incorrect because a statement that satisfies a firmly rooted hearsay exception (and state of mind probably qualifies) will normally satisfy the Confrontation Clause. **Answer (C) is incorrect** because the burden under FRE 403 is very heavily weighted against exclusion, and the prejudice here doesn't seem terribly great. **Answer (D) is incorrect** because the statement did seem to be a direct statement of state of mind.

111. **Answer (B) is correct.** The statement is hearsay and relevant to show who did it. Because it is against X's penal interests, and X is now unavailable, it can be admitted as a declaration against interest.

    Answer (A) is incorrect because X is not a party. **Answer (C) is incorrect** because the statement did not concern the cause or circumstances of impending death, and there is no indication X believed he was about to die when he made the statement. **Answer (D) is incorrect** because the evidence is relevant.

112. **Answer (A) is correct.** V testified at the trial or hearing. Under *United States v. Owens*, 484 U.S. 554 (1988), he would be "subject to cross examination concerning the statement." (The facts here are very similar to those in *Owens*.) The statement was one of identification of a person made after perceiving the person. Under the rule, it doesn't matter that PO is the one who actually testifies about who V identified.

Answer (B) is incorrect under the rule in *Owens*. **Answer (C) is incorrect** because PO need not have personal knowledge of the correctness of the identification, only of who V identified. **Answer (D) is incorrect** because there was sufficient evidence to support a finding that V had personal knowledge. The standard under FRE 602 is very easy to satisfy.

113. **Answer (C) is correct.** W's notes impliedly indicate that P said these things, and this is what the notes are offered to prove. (They are not offered to prove the truth of what he said about quantum theory.) Thus, the notes are hearsay. But because W states that the notes were taken during the class, that they accurately reflect what was said, that she no longer remembers what was said, the notes can be read to the jury under the doctrine of past recollection recorded.

Answer (A) is incorrect because it misconstrues the purpose for which the notes are offered. **Answer (B) is incorrect** because there is no requirement that W had a "legal duty" to record accurately. **Answer (D) is incorrect** because the attorney is not using the notes merely to refresh W's recollection.

114. **Answer (D) is correct.** The statement is hearsay because it is offered to prove the truth of what it asserts (that P suffered certain injuries). Facts are given that would justify its admission under exceptions for excited utterances, present sense impressions, statements of then existing physical condition, and statements for purposes of medical diagnosis or treatment.

Answer (A) is incorrect because it is not an admission. P is offering her own statement. **Answers (B) and (C) are incorrect** because they are not as complete as answer (D).

115. **Answer (C) is correct.** The prosecution's best response would be to argue that the preliminary fact of whether D heard the accusation should be decided by the jury under FRE 104(b)—that this is a case of "conditional relevancy." That argument would be fairly strong here because W's statement to D is independently admissible as a non-hearsay prior identification under FRE 801(d)(1)(C). Thus, there is little danger in allowing the jury to decide the preliminary fact of whether D heard the accusation; even if he did not, the accusation is admissible independently.

Answer (A) is incorrect because the facts do not indicate that W was speaking under the stress of excitement caused by a startling event. Also, the prosecution would be better off with an argument that the jury should decide the preliminary fact. That way, the jury would be more likely to hear the evidence. **Answer (B) is incorrect** for the same reason. **Answer (D) is incorrect** because the preliminary facts for prior identifications are for the court under FRE 104(a).

116. **Answer (D) is correct.** This is a typical case of former testimony. D's motive to cross-examine W now would be the same as at the civil trial (to shake W's story). D had the opportunity to conduct that cross-examination at the civil trial (and in fact did so, though the rule does not seem to require that he did). W is now unavailable.

Answer (A) is incorrect because the courts do not generally view the different stakes in criminal cases and civil cases as sufficient to make the motive different under this rule. **Answer (B) is incorrect** because it doesn't matter which trial came first as long as the rule's other requirements are met. **Answer (C) is incorrect** because D did have an opportunity to confront W, and in fact had that chance when W was under oath and subject to the penalty for perjury.

117.   **Answer (B) is correct.** The former testimony exception does not apply because X, a criminal defendant, *never* had the opportunity to confront W, and the "predecessor in interest" language of the former testimony exception does not apply to this situation (see the rule). **Answer (A) is incorrect** because the facts do not indicate that her motive would be different from the motive D had in the civil trial. **Answer (C) is incorrect** because the "predecessor in interest" language of the rule does not apply here. **Answer (D) is silly.** Evidence admissible against one party is not necessarily admissible against another party.

118.   **Answer (A) is correct.** X is unavailable even though she is on the stand. (See FRE 804(a).) The statement is against X's interest in that it might subject her to civil liability.

    Answer (B) is incorrect because X is not a party. **Answer (C) is incorrect** because the facts do not support the foundation for excited utterances. **Answer (D) is incorrect** because it wrongly assumes X is not unavailable.

119.   **Answer (D) is correct.** The problem states that X's statement is offered to prove D knew the substance was cocaine. Because it is not offered to prove the truth of the matter asserted by X (that this was cocaine), the statement is not hearsay. **Answers (A), (B), and (C) are incorrect** for the reasons given.

120.   **Answer (A) is correct.** Because X is not a party defendant, her statement cannot be an admission under FRE 801(d)(2)(A). The statement might be an admission of X's employer D under FRE 801(d)(2)(D). To qualify, three requirements must be met: (1) the statement must have been made by the party's agent; (2) it must concern a matter within the scope of the agent's employment; and (3) it must have been made while the agent was employed.

    Requirements (1) and (3) are easily satisfied here. X worked for D as service manager. That almost certainly makes X an agent of D. The problem also makes clear that at the time X spoke to P, X was working as the service manager. Thus, the statement was made during the course of X's employment.

    The real issue here is whether the statement concerned a matter within the scope of X's agency. To answer this, one would need to know something about the nature of X's job. As service manager, X probably was required to diagnose problems with vehicles brought to the dealership, but we can't really be sure of this without more information.

    That raises the second big question in this problem: Whose responsibility is it to decide whether the statement concerned a matter within the scope of X's employment? Under

FRE 104, most preliminary questions of fact are to be decided by the court (and the standard is preponderance of the evidence). However, if the relevance of the evidence depends on whether a condition of fact is satisfied (FRE 104(b)), the court's job is only to determine whether there is evidence sufficient to support a finding that the condition is satisfied. Here, the question would be as follows: Is X's statement relevant even if X's job did not include diagnosing problems with vehicles? The answer is yes. The statement, "the car's steering mechanism was not put together properly," is relevant even if X's job did not include diagnosis of the problems with cars brought to the dealership. The consequence is that this is *not* a problem that fits into FRE 104(b). That, in turn, means that the court must decide the preliminary fact question under FRE 104(a). **Answer (B) is incorrect** for this reason.

Note that under FRE 801(d)(2)(D), there is no requirement that the declarant be *authorized* to make the statement. This is a departure from the common law in many states, which did not recognize vicarious admissions unless the declarant was authorized to speak for the other person. The drafters of the Federal Rules decided that agency, scope of employment, and the making of the statement during the employment were sufficient in themselves to support admission of the evidence. The drafters created a second exemption, for authorized admissions. That exemption can be found in FRE 801(d)(2)(C).

Answer (C) is incorrect because courts tend not to apply the personal knowledge requirement to admissions. **Answer (D) is incorrect** because the statement is not hearsay if it is an admission under FRE 801(d).

121. **Answer (C) is correct.** X's statement essentially asserts that D did not commit the crimes. The statement is relevant because it increases the probability of D's innocence, so **answer (A) is incorrect.** X does not lack personal knowledge because she claims to know first-hand that D could not have committed the crimes, so **answer (B) is incorrect.** The statement is hearsay, however. Even if X was authorized to speak for D, the statement cannot qualify as an authorized admission under FRE 801(d)(2)(C) because the statement is being offered *by, not against* D.

Because the statement is inadmissible hearsay, there is no need to consider the application of FRE 403. That rule applies only to exclude otherwise admissible evidence. This evidence is inadmissible. Thus, **answer (D) is incorrect.**

122. **Answer (B) is correct.** This problem raises the question of how FRE 801(d)(2)(E), the co-conspirator rule, should be applied. There are several preliminary facts which must be found before a statement qualifies as a co-conspirator statement: (1) there must be a conspiracy; (2) the statement must have been made by a co-conspirator of the party against whom the statement is offered; (3) the statement must have been made "during the course" of the conspiracy; and (4) the statement must have been made "in furtherance" of the conspiracy. The third and fourth prerequisites are not really in issue here because the problem strongly suggests that the statement was made at a time when the conspiracy was still going on and that the statement helped further the conspiracy's goals.

The real questions here are whether there was in fact a conspiracy and whether the declarant, X, was a member of the conspiracy. Once again, we are faced with a problem involving the decision-making authority with respect to preliminary facts. Consider first the question whether there was a conspiracy. Is the statement (which asserts among other things that D was involved) relevant even if there was no conspiracy? Yes. Even if there was no conspiracy, the statement still increases the likelihood of D's guilt on the ground that D could have acted alone in importing the software. Thus, the existence of the conspiracy must be decided by the court under FRE 104(a).

Moving to the second question: Was the declarant (X) a co-conspirator? Even if X was not a co-conspirator, the statement is relevant because, once again, it increases the likelihood of D's guilt. So, again, the court must decide this question of preliminary fact under FRE 104(a).

Based on these considerations, answer (B) is correct because it recognizes that the court must decide the preliminary facts. **Answer (A) is incorrect** because it assumes FRE 104(b) applies, which it does not.

Answer (D) is incorrect because, even if X is a defendant (and the problem does not state whether that is true), X's statement would only be an admission of X, not of D, unless the statement qualifies under the co-conspirator rule. One cannot use a personal admission of one party as an admission of another party unless the statement qualifies under FRE 801(d)(2)(C), (D), or (E).

Answer (C) is incorrect as well. The answer is attractive on its face because it is true that the jury must eventually decide whether there was a conspiracy. That's one of the charges against D. But there is a fundamental difference between the following two things: (1) deciding the existence of a fact for purposes of determining guilt; and (2) deciding the existence of a fact merely as a prerequisite to the admission of a piece of evidence. When the court decides the question for purposes of admitting the evidence (applying the preponderance of the evidence standard), all it is doing is admitting the evidence. And there is no reason for the court to inform the jury that it made that finding. By not saying anything about the facts the court had to decide in order to admit the evidence, the court avoids unduly swaying the jury.

123.   **Answer (B) is correct.** FRE 602 tells us that a witness may not testify to a fact "unless evidence is introduced sufficient to support a finding that the witness has personal knowledge of the matter." (Of course, this rule does not apply to experts in most situations.) Compare this standard to the one in FRE 104(b), and it should be clear that they are the same. Thus, FRE 602 treats issues concerning personal knowledge as problems of conditional relevance. Under that standard, the court does not decide whether the witness had personal knowledge; it merely decides whether there is "evidence . . . sufficient to support a finding" of personal knowledge. This is the essence of answer (B), and it explains why **answer (A) is incorrect.**

Answer (C) is incorrect because FRE 602 makes clear that the witness's own testimony may be considered in determining whether there is evidence sufficient to support a finding of personal knowledge. ("Evidence to prove personal knowledge may, but need not, consist of the witness's own testimony.") That the witness's testimony might be self-serving does not mean the court (and ultimately the jury) may not consider it.

Answer (D) is incorrect because the problem does not supply sufficient facts to determine whether the court should admit the evidence.

124. **Answer (D) is correct.** The preliminary facts necessary to the admission of a statement as a dying declaration under FRE 804(b)(2) are for the court under FRE 104(a). (That is because the statement will be relevant even if those facts are not true.) The last sentence of FRE 104(a) states that "in making its determination [the court] is not bound by the rules of evidence except those with respect to privileges." That means the court may consider all of the items listed in answers (A) and (B). (Even the statement itself may be used to support its own admissibility.)

As the language quoted above indicates, the only constraint on the court is the application of evidentiary privileges. In *United States v. Zolin*, 491 U.S. 554 (1989), the Supreme Court held that in making preliminary determinations concerning the application of the crime-fraud exception to the attorney-client privilege, the court was permitted to consider any evidence that had not already been found privileged. Thus, the type of evidence referred to in answer (C) may be considered as well as the types mentioned in answers (A) and (B).

125. **Answer (C) is correct.** X's statement is hearsay because it asserts that X committed the crime, and it is offered to prove that fact, which decreases the likelihood that D committed it. However, the statement qualifies as a declaration against interest. FRE 804(b)(3) sets forth a number of prerequisites to the admission of hearsay under this exception. All of the prerequisites are for the court to decide under FRE 104(a).

First, the declarant must be unavailable. Under FRE 804(a)(2), a person is unavailable if she "persists in refusing to testify concerning the subject matter of the . . . statement despite an order of the court to do so." That is what X has done here. Thus, for purposes of the rule she is unavailable, even though she is sitting on the witness stand.

Next, "at the time of its making, [the statement must have been] so far contrary to" any of a number of interests "that a reasonable person in the declarant's position would not have made the statement unless believing it to be true." Here, the statement is clearly against X's penal interest. There is every reason to believe that in these circumstances, a reasonable person would believe that admitting to the commission of a crime might subject her to prosecution. Even though the statement was made to a friend, most people would feel that it is risky to make such a statement.

Next, "[a] statement is one tending to expose the declarant to criminal liability and offered to exculpate the accused is not admissible unless corroborating circumstances clearly indicate the trustworthiness of the statement." Here, the statement does expose X to criminal liability, and it is being offered to exculpate D, the accused. But the facts indicate that D offers "substantial" evidence that links X to the crime. Thus, this requirement has been satisfied.

Answer (A) is incorrect because to be an admission, a statement must have been made by a party. **Answer (B) is incorrect** because, as explained above, the statement qualifies as a declaration against interest. **Answer (D) is incorrect** because, even if the friend to whom X made the statement testifies, the statement will still be hearsay. (Remember that the question whether a statement is hearsay does not depend on who the *witness* is. It depends on who the *declarant* is.)

126. **Answer (D) is correct.** The declarant is P. P stated that D was not planning to deliver the CDs on time. The statement is offered to prove that D was not planning to deliver the CDs on time. From that, it can be inferred that D did not in fact deliver the CDs on time. (Note the difference between the phrase "to prove" for relevance purposes, and the same statement for hearsay purposes. For relevance, one must consider the entire chain of reasoning. If the chain leads to a conclusion of fact that is of consequence to the action, the evidence is relevant. For hearsay purposes, however, "to prove" only requires looking at the first inference. The first inference from the statement here is the same as the fact it asserts—that D was not planning to deliver the CDs on time. The statement is therefore hearsay.)

The question here is whether the statement satisfies any exception or fits into an exemption. **Answer (A) is incorrect** because, even though P's out-of-court statement implies something that D said, P did not tell her secretary, "D says. . . ." Thus, D is not a declarant, and the statement is not admissible as an admission because P is offering her own statement, not that of D.

Still, we would want the law of evidence to be rational, and not to reach different conclusions based on tiny differences in wording. So, even if P had said, "D told me, 'I'm not going to deliver the CDs on time,' " there would still be a hearsay problem here. D's admission, in a sense, would be "trapped" within P's assertion that D made the statement. Because P's assertion is also hearsay (it must be true that D made the statement for the whole thing to be relevant), there must be a hearsay exception for P's statement or the whole thing will be excluded unless P's statement fits within an exception or exemption.

Answer (B) is incorrect because the state of mind exception (FRE 803(3)) does not apply. That is because what P *thinks* about what D plans to do is not relevant. What matters is what D *in fact* plans to do.

Answer (C) is incorrect because P's statement does not constitute words of independent legal significance. It is merely *evidence of* D's repudiation, just as D's own statement, "I'm not going to deliver the CDs" would be.

127. **Answer (C) is correct.** There are two layers of hearsay in this case. The inner layer is W's testimony, which was that X was not paying attention and was swerving from side to side as she drove. It is hearsay because it is offered to prove the truth of the matter asserted—that X was driving that way.

The outer layer is the transcript, which amounts to the court reporter's statement that this is what W testified at the trial. That statement is also hearsay because it is offered to prove that W in fact gave that testimony. (If W did not give that testimony, the transcript would be irrelevant.)

The transcript almost certainly qualifies as a business record of the court reporter under FRE 803(6). The transcript might also serve as the court reporter's recorded recollection under FRE 803(5).

Starting from the inside and working outward, the question is whether W's testimony qualifies under the former testimony exception in FRE 804(b)(1). To qualify, (1) the declarant must be unavailable; (2) the statement must have been given as a witness at another hearing of the same or a different proceeding, or in a deposition taken in compliance with law in the course of the same or another proceeding"; and (3) "the party against whom the testimony is now offered, or, in a civil action, a predecessor in interest, had an opportunity and similar motive to develop the testimony by direct, cross, or redirect examination."

W is dead, so W is unavailable to testify at the current trial. The statement was given by W as a witness in the criminal trial. The first two requirements are therefore satisfied. The real question concerns "opportunity and similar motive to develop the testimony. . . ." It is vital to consider separately each party against whom the evidence is offered. As to X, there is no problem. X was a party to the criminal prosecution (X was the defendant), and had an opportunity to cross-examine W at that time. X's motive at the criminal trial would have been to impeach W's testimony by showing that W was wrong when she said X was not paying attention and was swerving. That is exactly the same thing X would seek to do if W were present to testify at the civil trial. Thus, the transcript is admissible against X.

Is the transcript admissible against D Corp.? Because D Corp. was not a party to the criminal prosecution, it had no opportunity to cross-examine W at that trial. But because the present action is a civil case, the "predecessor in interest" language of FRE 804(b)(1) might apply. The courts have generally interpreted the phrase broadly, and not limited "predecessor in interest" only to a party that would qualify under the law of property. Instead, courts tend to treat a party as a predecessor in interest under this rule if that party's interests are a good proxy for those of the current party. In other words, the courts tend to ask whether there was a party who had an opportunity to cross-examine the witness at the prior trial and whether that party would have used cross-examination for the same purposes as would the current party. That translates to the following question in the present case: Were X's interests in cross-examining W in the criminal trial the same as D Corp.'s interests in the current trial? The answer is yes because D Corp. claims that X was not driving recklessly. That was exactly X's defense in the first trial. Thus, the courts hold that X's cross-examination adequately protects D Corp.'s interests. (If X's lawyer did an egregiously bad job cross-examining W in the criminal trial, there is a chance that the current court will not apply the rule. Otherwise, D Corp. is pretty much stuck with the cross-examination X's lawyer conducted.)

The bottom line, therefore, is that the transcript is admissible against both D Corp. and X. **Answer (C) is correct.**

Answer (A) is incorrect because the transcript is offered to prove the truth of the matter asserted. In fact, both statements are offered to prove the truth of the matter asserted, as explained above. **Answer (B) is incorrect** because both statements were made out of court. **Answer (D) is incorrect** because, as explained, the transcript qualifies under the former testimony hearsay exception.

128. **Answer (C) is correct.** Under FRE 801(d)(2)(B), a party may adopt another's statement as her own, making it an admission. This will be the case if "the party has manifested an adoption or belief in its truth." That fact, in turn, depends on whether the party heard and understood the statement and whether, under the circumstances, a reasonable person in the position of the party would deny the truth of the statement if it isn't true.

The problem here is that X is not a party. As a result, the adoptive admission rule does not apply. Therefore, **answer (A) is incorrect.**

Answer (B) is incorrect because the facts do not support the conclusion that D's statement is an excited utterance. D does not seem to have been under the influence of stress caused by a startling event, and some time had passed since D was placed under arrest. This was probably enough time to allow for reflection about the situation.

Answer (D) is incorrect because there has not been a showing that X is unavailable.

That leaves answer (C). D's statement is hearsay for which no exception applies, and if the jury does not hear D's statement, X's response is irrelevant.

129. **Answer (A) is correct.** The document is hearsay because it asserts that the lumber was delivered on a certain date (two weeks later than it was supposed to arrive), and it is offered to prove that the lumber was delivered on that date. The question is whether any exception applies.

Answer (A) assumes the business records exception (FRE 803(6)) applies, which is correct. The preliminary facts are for the judge under FRE 104(a). The document, on its face, appears to be a "memorandum, report, record, or data compilation, in any form, of . . . events." The witness's testimony tends to show that records of this kind are made by the job foreperson (a person with knowledge) when building supplies arrive. The witness has testified that the document was kept in the place the company customarily keeps such records. That the document was written by a person who was unaware of any potential dispute between P and D means there are no meaningful indicia of lack of trustworthiness. The document qualifies as a business record.

Answer (B) is incorrect because the past recollection recorded doctrine only applies when a writing made or adopted by a witness with knowledge of the facts, but who now lacks sufficient recollection to testify fully, is used as a substitute for the witness's testimony. The custodian of records never had a personal knowledge of the lumber delivery date, so the record cannot be used as a substitute for her testimony.

Answer (C) is incorrect because the witness laying the foundation for business records is not required to have personal knowledge of the truth of the facts recited in the record.

Answer (D) is incorrect because the witness has no recollection of the delivery of the lumber that can be refreshed by the document.

130. **Answer (C) is correct.** Testimony concerning what P said at the earlier civil trial is hearsay. P is the declarant, and her statements about losing money to X in the scheme are offered in the present trial for the same purpose they were offered in the earlier trial: to prove that X in fact committed those acts.

The basic approach to the former testimony exception has already been discussed. From that discussion it should be clear that P's testimony, offered through the recollections of W, is admissible against X. X had an opportunity to cross-examine P in the earlier trial, and X's motive at that time was the same as it would be at the current trial if P were available: presumably to impeach P by showing she was wrong or being untruthful. There is no second layer of hearsay in this case because P's former testimony is being offered through a live witness who was present and can recount what P said.

The evidence is not admissible against D, however. D was not a party to the earlier action. Because the current case is a criminal prosecution, the "predecessor in interest" provision of FRE 804(b)(1) does not apply. That means the evidence may not be offered against D.

Answers (A), (B), and (D) are incorrect for the reasons given.

131. **Answer (B) is correct.** There are two layers of hearsay in this problem. Because V's statement is offered to prove that another person committed the crime, it is hearsay unless it qualifies under the prior identification rule (FRE 801(d)(1)(C)). That statement is contained within a police report, which is also hearsay because it is offered to prove the truth of the matters asserted (that V made the identification, and that the other facts recited in the report are true).

Is V's statement "one of identification of a person after perceiving the person"? It appears to be. An identification of a person's photo qualifies. Other requirements must be satisfied as well, however. The declarant (V) must testify at the trial or hearing and be subject to cross-examination concerning the statement. Here, V has not yet testified, but D has represented that she will call V. There is no requirement that the declarant testify before the statement is offered. (If V never testifies at the trial, the court, on the prosecution's motion, will strike the testimony about V's identification from the record and instruct the jury to ignore it.) In *United States v. Owens*, 484 U.S. 554 (1988), the Supreme Court read "subject to cross-examination concerning the statement" very loosely. Basically, as long as V takes the stand and willingly answers questions about the statement, the requirement will be satisfied. (Even if V proves forgetful about the incident or the photo identification, it appears that she will be deemed "subject to cross-examination concerning the statement.") Thus, V's statement qualifies as a non-hearsay statement of prior identification.

PO's report is hearsay, as noted above, but it appears to qualify as a public record or report under FRE 803(8). It is a report of a public office that sets forth "matters observed pursuant to duty imposed by law as to which matters there was a duty to observe," and "factual findings resulting from an investigation made pursuant to authority granted by law." On its face, the "matters observed" requirement, on its face, does not apply in criminal cases to matters observed by police and other law enforcement personnel. But courts have read this rule as applying only when the report is offered against the defendant, not the government. The "factual findings" part of the report is clearly admissible because the exclusion (the exception to the exceptions in part (c)) does not apply when the record is offered against the government.

The hearsay rule therefore does not exclude the report, including the part that tells about V's identification. Answer (B) states the law correctly as applied to this problem.

Answers (A), (C), and (D) are incorrect for the reasons given.

132. **Answer (D) is correct.** The Supreme Court's current confrontation-hearsay jurisprudence applicable to this situation basically boils down to this: If hearsay satisfies a "firmly rooted" hearsay exception, no further inquiry is needed to determine whether it satisfies the confrontation clause. Not all exceptions are "firmly rooted," however. The Court has not made clear how to determine what exceptions are in this category, but the Court has hinted that the length of time an exception has been around and the number of jurisdictions that have adopted it are relevant factors. The residual exception, which is relatively new and still somewhat controversial, is not firmly rooted.

If the evidence does not fit within a "firmly rooted" exception, the trial court must determine whether there are adequate "indicia of reliability." In making that determination, the court may take into account such factors as the circumstances in which the statement was made, but may *not* consider whether the assertion in the statement is corroborated by other evidence.

Based on these criteria, answer (D) is correct. **Answers (A), (B), and (C) are incorrect** for the reasons given.

133. **Answer (D) is correct.** The first issue here is one of personal knowledge. That prerequisite applies to hearsay declarants, not just witnesses. (The courts do not apply the personal knowledge requirement to party admissions, but this is not a party admission.) Under FRE 602, personal knowledge is a 104(b)-type fact, meaning that the court need only determine whether there is evidence sufficient to support a finding that the person had personal knowledge.

If the court determines that there is evidence sufficient to support a finding that X had personal knowledge, it must next deal with the hearsay issue. X's statement is hearsay if offered to prove that the blue car ran the light and struck the red car. It might be an excited utterance, however, if there was a startling event, if declarant (X) was under the stress of excitement caused by the event, and if the statement concerns the event. These are facts for the court to decide under FRE 104(a).

Answer (A) is incorrect because it is permissible—and usually wise practice—to lead a witness on cross-examination. **Answer (B) is incorrect** because the prior inconsistent statement rules apply when the same person has made inconsistent statements. That is not the case here. **Answer (C) is incorrect** because we do not have sufficient information to determine whether the excited utterance exception is satisfied. In addition, as noted above, the court will not reach the hearsay issue unless it determines that there is evidence sufficient to support a finding that the declarant had personal knowledge.

134. **Answer (B) is correct.** D's statement is hearsay because it was made out of court, it asserts that D is planning to fill P's order, and it is offered to prove that D did in fact fill P's order. The statement satisfies the state of mind exception (FRE 803(3)) because it was a statement of D's then-existing state of mind (here, the intention to do something in the future, an application of the *Hillmon* doctrine). Note that this is a very self-serving statement, but that does not matter for purposes of the application of FRE 803(3). That rule contains no specific trustworthiness requirement.

Answer (A) is incorrect because a statement of a party is not an admission unless offered *against* the party who made it. This statement was offered *by* the party who made it.

Answer (C) is incorrect because as long as it is reasonable to conclude that D was referring to the order at issue, the statement is relevant. It will be up to the jury to decide, ultimately, whether this is what D meant, and the amount of probative value the statement has.

Answer (D) is incorrect because it is very difficult to discern any *unfair* prejudice to P from the evidence. True, the evidence hurts P's case, but it does not appear to do so improperly. Even if there is some potential for prejudice (perhaps the jury will over-value the evidence as an indication of D's performance of the contract), it is extremely unlikely that the unfair prejudice will substantially outweigh the statement's legitimate probative value.

135. **Answer (A) is correct.** The father's statement is hearsay because it was made out of court, it asserts that P's arm hurt and that she cannot move it, and the statement is offered to prove those facts. The statement appears to qualify as a statement for purposes of medical diagnosis or treatment under FRE 803(4). That rule applies even if the declarant is seeking diagnosis or treatment for somebody other than herself. Here, as long as the father's purpose in making the statement to the admitting nurse was to obtain diagnosis or treatment for P, the statement will qualify. The preliminary facts are for the judge under FRE 104(a).

Answer (B) is incorrect because the facts do not suggest that the father was speaking while under the stress of excitement caused by a startling event or condition.

Answer (C) is incorrect because, as discussed above, the statement is hearsay.

Answer (D) is incorrect because, as discussed above, the statement almost certainly satisfies the exception in FRE 803(4).

136. **Answer (B) is correct.** There are two statements here. The "inner" statement is P's statement to the doctor, "My arm hurt a lot after I collided with another person." That statement is hearsay because it asserts that P suffered a collision with another person and that arm pain followed. The statement appears to satisfy the requirements of FRE 803(4), however, because P probably made the statement for purposes of obtaining treatment. This statement is "trapped," however, because it is contained within another statement: that of the doctor, who wrote that P made the statement just discussed. That statement, too, is hearsay because it asserts that P made the statement and is offered to prove that P made the statement.

FRE 805 provides that hearsay within hearsay is admissible if both levels of hearsay fit within an exception. In this case, the exception covering the doctor's statement is probably the business records exception. The requirements of FRE 803(6) have been discussed previously. The only real issue seems to be whether "the sources of information or the method or circumstances of preparation indicate lack of reliability." Whether that is the case here depends on whether the doctor has a business duty to listen and record accurately everything the patient said. Certainly, there is no problem with the part of P's statement that asserts that he had a lot of pain in his arm after the collision. The existence of pain in a particular part of the body would be something a doctor would want to know about. As a result, she is likely to listen carefully and to record accurately what the patient says about the pain. The same is probably true with the word "collision." A doctor would be interested not only in the existence of pain, but also about the general source of the pain. What about the patient's statement that the collision was with "another person"? Would that be "reasonably pertinent" to medical diagnosis or treatment (to borrow a phrase from FRE 803(4))? This might be the subject of argument, and perhaps testimony to the court, but it seems entirely likely that a doctor would consider it important to know whether a person's injury derived from a collision with another person or, for example, an automobile. That information might affect the diagnosis or treatment protocols the doctor follows. (If the patient had given the name of the person with whom she collided, it is unlikely the doctor would listen carefully to that information or take the trouble to record it accurately. The same would be true if the patient's injury derived from an automobile collision and the patient gave the make and color of the other car.)

Because it appears the business records exception would cover all parts of what the doctor recorded, and the "medical diagnosis or treatment" exception covers all parts of the patient's statement, it appears the document is admissible. All of the other answers are flawed. **Answer (A) is incorrect** because it asserts that no exception applies to the document. **Answer (C) is incorrect** because it identifies the doctor's statement about what the patient said as non-hearsay. **Answer (D) is incorrect** because, while it is true that the patient's statement might be self-serving, that is not a reason for the court to exclude it under FRE 803(4). (Moreover, in the circumstances, there was probably no reason for the patient to lie about the injury or exaggerate its effects.)

137. **Answer (A) is correct.** X's statement is hearsay because it asserts that D was the aggressor in the fight, which is what the prosecution is offering it to prove. It appears to satisfy the requirements of FRE 803(2), however, for excited utterances because there was a startling event (D's alleged attack on V), and the circumstances suggest that the statement was made under the stress of excitement caused by the event, which had just occurred.

The next question is whether the confrontation clause requires further inquiry into the reliability of the statement. The answer almost certainly is no. The Supreme Court has held that evidence that meets the requirements of "firmly rooted" hearsay exceptions satisfies the confrontation clause. In *White v. Illinois*, 502 U.S. 346 (1992), the Supreme Court held that the hearsay exception for "spontaneous declarations" was firmly rooted. Thus, no further inquiry into reliability is required.

Answer (B) is incorrect because it assumes further inquiry into reliability is required. **Answer (C) is incorrect** because it asserts that the statement is not hearsay. **Answer (D) is incorrect** because, although there is some doubt about the point after the Supreme Court's 2004 decision in *Crawford v. Washington*, 2004 WL 413301 (Mar. 8, 2004), to date the Court has held that the confrontation clause has made clear that the confrontation clause does not require that the declarant be shown to be unavailable or that she be produced. (Of course, if unavailability is a prerequisite for application of a particular exception, the confrontation clause would also presumably require that the government demonstrate the declarant's unavailability.)

138. **Answer (D) is correct.** There are two statements. The "inner" statement is the Chairperson's statement, "What a piece of junk!" The "outer" statement is the secretary's assertion that this is what the Chairperson said. The Chairperson's statement is not hearsay because it is *not* offered to prove that the ad was in fact terrible (which is what the Chairperson probably meant to assert). Instead, it is offered as circumstantial evidence that the board later rejected the ad (and thus that the corporation was not required to pay for it). That is why the Chairperson's statement is relevant. The "outer" statement (the secretary's statement) is hearsay because it is an assertion that the Chairperson made the other statement, and is offered to prove that the Chairperson in fact did make that statement. The secretary's statement certainly qualifies as a business record, however. It is the ordinary course of the business to take minutes of board meetings, and the secretary is required to keep and file those minutes in a certain way. Although it is true that the statement serves the interest of the party offering it, there is no real indication that at the time it was made, the company had reason to think there would be litigation over payment for the ad. Thus, this portion of the minutes is probably admissible.

Answers (A), (B), and (C) are incorrect for the reasons given.

139.   **Answer (B) is correct.** The report is relevant because it tends to show that P had in fact suffered liver damage as of a certain time. The doctor's statement is hearsay, however, because it asserts that P has suffered liver damage and it is offered to prove that fact. The doctor's testimony appears to satisfy all prerequisites for the business records exception. As to the trustworthiness issue, the report does not appear to lack trustworthiness when considered in context. The doctor prepared the report in connection with P's application to obtain health insurance. No litigation was anticipated at that time. In fact, if one wants to obtain medical insurance, any incentive to be dishonest would be to not disclose the patient's medical problems, or to minimize rather than exaggerate them. Thus, there are no indicia of lack of trustworthiness.

   Answer (A) is incorrect because, even if the doctor was speaking for P, the statement is being offered by P rather than against her. **Answer (C) is incorrect** because courts tend to hold that statements made by the medical professional are not within the FRE 803(4) exception. (Thus, statements made to obtain medical diagnosis or treatment are admissible under the exception, not statements that constitute medical diagnosis.) **Answer (D) is incorrect** because the report is admissible hearsay.

140.   **Answer (D) is correct.** There are actually three statements here: D's statement, Officer X's statement about what D said, and W's report stating what Officer X said. All three statements were made out of court. The innermost statement (that of D) is not hearsay because it is a party admission under FRE 801(d)(2)(A). That means Officer X, who heard D make the statement, could certainly testify that D made the statement.

   Officer X's statement was made in her capacity as a police officer involved in the case, and thus appears to be the type of statement that qualifies for inclusion in a business or public record. And as the author of the police report, W is a person required to make such reports in the ordinary course of police work. This is probably the type of report envisioned by FRE 803(8)(C) ("factual findings resulting from an investigation made pursuant to authority granted by law").

   So far so good. There is one big problem, however: FRE 803(8)(C) only applies in civil cases and against the government in criminal cases. The purpose of this limitation is to prevent trial by affidavit (trials at which the government presents reports rather than percipient witnesses who can be cross-examined). Thus, FRE 803(8) is not available here. But what about FRE 803(6), the business records exception? Most courts that have considered this issue have held that because FRE 803(8) establishes a clear prohibition of using certain types of police reports against criminal defendants, admitting the reports under the more general business records exception would improperly circumvent that rule. So the report is inadmissible hearsay.

   Because D's statement is "trapped" within an inadmissible police report, it is inadmissible in the manner offered. But recall what was said above: The government may still call Officer X to testify to what D said. This makes Officer X subject to cross-examination to test whether she correctly reported D's statements, which is what the drafters of the rules wanted to happen.

Answer (A) is incorrect for the reasons just given. **Answer (B) is incorrect** because the witness, W, never had personal knowledge of what D said. This means that although the report *might* be admissible to prove what Officer X said (assuming the requirements of FRE 803(5) can be satisfied), W has no way to verify the accuracy of Officer X's report of what D said. If Officer X was the witness, and Officer X could not remember what D said, the police report *might* be admissible under the recorded recollection doctrine *if*, at a time when she still remembered well what D said, Officer X adopted the report as an accurate reflection of D's statement. Even then, there might be a problem, as some courts have held that because FRE 803(8) seeks to prevent most police reports from being used against criminal defendants, those reports cannot be admitted under *any* hearsay exception, including the exception for recorded recollection.

Answer (C) is incorrect because D's statement, while against her interest, does not qualify under FRE 804(b)(3). This is because D is not unavailable.

141.   **Answer (D) is correct.** Suppose the note simply said, "I examined P's car and noticed a large dent on the right front door." In that situation, the note almost certainly would satisfy the recorded recollection doctrine because W will testify that she no longer remembers the facts recorded in the note, but that at the time she wrote the note, she remembered the condition of the car well, and that she recorded the facts accurately. The problem here is that the note records the statement of another person, who asserted that D ran the red light. W, the writer of the note, has no personal knowledge of the truth of this witness's statement. That statement is hearsay when offered to prove that D ran the red light, and on the facts given, no exception applies to it. Thus, the note is inadmissible.

Answer (A) is incorrect for the reasons just given. **Answer (B) is incorrect** both for the reasons just given and because when the recorded recollection exception applies, the writing may not be admitted as an exhibit unless offered by the adverse party. **Answer (C) is incorrect** because W has not laid the foundation for business records. This was an informal note written by the witness and kept at home, not the type of record "kept in the ordinary course" of W's business.

142.   The statement constitutes hearsay if offered to prove that X and a person other than D committed the crime, but it might be admissible as a declaration against interest under FRE 804(b)(3). X is unavailable because he is dead. The final sentence of that rule states, "A statement tending to expose the declarant to criminal liability and offered to exculpate the accused is not admissible unless corroborating circumstances clearly indicate the trustworthiness of the statement." In *Williamson v. United States*, 512 U.S. 594 (1994), the Supreme Court held that each part of a statement offered under this provision must be against the interest of the declarant. Here, the part taking responsibility is certainly against X's interest. Arguably, X's statement that he and another person committed the crime, and that the other person was not D, is against X's interest because it shows familiarity with certain details of the crime. The same is true for the statement about where the body was dumped, something that might only have been

known to a few people at the time X told the police about it. This is a close case. Some courts are likely to hold that the entire statement comes in as against X's interest, while others are likely to hold that the part stating that D was not involved is not against X's interest because, for one thing, X and D were friends, giving X a motive to protect D.

Finally, there must be "corroborating circumstances [that] clearly indicate the trustworthiness of the statement." X's knowledge of the number of people involved and the location of the body is one such circumstance. More information is needed to determine if this requirement is met, though it probably is satisfied.

143. The court probably should sustain P's objection. The document is hearsay because it asserts that P was responsible for the accident and it is offered to prove that fact. The closest fit among the hearsay exceptions is FRE 803(6), the business records exception. Most of the requirements of that rule have been satisfied. From the custodian's testimony and the document itself, this appears to be a report of a type regularly made, kept in the regular course of the business, containing information from a person with knowledge of the facts. But the document will be inadmissible if "the source of information or the method or circumstances of preparation indicate lack of trustworthiness." The person who supplied the information in the report was the driver whose conduct was at issue, and who thus had a significant incentive to give a version that would suggest she was not responsible for the accident. In addition, a key purpose of such reports is probably to help prepare for litigation arising from accidents. In *Palmer v. Hoffman*, 318 U.S. 109 (1943), the Supreme Court held that a report analogous to the one in this problem was inadmissible for the same reason. Though *Palmer* has been criticized and its precedential value narrowed, it has never been overruled. If there is anything left of the *Palmer* rule, it would certainly cover the facts of this case.

144. The court should overrule the objection. The "order log" is hearsay because it is an assertion of all orders placed between certain dates, offered to prove that these were the only orders placed. Because P's name does not appear in the log, the log tends to show that D received no order from P. The log is probably admissible as a business record under FRE 803(7) ("[a]bsence of entry in records kept in accordance with the provisions of [FRE 803(6)]"). The custodian's testimony shows that this was a record of a type regularly made, kept in the regular course of the business, containing information from a person with knowledge of the facts. In addition, even though the report is to some extent self-serving, it is routine and almost certainly not made in anticipation of litigation. Rather, it was made as an important part of the day-to-day conduct of D's business. The business probably relies on this record. Thus, the circumstances do not suggest lack of trustworthiness. The *Palmer v. Hoffman* rule will not exclude the record.

145. The court should overrule X's objection but sustain D's objection. The transcript of W's testimony from the earlier civil trial will be used to show that X ran a red light and struck V in a crosswalk. The transcript is hearsay within hearsay. The testimony

of W will be offered to prove the facts W stated, and the transcript itself is an assertion of the court reporter that W in fact made those statements. The transcript is admissable hearsay because it is the court reporter's business record.

The real problem is with W's testimony. FRE 804(b)(1), the former testimony exception, may be used to admit the testimony against X because X had an opportunity to cross-examine W at the civil trial, and X's motive in that cross-examination was the same as it would be if W were available to testify at the criminal trial (to show that W was wrong about aspects of her testimony). D, however, was not a party to the civil trial, and the "predecessor in interest" language of the rule only applies in civil trials. Thus, the transcript may not be offered against D, who never had an opportunity to cross-examine W at the civil trial.

146. **Answer (A) is correct.** X's statement is hearsay because it asserts that a blue Exterminator was weaving all over the road, and it is offered to prove that fact. (It is relevant because if D was weaving "in and out of lanes like it's a sports car" just before the accident, D might have been behaving in the same way at the time of the accident as well.) The evidence fits within FRE 803(1), the present sense impression exception, because the circumstances strongly suggest that X made the statement while observing an event, or immediately after observing it, and the statement concerned the event.

Answer (B) is incorrect because there is no requirement that anybody be present to verify the accuracy of the declarant's statement. **Answer (C) is incorrect** because X's statement, while implicitly containing an opinion, is primarily descriptive of the facts. Also, it is "rationally based on the perception of the witness" and will help the jury understand the facts. **Answer (D) is incorrect** because there is no suggestion that this was a "startling event or condition" and that X was speaking while under the stress of excitement caused by such a condition.

147. **Answer (B) is correct.** FRE 404(a) forbids a party from offering evidence of another person's character or a trait of her character to prove "action in conformity therewith on a particular occasion." There are several exceptions, none of which apply here. The government is seeking to infer guilt by showing that D's character would lead her to be the aggressor in the fight. This is exactly what the rule forbids.

     Answer (A) is incorrect. Although the evidence is hearsay (reputation is what the community says about a person; when offered to prove what the community says, it is hearsay), FRE 803(21) provides an exception for "reputation of a person's character among associates or in the community." The character rule is what bars the evidence here.

     Answer (C) is incorrect because character is not in issue. For character to be in issue ("an essential element of a charge, claim or defense," to use the language of FRE 405(b)), a person's character must be a required element. It is not an element of self-defense. True, a character for violent behavior might make self-defense less probable, but this is merely the use of character as circumstantial evidence of behavior. To determine whether character is in issue, ask yourself the following question: Does the law require proof of character in order to establish this charge, claim, or defense? If not, character is not in issue.

     Answer (D) is incorrect because, when evidence is barred by a specific rule, the court does not have discretion to admit it if it has particularly high probative value. In other words, there is no "reverse-403" rule.

148. **Answer (B) is correct.** Until the Federal Rules were amended in the mid-1990s, there was no exception to the ban on character evidence that would allow the court to admit evidence of a defendant's character to prove action in conformity in sexual assault or child molestation cases. The enactment of FRE 413–415 changed that situation by adding exceptions for these types of cases, both civil and criminal. In this hypothetical, the prosecution wishes to offer evidence that the defendant committed another act of child molestation. The purpose of the evidence is to prove, circumstantially, that the defendant committed the charged crime. FRE 414 specifically makes this evidence admissible "for its bearing on any matter to which it is relevant." Thus, the prosecution may ask the jury to infer from D's prior act of child molestation that D is the kind of person who would commit such crimes, and that D therefore committed the charged crime. That is why **answer (A) is incorrect.**

The courts have held, however, that FRE 413–415 do not *require* admission of the evidence, and that trial courts may exclude the evidence if its probative value is substantially outweighed by the danger of unfair prejudice. That is why **answer (D) is incorrect**.

Answer (C) is incorrect because, even though the *modus operandi* theory is still available after the enactment of FRE 413–415, the facts here do not show such a distinctive method as to earmark the charged crime as having been committed by D. Thus, *modus operandi* is not a legitimate theory on the facts given.

149. **Answer (D) is correct.** Character evidence is not admissible here because this is a civil action, and none of the exceptions in FRE 404(a) apply. (FRE 415 applies to civil cases, but only ones dealing with sexual assault and child molestation.) Thus, **answer (A) is incorrect**.

Answer (B) is incorrect because there is insufficient evidence to establish the existence of a habit. Habit is a specific reaction to a specific stimulus, and the person must have encountered the stimulus enough times to show that she acts in that specific way almost every time. It need not be an unconscious reaction, but there must be a sufficient number of instances to show that this is how the person reacts almost all the time.

Answer (C) is incorrect because character is not admissible to prove conduct in this situation. It is true that usually, when character may be offered as circumstantial evidence of a person's behavior, the party may use only reputation and opinion evidence on direct examination. But that question is never reached here because evidence of character is simply not admissible.

150. **Answer (D) is correct.** In this example, D is trying to show that P committed the burglaries mentioned in the newspaper article by showing that P committed other burglaries. The inference from the older burglaries is being used to show that P has the character of a burglar, and that P committed the burglaries mentioned in the article. That use is forbidden by FRE 404(a). Thus, the evidence is inadmissible. **Answer (C) is incorrect** because the question of what form of character evidence may be used is never reached; character evidence in any form is forbidden here.

Answer (A) is incorrect because character is not in issue. In many defamation cases, reputation is in issue, and thus reputation may be proven. But D's defense does not put reputation in issue. D is simply asserting that the story was true. There are many ways D can prove that fact; character is not required. Thus, character is not "an essential element of a charge, claim, or defense."

Answer (B) is incorrect because good faith is not D's defense. D claims the article was true, not that she published an untrue article in good faith.

151. **Answer (C) is correct.** Evidence concerning D's tendency to drive through that particular intersection without yielding might constitute habit evidence, but the way in which it is being offered here is hearsay for which no exception applies. W is not

testifying that D has a habit of driving through that intersection without yielding. W is testifying that people tell her D does this. If P wishes to prove D's habit, P should call as witnesses the people familiar with D's behavior. That would allow them to be subjected to cross-examination. For these reasons, **answer (D) is incorrect.**

Answer (A) is incorrect because the evidence probably does amount to habit rather than character. As explained above, it is not being offered in an appropriate way.

Answer (B) is incorrect because the habit rule is not so harsh as to require that a person *invariably* acts in a certain way. A court may conclude that it is sufficient that a person almost always reacts to the same stimulus in the same way.

152. **Answer (D) is correct.** FRE 404(a)(1) allows an "accused" (most courts have held this means a criminal defendant) to offer evidence of a pertinent trait of her character to prove action in conformity with that trait. A person with a character trait of peacefulness is less likely to commit murder than is one with a violent character. Thus, the evidence is relevant. FRE 405(a) allows D to use evidence of reputation or opinion on direct examination of the character witness. This discussion shows why **answers (A) and (B) are incorrect**.

Answer (C) is incorrect because bias does not render a witness incompetent to offer her opinion. The jury may consider bias as it assesses W's credibility, but the court may not exclude the evidence simply because of the witness's bias.

153. **Answer (A) is correct.** FRE 405(a) allows a party cross-examining a character witness to refer to specific instances of conduct. The main purpose is to impeach the character witness by demonstrating that she lacks adequate information on which to base her testimony on direct examination. Here, if W was unaware of D's involvement in a barroom brawl, W's opinion about D's peacefulness would carry less value with the fact-finder.

Answer (B) is incorrect for the reasons just given. **Answer (C) is incorrect** because leading questions are permissible, and usually favored, on cross-examination. **Answer (D) is incorrect** because for these purposes, the court may admit the evidence even if the two events are not very similar. If the incident in the bar is something a person would use to inform herself about D's character for peacefulness, W's possible ignorance of that event casts doubt on W's assessment of D's character.

154. **Answer (A) is correct.** In *Michelson v. United States*, 335 U.S. 469 (1948), the Supreme Court approved limits the common law had placed on a character evidence offered by a criminal defendant and on the rebuttal the prosecution is allowed to make. One rule provided that if the prosecutor seeks to cross-examine a character witness by inquiring about whether the witness has heard about an event inconsistent with the witness's character testimony, the prosecutor must show the court that it has a good faith belief that the event actually occurred. The Court noted that this is somewhat illogical because what should matter is that stories were circulating, even if untrue. (The witness's ignorance of those stories would show that her reputation testimony

is questionable.) Nevertheless, to keep the inquiry within reasonable bounds and protect the defendant from unfair prejudice, the Court approved the requirement that the prosecutor show a good faith belief that the event occurred.

Answer (B) is incorrect because a reputation witness is more properly asked the "have you heard" form of question rather than the "did you know" form. This is because reputation is what one has heard, not what one knows about the individual personally. (In any event, today, as both reputation and opinion are admissible, the courts will not usually reverse on such a technicality.)

Answer (C) is incorrect because the last sentence of FRE 405(a) allows a cross-examiner to mention "relevant specific instances of conduct."

Answer (D) is incorrect because, as noted above, the evidence is not admissible if the prosecutor does not have a good faith belief that the event occurred. Here, the prosecutor knows that D was not in fact involved. Thus, the evidence is inadmissible.

155.   The court should overrule the objection as long as D shows that W has sufficient knowledge of V's community reputation. FRE 404(a)(2) allows an "accused" (most courts interpret this to mean criminal defendant) to offer evidence of a pertinent trait of the character of a crime victim for the purpose of showing action in conformity with that trait on a specific occasion. Peacefulness or lack of peacefulness is a pertinent trait because P alleges that V was the aggressor in the fight. FRE 405(a) allows evidence of reputation or opinion on direct examination of a character witness. As long as W has sufficient knowledge of V's community reputation for peacefulness or lack of peacefulness, the testimony is proper.

156.   The court should overrule D's objection as long as W2 has sufficient knowledge of V's character for peacefulness to be able to offer a valid opinion. FRE 404(a)(2) actually provides two exceptions, the second of which applies here. In prosecutions for homicide where the defendant claims the victim was the first aggressor, the prosecution may rebut the defendant's evidence by offering evidence of the victim's character for peacefulness. It does not matter that D did not try to prove V's action using character evidence. The rule only requires that D try to prove that the victim was the first aggressor. FRE 405(a) limits the direct examination of character witnesses to reputation or opinion. Here, the prosecution is offering opinion evidence.

157.   **Answer (A) is correct.** FRE 404 only forbids the use of other crimes, wrongs, or acts when their relevance depends on an inference of the actor's character. Here, the evidence appears to be relevant to D's identity as the embezzler by means other than character. The theory is *plan*. A person who has a plan to act in a certain way is more likely to act in that way than is a person chosen randomly. In theory, this is not character-based propensity reasoning. Here, the existence of the plan may be inferred from D's subsequent embezzlement from the same trust. This explains why **answer (D) is incorrect**.

Answer (B) is incorrect because evidence of D's subsequent embezzlement does not contradict her claim that somebody else committed the charged crime.

Answer (C) is incorrect because the relevance of the plan theory as used here does not depend on the other crime having occurred before the charged crime.

158. The court should overrule D's objection because W3's testimony is proper to rebut D's claim that she does not have the character of an embezzler, and thus did not commit the crime. The trait of honesty is "pertinent" to the charge of embezzlement, which is a crime involving dishonesty. The prosecution has presented W3's testimony in the form of opinion, which is permissible under FRE 405(a). Because the prosecution has not offered W3's testimony to impeach D, it does not matter that D never testified.

159. **Answer (D) is correct.** Until a recent amendment to FRE 404(a), the rule appeared to deny the prosecution the right to meet D's evidence concerning the victim's character with evidence of the same trait of D's character. (This assumes D has not offered evidence of her own character.) The amendment gives the prosecution that right. It may now offer evidence of the same trait of character of D that D has offered concerning the victim. **Answer (A) is incorrect** for the reasons just explained.

Answer (B) is incorrect because FRE 803(21) provides a hearsay exception for evidence of a person's reputation.

Answer (C) is incorrect because the prosecution may rebut both by cross-examining D's character witnesses and by calling its own witnesses.

160. **Answer (C) is correct.** The evidence in this case is potentially admissible under FRE 404(b), which would allow a *modus operandi* theory to show identity—that D is the person who committed the charged crime. The theory is that the method D used in the uncharged prior robbery was so distinctive as to mark the robbery as his, and that the later robbery, committed in the same distinctive way, bore that mark. The evidence does not offend the character ban of FRE 404(a) because the courts hold that the *modus operandi* theory does not depend on an inference of the person's character.

Though the *modus operandi* theory potentially applies, the Supreme Court held in *Huddleston v. United States*, 485 U.S. 681 (1988), that when there is a dispute about the person's commission of the uncharged act, the standard of FRE 104(b) applies. That means the court may admit the evidence if it finds that there is evidence sufficient to support a finding that the person committed the uncharged act.

Answer (C) tracks the law as just discussed. **Answer (A) is incorrect** because FRE 404(b) admits "other crimes, wrongs, or acts" without regard to whether the person was charged criminally. **Answers (B) and (D) are incorrect** because they misconstrue the rules of law discussed above.

161. **Answer (B) is correct.** The theory here is that the evidence, though relevant on an impermissible character-propensity basis, is also relevant on a non-character basis supplied by the doctrine of chances. To state that theory in a common-sense way: What is the probability that four home care patients would die of poisoning while in D's care and without D's involvement? One would think the odds would be overwhelmingly

against such an event happening four times. Though one patient might die of poisoning without D's involvement, four seems beyond the realm of coincidence. (The point is not that this *couldn't* happen. It is that such a chain of events is extremely unlikely to happen without wrongdoing on D's part.)

Note that this theory applies even without specific proof that D poisoned the other three patients. The jury is being asked to put all four incidents together and to determine the likelihood of guilt based on the informal probability reasoning discussed above. Thus, **answer (D) is incorrect** because admissibility does not depend on the prosecution proving D's guilt in each of the three prior incidents.

Answer (A) is incorrect because although the prosecution may rebut D's good character evidence by calling its own witnesses, those witnesses would be limited to testifying on direct examination in the form of reputation and opinion evidence, not specific instances of conduct.

Answer (C) is incorrect because FRE 608(b) only allows specific instances of a witness's conduct to impeach the witness's credibility if those instances are "probative of truthfulness or untruthfulness." The courts do not consider murder to be probative of truthfulness or untruthfulness.

162.   **Answer (B) is correct.** FRE 412, the rape-shield rule, severely restricts the defendant's introduction of evidence of a rape victim's sexual history. There are some exceptions, but none apply here. FRE 412(b)(1)(C) states an exception for situations in which exclusion of the evidence would violate defendant's constitutional rights, but that is not the case here. That rule would apply only when the evidence has powerful probative value on the facts, or seriously undermines the victim's credibility. This requires a case-by-case determination, but the evidence in this case has little value either to show consent or to undercut V's credibility. Thus, **answer (D) is incorrect**.

Answer (A) is incorrect because the evidence is simply inadmissible. One need not reach the question of the proper form the evidence should take. (If the evidence were admissible, however, it would be in the form of specific instances of conduct such as used here, not in the form of opinion or reputation.)

Answer (C) is incorrect because the rule forbids the use of the victim's sexual history unless it falls within one of the exceptions, even if the defendant argues that the evidence is not being offered on a character basis. As noted above, the evidence does not fall within any exception in FRE 412(b)(1).

163.   The court should overrule D's objection for at least two reasons. First, evidence that D tried to spend the money the day before and that D was told the money was phony is arguably not another "crime, wrong, or act." It is an act, of course, but it is not a culpable act, which is what the rule almost certainly regulates. Even if this qualifies as another "crime, wrong, or act," however, the evidence is admissible to show D's knowledge that the bill was counterfeit when she tried to pass it on the charged occasion. The inference is not based on character. It derives from the simple

generalization that a person will tend to retain knowledge learned fairly recently. This applies regardless of the person's character. Thus, the evidence is likely admissible to prove knowledge under FRE 404(b).

164. **Answer (D) is correct.** This is not a situation in which character is in issue because neither P's claim nor D's defense requires proof of D's character for care. Thus, **answer (B) is incorrect**. Evidence of character is also not admissible here as circumstantial evidence of D's conduct because the case does not fit within any of the exceptions in FRE 404(a). Thus, **answer (C) is incorrect**.

If the evidence is to be admitted, it must be on the basis that the evidence is being used to show a habit, not character. That argument will fail, however. Habit under FRE 406 is a specific response to a specific stimulus. It is not a general tendency. That D tends to be "a careful driver who always pays attention" is not a specific response to a specific stimulus; it is far too general to be evidence of habit. Rather, it is evidence of D's character for care as a driver. Thus, **answer (A) is incorrect**.

165. **Answer (B) is correct.** This problem presents a simple example of motive evidence. FRE 404 is not implicated because the evidence is not about D1 and D2, but about the victims, and is not being offered to prove how anyone acted, but merely to show a basis for the existence of a motive to kill the victims.

Answer (A) is incorrect because the evidence is not being offered to show a tendency toward violence. **Answer (C) is incorrect** because the evidence does not include any out-of-court statement. **Answer (D) is incorrect** because it is difficult to discern any unfair prejudice to the four victims, who are not parties to the action. There is a possibility the evidence would unfairly prejudice the prosecution in that the jury might acquit thinking that the victims deserved to die, but that seems highly unlikely.

166. **Answer (C) is correct.** D, a criminal defendant, is permitted to offer evidence of a pertinent trait of her character to prove that she did not commit the crime. Here, however, that evidence is being offered by way of an out-of-court statement asserting the declarant's opinion of D's character for peacefulness. No exception applies. Thus, **answer (A) is incorrect**.

Answer (B) is incorrect because the evidence reveals no pattern of behavior. It is simply a general opinion.

Answer (D) is incorrect because the reliability of the evidence is a question for the fact-finder, not for the court in deciding admissibility.

167. **Answer (D) is correct.** The issue here is identity—whether D is the person who shot V. Thus, **answer (B) is incorrect**, as the evidence will not be admissible to prove the perpetrator's intent. The evidence does not show conduct specific enough, nor are there enough incidents, to prove the existence of a habit. **Answer (A) is incorrect** for this reason.

Answer (C) is incorrect because it misconstrues the scope of "pattern" or "common scheme or plan." It is true that D has exhibited a sort of pattern, and that the two prior and one currently charged offenses have something in common. Two similar incidents in the past do show a tendency to act in that way. However, if FRE 404(b) is read to permit the admission of evidence of prior similar acts in a situation as this, without showing some connection among the acts other than their similarity, FRE 404(b) would pretty much swallow the rule excluding character whenever a person is charged with a crime of the same sort she has committed previously. If a person is charged with bank robbery, for example, evidence that she has robbed a bank before would be admissible. Though some courts have taken a very broad view of the ideas of "pattern" and "common scheme or plan," the better view is that some connection is required before the evidence should be admitted. Such a connection might be shown, for example, if the person has figured out a scheme that involves all of the charged and uncharged acts. (But the scheme must be more than a desire to rob banks. There must be a specific connection among the robberies.) For these reasons, the court should sustain the objection in the present case.

168. **Answer (A) is correct.** Unlike the facts of the previous problem, this case shows a real connection between the events. The evidence strongly suggests that the salesperson developed a scheme to defraud customers that involved a particular type of lie. The evidence carries significant probative value on that score.

Answer (B) is incorrect because in this situation, even five similar incidents of this kind probably do not constitute sufficient evidence to establish a habit. Though behavior does not need to be unconscious to be classified as habitual, neither should it be the type of behavior that a person needs to think about carefully each time she engages in it. Courts would be very reluctant to call this behavior habitual.

Answer (C) is incorrect for the reasons given above. The evidence is not being offered on a character-based theory. The relevance of the evidence does not depend on an inference that D has a particular character trait.

Answer (D) is incorrect because FRE 404(b) applies in both civil and criminal cases.

169. Evidence of similar events is admissible if the events occurred under substantially the same circumstances as those involved in the present case. Here, the court would want to know whether the escalator was maintained in the same way when the other people fell, whether the other people were riding the escalator in the same way as P, whether the conditions on the escalator were the same (number of people, for example), and perhaps other facts. If the court concludes that the circumstances are substantially similar, the court will admit the evidence. If D requests a limiting instruction, the court is obligated to give it. The instruction would inform the jury that it may not use the evidence to infer negligence on the basis that the department store operators have a character for carelessness, but merely to show that the condition is dangerous.

170. The court would need to know whether there were any changes to the condition of the stairs during the two-year period prior to P's accident, whether the stadium manager

was in a position to receive reports of injuries if any occurred, whether the circumstances surrounding the accident differed meaningfully from the circumstances of the prior two-year period, and anything else that might affect the relevance and probative value of the stadium manager's proposed testimony. If the circumstances of the prior two years were similar enough to those in which P fell, the evidence would be relevant. It might also possess significant probative value, making it unlikely the court would exclude the evidence because of the danger of jury confusion.

171. **Answer (C) is correct.** The act of patrolling for spills more often than before the accident qualifies as a subsequent remedial measure because it is a step that, if taken earlier, would have made the accident less likely to occur. Evidence of subsequent remedial measures is relevant because it is rational to infer that one who undertakes such a measure believes herself to be responsible for the accident. Thus, it is an implied recognition of responsibility. (Of course, there could be many explanations other than this in a given case. For example, the person might simply have acted to reduce what was already a very low risk. But that does not mean the evidence is irrelevant. As long as it is rational to conclude that the taking of the measure represents an implied recognition of responsibility, it is relevant evidence.) This means **answer (B) is incorrect**.

FRE 407, however, excludes the evidence when offered to prove fault in this way. In the present problem, the facts disclose no other possible purpose for the evidence. As a result, the court must exclude it. **Answer (D) is incorrect** because it fails to account for the subsequent remedial measures rule.

Answer (A) is incorrect because, under the modern definition of hearsay as recognized in the Federal Rules, conduct is not hearsay unless the actor *intended the conduct as an assertion of the matter the conduct is offered to prove*. Here, there is no reason to believe that by having her employees patrol for spills more often, D intended to assert that the condition at the time of the accident was unreasonably unsafe.

172. **Answer (D) is correct.** In this case, the evidence concerning D's subsequent remedial measure, while not admissible to prove D's negligence in patrolling only as often as was done before the accident, is admissible to impeach the testimony of D's manager. The method of impeachment is impeachment by contradiction. While that theory arguably has been applied too broadly by some courts, in this case it is appropriate to admit the evidence because it very directly contradicts the manager's testimony. The manager has left the clear impression that everything is fine with the store's operations, but the manager's own conduct contradicts her. This potentially calls into question the whole of the manager's testimony, and the jury should hear the evidence to help it evaluate the manager's credibility.

Answers (A) and (B) are incorrect for the reasons discussed in connection with the previous problem. **Answer (C) is incorrect** for the reasons just given.

173. **Answer (D) is correct.** In the previous problem, the evidence had a clear and intuitively strong tendency to impeach the witness by contradiction. That is not the situation here. The evidence, in fact, does not contradict W's testimony, nor is it inconsistent with it in any meaningful way. The only way in which the evidence is relevant is as an implied recognition of responsibility, and for that purpose it is inadmissible.

   Answers (A) and (B) are incorrect because they both involve the type of inference FRE 407 forbids. **Answer (C) is incorrect** for the reason just stated.

174. **Answer (C) is correct.** The evidence here is admissible for two reasons. First, it tends to impeach the expert witness by contradiction. The evidence suggests that the expert was wrong when she testified that this was the strongest, most wind-resistant available glass for this type of window. If she was wrong about that fact, she might have been wrong about other facts to which she testified. The evidence is also admissible to show the feasibility of precautionary measures. Evidence is only admissible for that purpose when the party whose conduct is at issue "controverts" feasibility (in other words, when the party argues that safer measures were not feasible). Here, the expert's testimony certainly contests feasibility. Hence, the evidence is admissible to prove feasibility.

   Answer (A) is incorrect because although FRE 407 initially was unclear about its application to product liability cases, an amendment to the rule makes clear that it does apply to such cases. **Answer (B) is incorrect** because it essentially states the forbidden use of the evidence. (A party who knows of a defect and who fails to fix it is more likely responsible than one who does not know of the defect.) **Answer (D) is incorrect** for the reasons given above.

175. D should argue that its claim concerning cost-effectiveness did not constitute contravention of feasibility. D should argue that feasibility is only controverted when a party claims something *could not have been done* for such reasons as lack of technology, and that feasibility is not controverted by cost-benefit arguments such as the one made here. D is not claiming the stronger glass could not have been used; D is only claiming it would have cost too much under the circumstances. D might conclude the argument by suggesting that if the court read the "feasibility" concept as broadly as P would like, it would practically subvert the policy of the exclusionary rule by making the evidence admissible in too many cases.

176. **Answer (D) is correct.** Evidence of subsequent remedial measures may be admitted if offered to prove the actor's ownership of or control over the instrumentality of the accident, where the actor denies ownership or control. Here, D has asserted that the road was private and that it had no authority to repair it. Evidence that a city road crew did in fact repair the pothole after the accident tends to show that the city did in fact have such authority.

   Answers (A) and (B) are incorrect for the reasons just discussed. **Answer (C) is incorrect** because the act is only evidence of ownership or control; it does not have "independent legal significance."

177.   **Answer (D) is correct.** FRE 408 excludes compromise evidence. Included are offers to compromise disputed claims, completed compromises of such claims, and statements made in the course of compromise negotiations. Here, a disputed claim exists. P's statement to D was both an offer to compromise (the offer to accept $5000) and a statement made in the course of compromise negotiations (the assertion that D was negligent but that P was distracted). On the facts given, the statement appears relevant only to prove "liability for or invalidity of the claim or its amount."

      Answers (A) and (B) are incorrect because even though P's statement (the entire statement) is a party admission, it is excluded by FRE 408. That evidence is not excluded by one rule does not mean it is admissible. Other rules might exclude it. **Answer (C) is incorrect** because the statement is not a declaration against interest (P is not unavailable). Even if the statement were a declaration against interest, the compromise rule would still exclude it.

178.   **Answer (A) is correct.** From the facts, it is clear that D was not disputing either the validity of the claim or its amount. (The statement, in fact, appears to concede liability.) Because FRE 408 only excludes offers and statements relating to disputed claims, the rule does not reach this statement. The hearsay rule also does not stand in the way of admission, because the statement is a party admission. **Answers (B), (C), and (D) are incorrect** for the reasons just given.

179.   **Answer (C) is correct.** Evidence that D settled with W is relevant to D's fault because a person who settles a case with another who has made a claim is more likely to believe herself liable than one who does not settle. However, when offered for this purpose, the evidence is excluded by FRE 408. **Answers (B) and (D) are incorrect** for this reason. The rule permits the court to admit compromise evidence when it is offered to prove "bias or prejudice of a witness." That is the case here. A person who accepts money from one against whom she has made a claim is more likely to act favorably toward that person than is one who has not settled. To help the jury assess W's credibility when she testified that P crossed the center line and struck D, the jury should hear that W and D settled W's claim. **Answer (A) is incorrect** because, as explained above, the evidence is admissible to prove W's bias.

180.   **Answer (B) is correct.** D's attorney's statement almost certainly was an authorized admission, and thus is not hearsay. Thus, **answer (A) is incorrect**. The compromise rule excludes statements made during negotiations to compromise "a claim which was disputed as to either validity or amount." Here, even though D did not dispute the validity of the basic claim, D did dispute the damages element. Thus, the statement by D's attorney falls within the prohibition of FRE 408. This explains why **answer (C) is incorrect**.

      Answer (D) is incorrect because there is no such thing as a "reverse-403" rule. That is, there is no rule that allows a court to admit otherwise inadmissible evidence if its probative value substantially outweighs unfair prejudice or other dangers the evidence might present. The court does not have the authority to admit this evidence if FRE 408 excludes it, which it does.

181. **Answer (D) is correct.** The evidence is relevant because it constitutes D's acknowledgment of guilt in the very situation for which she is now being sued for battery. FRE 410 excludes withdrawn guilty pleas and pleas of *nolo contendere*. It does not exclude pleas of guilty that were never withdrawn. The hearsay rule does not bar this evidence because the guilty plea is a statement by D. When offered by P, it is a party admission.

Answer (A) is incorrect because, on the facts, it is not possible to state that the probative value is substantially outweighed by the danger of unfair prejudice. In fact, the evidence appears to have significant probative value, and it is unlikely that the jury will use the evidence *improperly*, making it extremely unlikely that there is much potential for unfair prejudice.

Answer (B) is incorrect because the evidence is not offered for an impermissible character purpose. FRE 404(a) forbids character evidence when offered as circumstantial evidence of conduct on a particular occasion. The guilty plea here did not arise out of another incident from which the jury will be asked to infer conduct on the occasion in question. The evidence concerns the very conduct at issue, and D's guilty plea is an indication of guilt.

Answer (C) is incorrect because it misconstrues the nature of relevance analysis. The fact that an item of evidence might have several logical uses does not destroy its relevance if one of those uses is the one for which it is offered.

182. **Answer (A) is correct.** The prior guilty plea is relevant because it tends to show that at one time at least, D believed herself to be guilty of the crime charged. However, FRE 410 excludes guilty pleas that have been withdrawn. Evidence of the plea is not admissible to prove guilt or to impeach the pleader's credibility.

Answers (B), (C), and (D) are incorrect for the reasons given above.

183. The court should sustain D's objection. D's statement is a party admission, and thus not hearsay. However, the statement is made inadmissible by FRE 410(3), which excludes not only a withdrawn guilty plea, but any statements the person made during a hearing to enter the plea. The purposes for exclusion are primarily fairness and avoidance of unfair prejudice. If the court permits a person to withdraw a guilty plea, all consequences of the plea should also be removed. Allowing the prosecution to present evidence of the withdrawn plea would invite the jury to infer guilt from the very plea the court permitted the defendant to withdraw.

184. The court should overrule D's objection. D's statement is not hearsay because it constitutes a party admission. In addition, FRE 410 only excludes "any statement made in the course of plea discussions *with an attorney for the prosecuting authority* that do not result in a plea of guilty or which result in a plea of guilty later withdrawn." Statements made to police in an effort to plea bargain usually do not qualify because

police officers are not prosecutors. If the police officers were acting as agents of the prosecuting authority, D's statements might be excluded, but the problem supplies no facts on which to base that conclusion.

185. The court should overrule D's objection. Although many people pay traffic fines rather than take the trouble to contest them, the evidence is still relevant because one reasonable inference from the payment is that the person paying the fine believed herself to be guilty. In addition, FRE 410 does not exclude guilty pleas that were never withdrawn. D's best bet in this case is to argue that the jury should give the evidence very little weight because payment of traffic citations often is not an indication of guilt, but D should also be aware that the jury might consider the evidence to have significant probative value in light of the fact that D might have known that P was injured, that P might sue, and that a guilty plea would be used against D.

186. **Answer (C) is correct.** D's offer to take P to the hospital constitutes the type of conduct made inadmissible by FRE 409 because it is an offer "to pay medical, hospital, or similar expenses occasioned by an injury."

Answer (A) is incorrect because even if the statement is a party admission, it is still excluded by FRE 409. **Answer (D) is incorrect** because the evidence is relevant. It is somewhat more likely that a person who offers to pay for another person's medical or related expenses is responsible for the other's injuries than is one who does not make an offer.

Answer (B) is incorrect because there is no indication that this was an offer to settle a disputed claim.

187. **Answer (D) is correct.** The offer to pay P's medical bills is a party admission but is barred by FRE 409. The statement, "I didn't see you in the street" is not barred by that rule, however. Note that unlike the compromise rule (FRE 408), the medical payments rule does not exclude evidence of statements made in connection with the payment or offer to pay expenses. Thus, the statement accompanying the offer to pay is admissible. **Answer (A) is incorrect** because it assumes the entire statement is admissible as a party admission. **Answer (C) is incorrect** for the opposite reason; part of the statement is admissible.

Answer (B) is incorrect because there was no disputed claim at the time D made the statement. Thus, the evidence does not fit within the compromise rule.

188. **Answer (D) is correct.** What D did for P was nice, and the law likes to encourage nice gestures, but no rule would exclude this evidence. It was not an offer to pay hospital, medical, or related expenses. It was not an offer to compromise a disputed claim. And of course, the evidence is relevant because a person who replaces the property of another that was destroyed in an accident involving the two people is more likely responsible for the injury than is one who does not act in that way. **Answers (A), (B), and (C) are incorrect** for these reasons.

189. The court should sustain the objection. It is not likely that people who have liability insurance are more careless than people without liability insurance. In fact, the opposite might be true because having liability insurance shows a degree of responsibility. (Of course, many states require liability insurance, so having it might mean little or nothing.) Though relevant, FRE 411 makes the evidence inadmissible when offered to prove that the person "acted negligently or otherwise wrongfully." That is the only purpose for which the evidence might be relevant on the facts given. Thus, the evidence is inadmissible.

190. The court should sustain D's objection. FRE 411 only excludes evidence of liability insurance when it is offered to prove negligence or other wrongful conduct. Such evidence is admissible for other purposes, including proving a witness's bias. Here, P might argue that because D and D's expert witness both maintain malpractice insurance with the same company, D's expert might tend to favor D in order to keep her insurance company from having to pay P's claim. This, in turn, might keep premiums down. However, most courts would hold that having a common malpractice insurance carrier is not sufficient to establish bias, or even if it does show possible bias, the potential unfair prejudice from the evidence substantially exceeds any value to show bias.

191. The court should probably overrule D's objection. Technically, FRE 411 might not apply because this is jury selection, not a question of admissibility or inadmissibility of evidence offered formally at trial. Nevertheless, parties are entitled to an unbiased jury, and a person who works for a party's insurance company might favor the employer (and thus the party) in deliberations. The court should try to elicit this information as carefully as possible so as to avoid unduly emphasizing the existence of liability insurance, but P is probably entitled to determine if any jurors are employed by the insurer.

192. **Answer (D) is correct.** The character trait of peacefulness is not "pertinent" to whether a person has committed perjury. Thus, under FRE 404(a)(1), it is not admissible to prove her innocence, meaning that **answer (A) is incorrect.** The evidence is also inadmissible to support D's credibility by showing that she did not lie when she denied committing the crime. Under FRE 608(b), only specific instances of conduct that are "probative of truthfulness or untruthfulness" are admissible to attack or support the witness's character for truthfulness. Being a peaceable person is not probative of truthfulness or untruthfulness. Thus, **answer (B) is incorrect. Answer (C) is incorrect** for the same reasons.

193. **Answer (C) is correct.** The evidence probably qualifies as another "crime, wrong, or act" that might be admissible under FRE 404(b) to show a motive to rob a liquor store to obtain money with which to purchase drugs.

    Answer (A) is incorrect because being a drug addict with a $500 a day habit is not "probative of truthfulness or untruthfulness, and thus under FRE 608(b), the evidence is not admissible to impeach D's credibility.

    Answer (B) is incorrect because, without more, the evidence is not relevant to show D does not recollect accurately.

    Answer (D) is incorrect because questions going to a person's motive to commit a crime are not beyond the scope of the direct examination when the person testified that she did not commit the crime.

194. **Answer (B) is correct.** W testified that D was on the driveway at the time of the collision. Previously, W implied that D was on the sidewalk at that time. The prior statement is therefore inconsistent with the trial testimony, and is admissible to impeach W's credibility.

    Because the prior statement was not made under oath and subject to penalty of perjury, it is not admissible as non-hearsay under FRE 801(d)(1)(A). This means that **answers (A) and (C) are incorrect.** Because the evidence is admissible to impeach W, **answer (D) is incorrect.**

195. **Answer (A) is correct.** In this iteration of the skating problem, the prior inconsistent statement is being proven by extrinsic evidence. Under FRE 613(b), all that is required is that the witness be given the opportunity to explain or deny the statement. That was done here, because W was asked on cross-examination about the statement. (P was not required to do it this way. P could have avoided mentioning the prior

inconsistent statement on cross-examination, elicited the statement from X, and then re-called W to confront her with the statement.) Because the prior statement was not made under oath subject to penalty of perjury, it is not admissible substantively (to prove the truth of the matter asserted).

Answers (B), (C), and (D) are incorrect for the reasons just given and for those noted in the answer to the previous question.

196.   **Answer (D) is correct.** Begin with the purpose of the evidence. P wishes to do one or both of two things. First, P might wish to impeach W's credibility by means of a prior inconsistent statement. W, who testified that D was on the driveway, previously said that D was on the sidewalk. This is a prior inconsistent statement. Under FRE 613(b), a party may offer extrinsic evidence of a prior inconsistent statement as long as the witness being impeached is given an opportunity to explain or deny making the statement. W had that opportunity here, because she was confronted with the statement on cross-examination. If X had heard W's prior inconsistent statement, she could have testified about it.

The problem is that X did not hear the prior inconsistent statement. Z heard it. Z made the out-of-court statement to X that W had made the statement. This makes Z a hearsay declarant. (Z's statement asserting that W said, "D was just learning to skate and should not have been on the sidewalk" is offered to prove what it asserts—that W made that statement.) There is no exception covering Z's statement. Thus, X's testimony is inadmissible hearsay.

Answers (A), (B), and (C) are incorrect for the reasons just given.

197.   **Answer (A) is correct.** As in the previous problems involving these facts, the evidence at issue is a prior inconsistent statement. Here, the statement was made under oath in a deposition. That means it is admissible non-hearsay under FRE 801(d)(1)(A) if the declarant testifies at the trial or hearing and is subject to cross-examination concerning the statement. Those requirements are satisfied here. Thus, the prior statement is admissible to show that D was on the sidewalk (the truth of the matter asserted).

The prior inconsistent statement is also admissible to impeach. It is unlikely P will want to use it for that purpose, as P would like W to be believed when she made the prior statement. But technically, it is admissible to impeach.

Answers (B), (C), and (D) are incorrect for the reasons just given.

198.   **Answer (A) is correct.** Evidence that W testified incorrectly about what outfit she was wearing when she saw the crime take place is relevant because it suggests that she might be wrong about other things. Thus, this is impeachment by contradiction. There is no rule limiting the nature of contradictory matter raised *during the cross-examination of a witness.* Thus, it does not matter that the color of W's outfit is "collateral." The question is proper. This means that **answer (C) is incorrect.**

Answer (B) is incorrect because the question does not deal with W's ability to perceive.

Answer (D) is incorrect because a possible error concerning what the witness was wearing when she saw the crime take place does not tend to show that the witness has a bad character for truthfulness or untruthfulness.

199. **Answer (D) is correct.** Using a false identification is an act that is "probative of truthfulness or untruthfulness." Under FRE 608(b), such acts are admissible in the discretion of the court if not proven by extrinsic evidence. A question asked during cross-examination is not extrinsic to the witness. Thus, this is a proper attempt to impeach W by showing character for untruthfulness, meaning that **answer (A) is incorrect.**

Answer (B) is incorrect because the question does not suggest facts that contradict W's testimony.

Answer (C) is incorrect because questions going to the witness's credibility are not beyond the scope of the direct examination. It does not matter that the incident with the false identification was not mentioned during direct examination.

200. **Answer (A) is correct.** Under FRE 608(a), it is permissible to impeach a witness's truthful character using evidence of reputation for untruthfulness. That is what is happening in this problem. There is no "extrinsic evidence" rule; the party attacking the witness may call another witness to testify to the first witness's reputation for truthfulness.

Answer (B) is incorrect because FRE 608(a) contains no requirement that the witness's truthfulness has first been supported. In fact, the opposite is true: character for truthfulness may not be proven by reputation or opinion unless a witness's truthful character has been attacked.

Answer (C) is incorrect because it does not matter that this is a civil action.

Answer (D) is incorrect because the credibility of witnesses is relevant.

201. **Answer (C) is correct.** The purpose of the prosecutor's question is to impeach D with a prior conviction. This is governed by FRE 609. Under FRE 609(a), because murder is not a crime "involving dishonesty or false statement," evidence of the conviction is not admissible automatically. Thus, **answer (B) is incorrect**. Because murder is a crime "punishable by death or imprisonment in excess of a year," the crime *might* be admissible to impeach. Thus, **answer (A) is incorrect**. The standard depends on who the witness is. If the witness is the "accused," the evidence is only admissible if the probative value exceeds the danger of unfair prejudice. (Note that this is *not* the FRE 403 standard.) Thus, answer (C) is correct, and **answer (D) is incorrect**.

202. D should argue that the testimony undercuts W1's capacity to observe, recollect, and narrate accurately, and that it is not an attack on W1's character for truthfulness. If

it impeaches by capacity, there is no rule that specifically governs the evidence, and thus the court should simply decide whether the evidence is relevant and whether its potential for prejudice, consumption of time, or distraction of the jury substantially outweighs its probative value. (The court should also consider whether the evidence has too great a tendency to embarrass the witness, which would run afoul of FRE 611(a)(3), which provides that "[t]he court shall exercise reasonable control over the mode and order of interrogating witnesses and presenting evidence so as to . . . protect witnesses from harassment or undue embarrassment.") It would have been much better for D to call the psychiatrist rather than a lay person who happens to know that W1 is under the psychiatrist's care, but this does not make the evidence inadmissible per se. If the court characterizes the evidence as an attack on W1's character for truthfulness, the court will exclude the evidence because, under FRE 608(b), no extrinsic evidence is allowed for that purpose, and calling another witness constitutes extrinsic evidence.

203. **Answer (D) is correct.** D's question violates the common law rule, that one may not impeach a witness by contradiction on a collateral matter using extrinsic evidence (what a mouthful!). Even though the Federal Rules do not mention this rule, it is sensible because it avoids wasting time on matters the only purpose of which is to impeach by contradiction, and even then, involves matters so unimportant that the witness's error says virtually nothing about her credibility. Though the Federal Rules do not adopt the common law rule, many courts would exclude this evidence as a waste of time under FRE 403.

The problem here is not in asking whether W1 owns a blue raincoat, but in using extrinsic evidence to establish that she does not. If D wanted to show that W1 did not own a blue raincoat, D should have asked W1 that question. Unfortunately, however, if W1 had insisted that she did own a blue raincoat, D would have been stuck with that answer.

Answer (A) is incorrect for the reasons just given. **Answer (B) is incorrect** because whether W1 owns a blue raincoat or not does not affect her character for truthfulness. **Answer (C) is incorrect** because evidence that goes to the credibility of a witness is not irrelevant.

204. **Answer (D) is correct.** The prosecution is attempting to impeach W with a prior conviction. The conviction is not one for a crime involving dishonesty or false statement, so it is not automatically admissible. Thus, **answer (B) is incorrect**. Because murder is a crime "punishable by death or imprisonment in excess of a year," the court has discretion to admit the evidence. Thus, **answer (A) is incorrect**. Because the witness is a witness other than the accused, the evidence "shall be admitted, subject to Rule 403." That means the evidence is admissible unless the probative value is substantially outweighed by the danger of unfair prejudice. This is the test stated in answer (D). **Answer (C) is incorrect** because it states the standard that would apply if the witness being impeached were the accused.

205. **Answer (A) is correct.** D's goal is to impeach W1 by showing a motive to testify against D. There is no specific rule governing this type of impeachment, but the Supreme Court confirmed that this important form of impeachment is still available in *United States v. Abel*, 469 U.S. 45 (1984). The Court indicated that this method of impeachment is controlled by FRE 403. Because FRE 403 is heavily slanted toward admission (exclusion may only occur if the probative value of the evidence is substantially outweighed by the dangers mentioned in the rule), this form of impeachment is readily available. Here, the evidence will be admissible because the evidence carries substantial probative value and there is little danger of jury misuse of the evidence.

Answer (B) is incorrect because there is no prohibition of extrinsic evidence when the method of impeachment is bias or motive.

Answer (C) is incorrect because D's purpose is not to impeach W1's character for truthfulness. (If that was D's purpose, the evidence would not be admissible because FRE 608(b) does contain a prohibition on extrinsic evidence.)

Answer (D) is incorrect because FRE 408, the compromise rule, does not bar the evidence when used to impeach a witness by showing bias.

206. **Answer (C) is correct.** D's goal is to impeach W with a prior conviction. Medicare fraud is a crime involving dishonesty or false statement. Under FRE 609(a)(1), such a crime "shall be admitted" regardless of the punishment associated with it. Courts have held that the trial court has no discretion to exclude the evidence. Thus, the court must overrule the objection.

Answers (A), (B), and (D) are incorrect for the reasons just given.

207. **Answer (A) is correct.** P is attempting to offer her own prior *consistent* statement. Under FRE 801(d)(1)(B), a prior consistent statement is only admissible if the declarant testifies at the trial or hearing, is subject to cross-examination concerning the statement, and the statement "is offered to rebut an express or implied charge of recent fabrication or improper influence or motive." In *Tome v. United States*, 513 U.S. 150 (1995), the Supreme Court also held that the rule incorporates the additional common law requirement that the statement was made before the charge of fabrication was made or before the influence or motive came into being. Here, the problem is that P made the statement when she already had a motive to lie. Thus, the statement is inadmissible hearsay.

Answer (B) is incorrect because it is an overly broad statement. The rules only regulate some methods of enhancing the credibility of a witness. There is nothing impermissible about supporting a witness's credibility by showing that she has very good vision, for example.

Answer (C) is incorrect because a prior inconsistent statement, if admissible, does hot have to be proven by the declarant's testimony.

Answer (D) is incorrect because the evidence is inadmissible.

208.   **Answer (A) is correct.** W's prior statement that he was at the movies for the entire night is inconsistent with his trial testimony that he was across the street from the car dealer at the crucial time that night. Because the statement was not made under oath subject to penalty of perjury, the statement is not admissible to prove the truth of the matter asserted (FRE 801(d)(1)(A)). It is only admissible to impeach. The requirements of FRE 613(a) have been satisfied.

   Answers (B), (C), and (D) are incorrect for the reasons just given.

209.   **Answer (C) is correct.** As in the previous problem, the method of impeachment being used here is prior inconsistent statement. FRE 613(b) provides that if extrinsic evidence of a prior statement is offered, the declarant must be given the opportunity to explain or deny the statement. That occurred here, during W's cross-examination. Thus, the evidence is admissible to impeach W by prior inconsistent statement.

   Answer (A) is incorrect because, as just shown, the rules governing the use of prior statements do not contain an extrinsic evidence prohibition.

   Answer (B) is incorrect because the matter of W's whereabouts at the crucial time is not collateral.

   Answer (D) is incorrect because D is not offering the evidence to prove that W has a bad character for truthfulness.

210.   **Answer (C) is correct.** The prosecution is using a prior *consistent* statement in this problem. The requirements of FRE 801(d)(1)(B) have been satisfied. W has testified at the trial, is subject to cross-examination concerning the prior consistent statement, the statement is being offered to rebut a charge of recent fabrication (as raised by the defense), and W made the statement before that charge had been leveled. This means answer (A) is correct: the question is a permissible attempt to establish W's credibility.

   When a prior consistent statement satisfies the requirements of FRE 801(d)(1)(B), it can be used both to support the witness's credibility and to prove the truth of the matter asserted (here, that W was at Mel's Diner at the crucial time). Thus, answer (B) is also correct: the question is a permissible attempt to establish W's whereabouts on the evening of February 6.

   Because the evidence is admissible for both credibility and substantive purposes, answer (C) is the correct answer. **Answer (D) is incorrect** for the reasons just given.

211.   **Answer (C) is correct.** If D hates poodles, it is not likely he would travel to another city to attend a poodle show. This is therefore an attempt to impeach D by showing the implausibility of his alibi. There is no specific provision in the Federal Rules governing this type of impeachment. Therefore, it is subject only to the general requirements of FRE 102 and 611(a) (which deal with such things as fairness, witness harassment, and needless consumption of time), and to FRE 403. There is no reason

to think that the probative value of the evidence for its legitimate purpose of impeaching D's credibility is substantially outweighed by the danger of unfair prejudice or other dangers mentioned in FRE 403.

Answer (A) is incorrect because evidence going to the credibility of a witness is not irrelevant.

Answer (B) is incorrect because hating poodles does not affect a person's character for truthfulness.

Answer (D) is incorrect because a bias against poodles is not relevant to D's credibility in this instance. (Had D been on trial for attacking a poodle, and D denied doing so, the evidence might be admissible to impeach by showing a bias against poodles or a motive to hurt them.)

212. **Answer (C) is correct.** The applicable standard for admission of the evidence is in FRE 609(a)(1). If the witness being impeached with a prior conviction is the criminal defendant, the evidence is admissible only if the probative value exceeds the risk of unfair prejudice. The fact that the conviction was for the same crime as the one for which D is now on trial increases the risk of unfair prejudice, but does not make the evidence per se inadmissible. Thus, **answer (A) is incorrect.**

Answer (B) is incorrect because it is based on the wrong standard.

Answer (D) is incorrect because battery is not a crime involving dishonesty or false statement, so the conviction is not automatically admissible to impeach D.

213. **Answer (C) is correct.** The evidence is relevant on two grounds. First, it supplies a motive for D to attack V. If D was having an affair with W, D might have had a motive to kill V to remove her from the picture. Thus, the evidence is admissible substantively. Second, the evidence tends to supply a motive for W to lie. W might want to protect D to preserve their relationship.

Answers (A), (B), and (D) are incorrect for the reasons just stated.

214. **Answer (A) is correct.** Evidence that W1 was watching "Beetleman" instead of "Bar Wars" impeaches W1 by contradiction. But which movie W1 was attending has no value to the case except to impeach in this way. Thus, the matter of what movie W1 was watching is considered "collateral." Although the Federal Rules do not adopt the common law rule, most federal courts would exclude evidence that impeaches a witness by contradiction on a collateral matter *using extrinsic evidence* under FRE 403 because it is a waste of time. Calling another witness (W2) is extrinsic evidence. Thus, this was an improper attempt to impeach by contradiction.

Note that the result would be the same if the evidence was that W1 *told W2* that she had seen "Beetleman." This would be a prior inconsistent statement. Because the matter about which W1 spoke inconsistently is collateral, most courts would forbid the use of extrinsic evidence to prove the prior inconsistent statement. This rule is not contained in the Federal Rules, but it follows naturally from the common law rule just discussed, and most federal courts today would exclude the evidence as a waste of time under FRE 403.

Answers (B), (C), and (D) are incorrect for the reasons just given.

215. **Answer (D) is correct.** The statement by X was admissible as an excited utterance. Thus, even though X has not testified at the trial, X's credibility is on the table. FRE 806 provides that "[w]hen a hearsay statement, or a statement defined in FRE 801(d)(2)(C), (D), or (E), has been admitted in evidence, the credibility of the declarant may be attacked, and if attacked may be supported, by any evidence which would be admissible for those purposes if declarant had testified as a witness." That rule would make X's prior conviction admissible if it satisfies the requirements of FRE 609. Because forgery is a crime involving dishonesty or false statement, it is admissible per se pursuant to FRE 609(a)(2).

Answers (A), (B), and (C) are incorrect for the reasons just stated.

216. **Answer (B) is correct.** The evidence seeks to support D's credibility by showing a good character for truthfulness. FRE 608(a) provides that such evidence in the form of reputation or opinion is only admissible "after the character of the witness for truthfulness has been attacked by opinion or reputation evidence or otherwise." The facts do not reveal that the prosecution attacked D's character for truthfulness. Thus, the evidence is inadmissible. **Answers (A) and (C) are incorrect** for the reasons just stated. **Answer (D) is incorrect** because W's opinion, stated on the witness stand, is not hearsay.

Note that in this situation, the evidence would not be admissible under FRE 404(a) because honesty is not a "pertinent" trait of character in this situation. D allegedly stole the cards while the child was playing with them; she is not alleged to have used any fraud or other dishonesty to cause the child to part with the cards.

217. **Answer (C) is correct.** FRE 609(b) provides that if more than ten years have elapsed from the date of conviction or release from confinement, whichever is later, evidence of a prior conviction is inadmissible "unless the court determines, in the interests of justice, that the probative value of the conviction supported by specific facts and circumstances substantially outweighs its prejudicial effect." Note that this is the opposite of the FRE 403 standard. Here, the usual result will be exclusion, not admission. This rule applies even to crimes involving dishonesty or false statement, such as the perjury conviction in this case.

Answers (A) and (B) are incorrect for the reasons just stated. **Answer (D) is incorrect** because the facts given in the problem do not reveal whether the prosecution can meet its burden under FRE 609(b).

218. **Answer (D) is correct.** FRE 607 provides that "[t]he credibility of a witness may be attacked by any party, including the party calling the witness." The purpose of this

rule was to do away with the common law rule that a party vouches for her own witnesses and may not impeach her own witness unless the witness turns hostile. At the same time, the courts have held that there are limits to a party's rights under FRE 607. Specifically, a party may not abuse the intent of the rule by calling a witness for the sole purpose of impeaching her through a method that reveals otherwise inadmissible evidence.

That is what the prosecution has done in this case. If W never testified, the prosecution would have no legitimate way to introduce W's statement to her friend that incriminated D. It would not be admissible substantively because of the hearsay rule, and if W neither testifies nor is a prior statement of W admitted pursuant to an exception to or exemption from the hearsay rule, there would be no basis for impeachment of W. Here, the prosecutor's probable objective is to place before the jury the statement incriminating D. That statement would purportedly be offered only as a prior inconsistent statement to impeach W, but the prosecutor no doubt knows that the jury will have a hard time abiding by a limiting instruction, and will instead consider the evidence for what it asserts.

This answer assumes that the prosecution really does "know" that W will stick to the story she gave before the grand jury. The courts will not require absolute certainty, but a reasonably high standard of knowledge should be required in order to avoid losing potentially relevant information. Thus, if the prosecutor has a legitimate reason to believe that W will testify differently at trial than at the grand jury, the court should allow the prosecutor to call W.

Answers (A) and (C) are incorrect for the reasons given. **Answer B is incorrect** because the prosecutor had no reason to believe that W might change her testimony. The prosecutor is not entitled to place W before the jury, and introduce her prior inconsistent statement, on the sole ground that her demeanor will reveal that she is being untruthful. (In an extreme case this might be possible, but the facts here do not appear to support such a result.)

219. The court should overrule the objection. Even though Z never testified at the trial, Z's excited utterance was admitted to prove that D rammed X's car. Admission of that statement places Z's credibility in issue. FRE 806 provides that "[w]hen a hearsay statement, or a statement defined in FRE 801(d)(2)(C), (D), or (E), has been admitted in evidence, the credibility of the declarant may be attacked, and if attacked may be supported, by any evidence which would be admissible for those purposes if declarant had testified as a witness." The rule further provides that a prior inconsistent statement may be introduced for that purpose without being subject to the requirement that the declarant be afforded an opportunity to explain or deny the statement (a requirement contained in FRE 613(b)). In this case, D is availing herself of the opportunity to impeach Z with a prior inconsistent statement.

220. The court should sustain the objection. FRE 610 provides that "[e]vidence of the beliefs of a witness on matters of religion is not admissible for the purpose of showing that

by reason of their nature the witness's credibility is impaired or enhanced." D's question was designed to impeach W by virtue of her religious beliefs—to show that a person who believes all people with blue eyes are evil should not be believed. (This is a sort of character impeachment.) This falls within the prohibition of FRE 610.

221.   The court should overrule the objection. D is not attempting to impeach W by means of the nature of her religious beliefs, but trying to establish a possible bias or motive to testify in favor of the church to which W belongs. FRE 610 therefore does not apply. The court may still exclude the evidence under FRE 403, but that will be a difficult standard to satisfy, especially in light of the fact that the courts tend to treat bias or motive impeachment as strongly affecting the credibility of a witness. If the P church congregation is huge and W is not an active member, the probative value of the evidence to impeach by showing bias or motive is not as great as if the congregation was smaller and W was an active member. Even there, however, most courts would probably overrule the objection. Of course, if P requests a limiting instruction informing jurors of the limited purpose for which the court admitted the evidence, the court must grant the request.

222.   The court should overrule P's objection. Evidence that P is a "liar extraordinaire" is not relevant to whether D struck P or vice versa, but it does tend to impeach P's statement that D struck her. Normally, a person who does not testify at the trial is not subject to impeachment. However, FRE 806 provides that a hearsay declarant whose statement has been offered at trial may be impeached. That is the situation here. P's statement was admitted, probably as an excited utterance. This made P subject to impeachment. FRE 608(a) allows reputation or opinion evidence on the issue of a person's reputation for truthfulness. W2's proposed testimony fits into the reputation category, and is proper.

223.   The court should sustain the prosecutor's objection and not permit W1 to testify concerning the weather. D is attempting to impeach W1 by contradiction. The common law rule, is that one may not impeach a witness by contradiction on a collateral matter using extrinsic evidence. In this hypothetical, the weather is collateral because the events took place inside a bank, not outside. Thus, without more information, it does not appear that the fact that it was raining is relevant except insofar as it tends to impeach W1 by contradiction. (If D could show that most of the illumination in the bank was supplied by windows, and that it was dark in the bank because it was raining outside, the evidence concerning the weather might take on some value because it might have affected W1's ability to identify the robber. But those facts are not given.) Although the Federal Rules did not adopt the common law rule just described, federal courts will usually exclude evidence of this kind under FRE 403.

Because the weather is a collateral fact, D is restricted to cross-examination, and is stuck with W1's response. D may not use W2 to show that it was raining.

224. **Answer (D) is correct.** According to FRE 902(6), "printed materials purporting to be newspapers or periodicals" are self-authenticating, meaning that "[e]xtrinsic evidence of authenticity as a condition precedent to admissibility is not required with respect to" the item.

     Answer (A) is incorrect because it fails to recognize the application of the self-authentication doctrine, and because even under normal authentication doctrine (FRE 901(a)), this issue is to be decided according to a different standard: whether there is sufficient evidence to support a finding that the item is what its proponent claims.

     Answer (B) is incorrect because the objection was made on the basis of authentication, not the best evidence rule. Even if D had objected on best evidence rule grounds, the court should overrule the objection because that rule does not require a party to offer the "best evidence" to prove a point except when the issue is the contents of a writing and the party offers secondary evidence of the writing rather than the writing itself.

     Answer (C) is incorrect because it fails to recognize the application of the self-authentication doctrine. If this were a normal authentication situation, the answer would be correct.

     Note that if P had objected on hearsay grounds, the court probably would have sustained the objection. The article asserts that all the goods in D's warehouse were destroyed by flooding, and it is offered to prove that fact.

225. **Answer (A) is correct.** FRE 901(a) provides that a piece of evidence is authenticated if the court finds that there is sufficient evidence to support a finding that the evidence is what its proponent claims. FRE 901(b)(6) provides an illustration of authentication involving telephone conversations: "evidence that a call was made to the number assigned at the time by the telephone company to a particular person or business, if . . . (B) in the case of a business, the call was made to a place of business and the conversation related to the business reasonably transacted over the telephone." Here, P has testified that she placed the call to a number identified with D in the phone book, and that the answering party identified himself as a "heating service." This is sufficient evidence to support a finding that P actually placed the call to D.

     Answer (B) is incorrect because it assumes that the court must make the finding of whether the call was actually placed. This is not the standard of FRE 901(a).

     Answer (C) is incorrect because the answering party need not identify itself specifically as a particular business in order for there to be sufficient evidence to support a finding that the call was actually placed to the business.

Answer (D) is incorrect because the very purpose of a motion to strike is to remove evidence from consideration that the jury has already heard. Normally, the court will also instruct the jury to ignore the evidence.

226.   The prosecution will probably try to establish chain of custody. One or more witnesses will testify to the location of the bat from the time it was found (presumably in D's possession) until the time it was brought into court. Often, a police officer will testify that she marked the item at the scene and placed it in a secure location (such as an evidence locker). That witness or other witnesses will establish the movements (if any) of the item from the time it was discovered until the time of trial. Any breaks in the chain might be fatal, but need not be. The basic standard for authentication is the same as for all other situations: whether there is evidence sufficient to support a finding that the item is what its proponent claims (FRE 901(a)).

227.   **Answer (D) is correct.** P's testimony is sufficient to authenticate the photograph. P has personal knowledge of the positions of the cars immediately after the crash, and has testified that the photograph accurately depicts that scene. There is no requirement that the photographer testify.

Answer (A) is incorrect for the reason just given. The photographer is not a necessary witness as long as someone with personal knowledge testifies.

Answer (B) is incorrect because P's testimony is sufficient to support a finding that the cars were not moved between the accident and the time the photograph was taken.

Answer (C) is incorrect because the best evidence rule has not been violated in this situation. P is not testifying about the contents of the photograph without using the photograph. P has brought the photograph to court and will use it to prove its own contents.

228.   One way would be to obtain an expert's opinion, as discussed in FRE 901(b)(3). P could obtain a handwriting exemplar from D, which the court would order D to provide if D is unwilling to do so voluntarily. That exemplar could be authenticated simply by testimony, from someone with knowledge, that D provided it. The expert would then testify that she compared the exemplar with the questioned letter and concluded that they were written by the same person.

A second way to authenticate the letter would be by the testimony of a lay witness familiar with D's handwriting (and whose familiarity was not acquired for purposes of the litigation). *See* FRE 901(b)(2).

In either case, the evidence would be admissible if the court concludes that there is evidence sufficient to support a finding that D wrote the questioned letter. That is an easy standard to satisfy.

229. **Answer (D) is correct.** The best evidence rule only applies when a party seeks to prove the contents of a writing. In that situation, unless an exception applies, the party must offer the writing, not secondary evidence (such as testimony about what the writing says). Here, P has not testified about the contents of her medical records. She has merely testified that she suffered complications that required amputation. Though her testimony might not be the "best evidence" of the condition that led to the need for amputation, the best evidence rule does not require P to produce the "best evidence" to prove anything except the contents of a writing.

Answer (A) is incorrect for the reasons just stated.

Answer (B) is incorrect because, if the best evidence rule does not apply, there is no requirement that the party produce the writing that would support her testimony.

Answer (C) is incorrect because it lays out an exception to the best evidence rule. Exceptions are not needed if the rule itself does not apply, which is the case here.

230. **Answer (D) is correct** for the same reasons as in the previous question. Even though the transcript is clearly the "best evidence" of X's testimony, the best evidence rule does not apply for one simple reason: W is not testifying about the contents of the transcript; she is testifying about the contents of her memory of what X said at the trial. Thus, if W testifies that X testified at the first trial, "Defendant shot the victim," W's testimony does not violate the best evidence rule. If W had testified that the transcript reports that X testified, "Defendant shot the victim," that testimony would violate the best evidence rule because W will have testified about the contents of a writing.

Answers (A), (B), and (C) are incorrect for the same reasons as in the previous question.

231. **Answer (A) is correct.** An X-ray is a "photograph" as defined in FRE 1001(2), and photographs are covered by the best evidence rule. Dr. W will testify about the contents of the X-ray, which presumably shows the condition of the bones of P's leg. The best evidence rule requires that unless certain exceptions apply (and none are applicable on the facts given here), the writing itself must be offered to prove its contents.

Note that as long as the writing is offered, there is no rule forbidding secondary evidence from being offered as well. Thus, Dr. W could explain what the X-ray shows. She could also testify about other facts that led her to conclude that P's leg was broken. And of course, P is not required to use the X-ray to prove her leg was broken. The best evidence rule simply provides that if a party wishes to prove the contents of a writing, recording, or photograph, the item itself must be offered.

Answer (B) is incorrect for the reason given above. An X-ray is covered by the rule.

Answer (C) is incorrect because, although it seems illogical, there is no exception to the rule for writings, recordings, or photographs that a fact-finder would be unable to understand or interpret.

Answer (D) is incorrect because the proposed testimony is about what the X-ray shows, even if it requires some interpretation. As long as Dr. W will testify that the X-ray shows a break in P's leg, the X-ray must be produced (barring application of an exception).

232. **Answer (A) is correct.** The issue concerns the terms of the agreement. The agreement is in writing. If D wants to prove the terms, she must therefore offer the writing. It does not matter that a contract is actually something that exists between two minds and that the writing is only a memorandum. In law, the writing takes on special significance; its terms *become* the terms of the agreement.

Answers (B) and (C) are incorrect for the reasons just given. D is required to offer the writing to prove the terms of the contract.

Answer (D) is incorrect because there is no exception to the best evidence rule for situations in which the writing is central to the case. In fact, just the opposite is true; FRE 1004(4) sets forth an exception for situations in which the writing goes to a collateral matter (where it "is not closely related to a controlling issue").

233. The best evidence rule only applies if the witness is testifying about the "contents" of a writing, and not simply the writing's existence. If the only issue were whether there was a piece of paper on the car's windshield, there would be no best evidence rule problem. If the issue were the exact nature of the citation (the precise violation it states, for example), the best evidence rule certainly would apply. This case falls between. Though the parking ticket is a "writing," one argument is that the witness is simply identifying it as a parking ticket, not testifying to its contents. The opposite argument is that to testify that it was a parking ticket is to testify about its contents. The better argument is that this is not a best evidence rule violation, for the reason given above and one more—The importance of the ticket is its context in time: that it was on the car at that particular moment. The fact-finder would gain little by seeing the ticket in court.

An analogy: A witness will testify that the person who approached him was wearing a police badge. Probably, the testimony will not violate the best evidence rule.

234. A tombstone satisfies the definition of a "writing" in FRE 1001(1) because it consists of "letters, words, or numbers . . . set down by . . . other form of data compilation." Thus, it appears the best evidence rule applies. But it is not likely possible to produce the tombstone in court. FRE 1004(2) provides an exception for situations in which "no original can be obtained by any available judicial process or procedure." This is such a situation. The best evidence rule will not bar the witness's testimony.

The hearsay rule also would not prevent the testimony. The words "Elvis Aaron Presley" are hearsay because they are an assertion of a person, made other than while testifying at the trial or hearing, and they are offered in evidence to prove the truth of what they assert (that Elvis is dead). FRE 803(13), however, provides an exception for "[s]tatements of fact concerning personal or family history contained . . . on . . . tombstones."

235. **Answer (C) is correct.** A photocopy qualifies as a "duplicate" under FRE 1002(4) because it "is a counterpart produced by . . . photography, including enlargements or miniatures, or by mechanical or electronic re-recording, or by chemical reproduction, or by other equivalent technique which accurately reproduces the original." Photocopying qualifies under this definition. Normally, a duplicate is admissible to the same extent as the original (FRE 1003). However, the same rule provides that the court should exclude the duplicate if "(1) a genuine question is raised as to the authenticity of the original or (2) in the circumstances it would be unfair to admit the duplicate in lieu of the original." This case seems to satisfy the second test. D has claimed P tampered with the photocopy. It would be unfair to permit P to use the photocopy in lieu of the original.

Answer (A) is incorrect because it fails to take account of the exception in FRE 1003.

Answer (B) is incorrect because a photocopy does qualify as a duplicate.

Answer (D) is incorrect because it ignores the application of the best evidence rule, which is supposed to encourage the use of originals as a means of advancing the likelihood of learning the truth. In this case, requiring P to produce the original will serve that purpose. P may also produce the photocopy in addition to the original, but not in lieu of it.

236. **Answer (C) is correct.** FRE 201 governs the taking of judicial notice of adjudicative facts. FRE 201(a) provides that to be a proper subject of judicial notice, a fact "must be one not subject to reasonable dispute in that it is either (1) generally known within the territorial jurisdiction of the trial court or (2) capable of accurate and ready determination by resort to sources whose accuracy cannot reasonably be questioned."

Answer (A) is incorrect because it presents a fact that is subject to judicial notice under subpart (a)(2) of FRE 201. This fact is one that is not subject to reasonable dispute because there are authoritative horticultural sources that will clearly state that palm trees grow better in warm climates than in cold climates.

Answer (B) is incorrect because it falls into the same category as answer (A). Sources whose accuracy is not subject to dispute will verify the molecular structure of deuterium.

Answer (D) is incorrect because it presents a fact that is subject to judicial notice under subpart (a)(1) of FRE 201. If a certain state forbids the sale of packaged liquor on Sundays, this fact is very likely to be known generally within that state.

Barring additional facts not given in the problem, answer (C) does not state a fact of which judicial notice may be taken. It is quite unlikely that people within the court's territorial jurisdiction will generally be aware that a particular road was not plowed for twenty-four hours after a particular snow storm. It is possible that many people know this to be true, but it is very unlikely that the fact is "generally known." Also, this is not a fact that is likely to be found in a "source whose accuracy cannot reasonably be questioned." Even a contemporaneous newspaper account that stated the fact might be disputed because newspapers often contain inaccuracies.

237. **Answer (D) is correct.** FRE 201(g) provides that "[i]n a civil action or proceeding, the court shall instruct the jury to accept as conclusive any fact judicial noticed." The language makes clear that this is mandatory. If the court has taken notice, it *must* tell the jury that the fact is conclusively established.

Answer (A) is incorrect because, once the court has taken notice of the fact, no contrary evidence may be offered.

Answer (B) is incorrect because such an argument would run directly contrary to the provision of FRE 201(g) that the court's taking of notice is conclusive as to the fact. It is therefore improper to argue to the jury that it should make a contrary factual finding.

Answer (C) is incorrect because, as noted above, the court is *required* to give the instruction.

238. **Answer (A) is correct.** Certainly, the danger posed by AIDS is generally known within the territorial jurisdiction of the trial court. If for some reason it is not, D can certainly provide the court with authoritative sources establishing that fact.

    Answer (B) is incorrect because the importance of facts to the claim or defense does not affect the propriety of taking judicial notice.

    Answer (C) is incorrect because FRE 201(f) provides that "[j]judicial notice may be taken at any stage of the proceedings. Thus, notice may be taken even after the trial begins. (In fact, notice is sometimes taken at the appellate stage.)

    Answer (D) is incorrect because FRE 104(a) provides that the court may rely on any non-privileged evidence in making evidentiary rulings. Thus, even if D supports her judicial notice request with hearsay (the reliable source is likely hearsay, for example), the court may consider the hearsay in making its ruling.

239. **Answer (C) is correct.** FRE 201 does not forbid the taking of judicial notice in criminal cases, even against the defendant and even if the fact noticed constitutes an essential element of the crime. Thus, **answers (A) and (B) are incorrect.**

    If the court takes notice in a criminal case, however, FRE 201(g) states that "the court shall instruct the jury that it may, but is not required to, accept as conclusive [the] fact judicial noticed." The purpose of this rule is to preserve a criminal defendant's right to trial by jury. **Answer (D) is incorrect** because it is phrased in permissive terms (the court "may" instruct the jury). The instruction that the jury need not consider the fact conclusively established is a mandatory instruction.

240. The court may take notice of the fact, but not on the basis of FRE 201. This is not an "adjudicative fact," but a "legislative fact." In the words of the Advisory Committee note to FRE 201, legislative facts "are those which have relevance to legal reasoning and the lawmaking process, whether in the formulation of a legal principle or ruling by a judge or court or in the enactment of a legislative body." In other words, legislative facts are the kinds of "facts" that rule-makers take into consideration when deciding on the appropriate rule. Those facts often are disputable; indeed, they are often hotly contested. If legislatures and courts were not permitted to take such facts into account, lawmaking would be virtually impossible to undertake.

TOPIC 14:   ANSWERS
BURDENS OF PROOF AND PRESUMPTIONS

241. **Answer (A) is correct.** The party who has the burden of persuasion as to an issue generally must also bear the burden of producing evidence. Here, P has the burden of persuading the jury that D was negligent, and must also produce evidence of D's negligence. The testimony of P's witness is certainly sufficient to meet a burden of production. This does not mean, however, that P has met a burden of *persuasion*. It only means that P has produced sufficient evidence to *allow* the jury to render a verdict for P on the negligence issue. The burden of persuasion remains with P.

What happens if D fails to produce any contrary evidence on the negligence question? Barring very unusual circumstances in which the evidence presented by the party with the burden of persuasion (here P) is so overwhelming as to make a decision for the other party irrational, there is still a jury question. Thus, by failing to offer evidence of non-negligence, D has taken a risk that the jury will find in P's favor on that question, but no more. The burden of persuasion is still with P, and the court should not direct a verdict for P on the issue.

(A) is therefore the correct answer. The case goes to the jury on the negligence issue, and the jury should be instructed that P bears the burden of persuasion.

Answer (B) is incorrect because, as stated above, the effect of D's failure to offer evidence is not to order the issue decided for P, but to let the case go to the jury.

Answer (C) is incorrect because it assumes that the burden of persuasion has shifted to D. As explained above, it has not.

Answer (D) is incorrect because the evidence discussed only goes to the issue of negligence, not to the entire *prima facie* case.

242. **Answer (D) is correct.** P has the burden of persuasion on the negligence issue, and also has the burden of producing evidence on that issue. P has failed to produce any affirmative evidence of D's negligence. Thus, P has not met a burden of producing evidence on this essential element of the *prima facie* case. There is no reason to force D to present any evidence at all. The court should direct a verdict for D. Note that the directed verdict will be on the entire negligence claim; the failure of any essential element of the *prima facie* case means the entire claim fails.

Answer (A) is incorrect because, by failing to meet a burden of production, P has not earned the right to have the jury decide in her favor.

Answer (B) is incorrect because D has no obligation to present evidence if P has not met a burden of production on an essential element of her claim.

Answer (C) is incorrect because the court has sufficient information before it to rule on D's motion. Of course, the court may choose to give P another opportunity to present evidence as to D's negligence, but it should not force D to present a case unless, and until, P presents such evidence.

243. The court should still grant D's motion. P is arguing that even though she has no affirmative evidence of negligence, she should be given the opportunity to produce it from D's witnesses, or, even if not, show the jury by the witnesses' demeanor that they are lying. If the court were to allow the case to go forward based on this argument, directed verdicts would practically disappear. It is possible that granting such motions will work injustice occasionally, but that will not likely happen often. Remember that in civil cases, there is ample opportunity for discovery. P should use that opportunity to take the depositions of D's witnesses. If P really believes that she can show that D's witnesses are lying, or get them to change their stories, she can thus establish a record to place before the court in opposition to D's motion for directed verdict.

244. **Answer (C) is correct.** According to the "bursting bubble" theory of presumptions, a presumption only shifts the burden of production to the opponent, and when the opponent offers sufficient evidence of the non-existence of the *presumed fact* to meet a burden of production, the presumption disappears from the case. Here, P has produced sufficient evidence to meet her burden of production. This causes the presumption to come into being, and shifts the burden of production to D. However, D's blood test evidence is clearly sufficient to meet a burden of production. That causes the presumption to disappear, leaving only logical inferences. (Note that D's evidence destroys only the presumption, not the logical inference. In other words, D's evidence is not so overwhelming as to require a directed verdict for D.)

As a result of the evidence produced by P and D, the situation is as follows: P's cohabitation evidence gives rise to a logical inference that D is the father of the child, and D's blood test evidence gives rise to a logical inference that he was not the father of the child. The jury will simply decide whether D is the father taking into account all the evidence, as it normally would do.

Answer (A) is incorrect because, even though P has produced sufficient evidence to meet a burden of production as to the foundational facts, D's evidence destroys the presumption, making an instruction on the presumption inappropriate under the bursting bubble theory.

Answer (B) is incorrect because it assumes that P's evidence is so strong as to require a decision that D was the father. This is not true. P's evidence is only sufficient to meet a burden of production. And as explained above, under the bursting bubble theory of presumptions, D's evidence has destroyed the presumption, making an instruction about the presumption inappropriate.

Answer (D) is incorrect because, even though D's blood test evidence is rather strong, it is probably not strong enough to *require* a verdict in D's favor on the paternity issue. This is still a jury question.

245.   **Answer (A) is correct.** In this case, P's evidence is sufficient to meet a burden of production on all of the foundational facts (deed purports to create an interest in property, it is at least 30 years old, it is in such condition as to create no suspicion as to its authenticity, it was kept in a place where such a writing is likely to be found, and it has been acted on as authentic by persons having an interest in the matter). This meets a burden of production. D's evidence, in turn, only challenges one of the foundational facts (keeping the deed in a place where such a writing is likely to be found), and does not challenge the presumed fact (that the deed is authentic). That means P has caused the presumption to come into force. That means an instruction concerning the presumption is appropriate.

Note that it does not matter whether the jurisdiction follows the majority theory of presumptions (bursting bubble) theory or the minority theory (Morgan-McCormick). The theories operate the same way when the opponent does not produce evidence to challenge the presumed facts. That is the case here.

Answer (B) is incorrect because all P has done is to produce enough evidence to meet a burden of production as to the existence of the foundational facts. P has not produced such overwhelming evidence that a finding in P's favor is required. This is true even as to those foundational facts that D has not challenged. The jury can still choose to disbelieve P's evidence on one or more of the foundational facts.

Answer (C) is incorrect because, even though D may have produced sufficient evidence to meet a burden of production as to one of the foundational facts, this does not destroy the presumption. The court should still give the instruction.

Answer (D) is incorrect because D's evidence concerning where P kept the deed was not so strong as to compel a finding that it was kept in the car glove box rather than in a safe deposit box. All D has done is produce sufficient evidence to support such a conclusion.

246.   **Answer (B) is correct.** The Supreme Court has held that generally, true presumptions (what it called "mandatory presumptions") may not operate against a criminal defendant. At the same time, the Court has held that if the statutory device was presented to the jury in a *permissive* fashion, it does not violate the defendant's right to a trial by jury. The instruction in (B) mentions the statutory device but does not tell the jury that it *must* conclude that D was in possession if it finds that D was an occupant of the vehicle at the relevant time. The phrase "may, but need not" connotes a permissive inference.

Answer (A) is incorrect because it instructs the jury that the device is mandatory.

Answer (C) is incorrect because it suggests that D has a burden of proof with regard to an element of the crime. The Constitution forbids this.

Answer (D) is incorrect because the Supreme Court has not forbidden any mention of an inference that might arise from a statutory device, even if that device is written in "presumption" form. As long as the jury instruction does not suggest that the jury must make a finding from the existence of certain facts, it is not improper to issue the instruction. (Of course, one might argue that under some circumstances, it is unfair to mention one inference a jury might draw and not mention others, but that argument should be made in the context of a particular case in which the instruction might amount to an inappropriate comment on the evidence by the court.

247.   **Answer (D) is correct.** A "conclusive presumption" is really a rule of law that makes the foundational facts the important facts and renders the actual truth of the presumed fact irrelevant. So-called conclusive presumptions are enacted to serve an important social purpose. In this case, the presumption is probably designed to protect children born to married, cohabiting couples from having their legitimacy dragged before the courts. In effect, the presumption provides that if the conditions are met, it is no longer legally important whether the man is actually the biological father. That essentially renders evidence contesting whether D was the biological father irrelevant. In this case, D's evidence would attack the now-irrelevant factual issue of whether he was the biological father. The evidence should not be admitted.

There is still a question for the jury, however: whether the foundational facts are true. That D has not challenged P's evidence on the foundational facts does not mean they are established; the jury must still decide whether to accept P's evidence as accurate. The court should instruct the jury that if it finds that those foundational facts are true, it must find that D is the father.

Answer (A) is incorrect because it assumes D's blood test evidence is admissible, which it is not. Also, the answer assumes there is some means of weighing the presumption against D's evidence, which makes no sense.

Answer (B) is incorrect because it assumes D's blood test evidence is admissible, which it is not. Also, the answer assumes that the presumption shifts the burden of persuasion on the paternity issue to D. It does not do that.

Answer (C) is incorrect because it does not take into account that there is still a question for the jury considering the truth of the foundational facts. The presumption will only operate against D if the jury finds those facts to be true.

248. **Answer (D) is correct.** A client has a privilege for confidential attorney-client communications. Of course, the communications must deal with the legal matter on which the client has sought assistance. Without more information, there is no basis to conclude that this conversation was anything but confidential. It also dealt with the attorney's representation of D on the murder charge. The privilege covers a person's admission to wrongdoing. Unless there is some unknown code between D and this attorney, asking for help to "beat this charge" is not seeking the attorney's assistance to cover up the crime. The privilege applies.

   Answer (A) is incorrect because the mere fact that the prosecutor has learned of the conversation is not sufficient to prove waiver by D. The prosecutor has produced no evidence to show that D has manifested a desire to waive the privilege. Even if the jurisdiction still maintains the old "eavesdropper rule," by which overheard conversations are not privileged, we do not know that this is how the prosecutor learned of the statement.

   Answer (B) is incorrect because a guilty client—even one who admits guilt—is just as entitled to the attorney-client privilege as an innocent one, and asking for help to "beat this charge" is not tantamount to seeking the attorney's help to cover up the crime.

   Answer (C) is incorrect because, as discussed above, the entire communication is privileged.

249. **Answer (D) is correct.** The communication is still privileged despite the presence of D's spouse and the attorney's secretary. Explanations follow.

   Answer (A) is incorrect because, even if the husband is not the client, there is a privilege for confidential communications between spouses. The court would treat the communication between D and the attorney in the spouse's presence as within the scope of both privileges.

   Answer (B) is incorrect because the secretary is probably a party whose presence is part of the provision of legal services to D, the client. Thus, the secretary is within the scope of the privilege.

   Answer (C) is incorrect because, as explained above, it is the privilege for confidential spousal communications that draws the husband within the scope of privilege here.

250. Application of the crime-fraud exception is a question for the court under FRE 104(a). In *United States v. Zolin*, 491 U.S. 554 (1989), the Supreme Court held that even though FRE 104(a) provides that the court is bound by rules of privilege in deciding

223

preliminary facts, the court may still conduct an *in camera* inspection of allegedly privileged materials if it finds that there is a factual basis adequate to support a good faith belief that the crime-fraud exception applies. Here, the court may use the secretary's notes as well as any other material that has not already been found privileged to decide whether that standard has been met. If the judge decides that an adequate basis exists to conduct the *in camera* inspection, she will listen to the tape and decide whether the crime-fraud exception applies.

251.   **Answer (A) is correct.** Dr. X is serving as a conduit for the transmission of confidential information between P and P's attorney. In a sense, X is like an interpreter. Her participation is necessary in order for P to communicate fully with her attorney. As long as the examination was conducted in private and the report sent to the attorney in confidence, the attorney-client privilege will apply.

Answer (B) is incorrect because Dr. X's examination and report are not subject to the physician-patient privilege. The primary reason is that by bringing an action for personal injuries, P has waived any physician-patient privilege covering communications relevant to the condition for which she seeks compensation. This is often known as the "patient-litigant" exception.

Answer (C) is incorrect because it assumes a physician-patient privilege applies, which is incorrect.

Answer (D) is incorrect because it does not take account of the attorney-client privilege.

252.   **Answer (D) is correct.** Under federal law, a spouse has a privilege not to testify against her spouse in a criminal action. The testifying spouse is the only holder, meaning that even if the party spouse objects to her testimony, he cannot prevent her from testifying. This privilege is not based on confidential communications. It is simply a privilege not to testify against the spouse. Thus, it doesn't matter that W's friend also saw D's wet clothes and muddy shoes. Because W is willing to testify, D cannot prevent her from doing so.

Answer (A) is incorrect because the privilege for confidential spousal communications does not apply to this situation. There are two reasons. First, there is no indication of any communication in these facts; D's conduct was not communicative. Second, even if there was a communication, the fact that it was made in the presence of a third party (W's friend) means it was not confidential.

Answer (B) is incorrect because, as noted above, the adverse testimony privilege is held by the testifying spouse. If, as in this case, she is willing to testify, her spouse may not prevent her from doing so.

Answer (C) is incorrect because the privilege for confidential spousal communications does not apply here.

253.   **Answer (A) is correct.** In this situation, the privilege for confidential communications will apply. That privilege continues even after the marriage ends. It covers confidential

communications, which in this case would be the statement D made to W. The adverse spousal testimony privilege will not apply, however. That privilege ends when the marriage ends. Because D and W are not married at the time of the trial, D cannot prevent W from testifying against him.

Answers (B), (C), and (D) are incorrect for the reasons noted above.

254. **Answer (D) is correct.** In *Jaffe v. Redmond*, 518 U.S. 1 (1996), the Supreme Court recognized a psychotherapist-patient privilege under federal law, and applied that privilege to a licensed clinical social worker. There is little doubt that the privilege would extend to a psychiatric social worker as well. The privilege belongs to the patient, who has manifested her intention to maintain the privilege (by instructing PSW not to answer the questions).

Answer (A) is incorrect because privileges operate at all stages of a case, not only at trial.

Answer (B) is incorrect because privileges may be asserted by non-parties as well as parties.

Answer (C) is incorrect because, as noted above, there is a psychotherapist-patient privilege in federal court, and it would apply to the W-PSW relationship.

255. Privileges represent a compromise. On one side of the scale is the need for evidence in order to learn the truth. On the other side of the scale are several values, among them the encouragement of full and frank discussion between parties to certain relationships and the protection of privacy. Courts believe that parents and minor children are likely to communicate fully and frankly even without a privilege, and that the need for evidence to learn the truth outweighs both this value and the value in protecting the privacy of parents and minor children.

256. **Answer (B) is correct.** In *Upjohn Co. v. United States*, 449 U.S. 383 (1981), the Supreme Court declined to state a specific test for attorney-client privilege in the corporate context, but it did reject the "control group" test that some courts had used. Instead of adopting that test, the Court named a number of factors that made the communications at issue in the case privileged. Among those factors were (1) that the communications were made by corporate employees to corporate counsel at the direction of corporate superiors; (2) that the purpose of the communications was to secure legal advice for the corporation; (3) that upper-echelon management did not possess all the information necessary to obtain the advice; (4) that the communications concerned matters within the scope of the employees' duties; (5) that the employees knew the purpose of the communications was to obtain legal advice; and (6) that the employees were instructed that the communications were to be kept confidential. Most, if not all, of those factors are present in Answer (B).

Answer (A) is incorrect because it essentially states the control group test, which the Supreme Court rejected in *Upjohn*.

Answer (C) is incorrect because there is an attorney-client privilege for corporations.

Answer (D) is incorrect because it states too broad a test for covered communications. Not all communications between a corporate employee and the corporation's counsel are protected by the privilege.

257. **Answer (C) is correct.** When the attorney brings an action against the client for breach of duty (such as failure to pay the attorney's fees), or the client sues the attorney for breach of duty (such as legal malpractice), there is no privilege between the attorney and the client as to communications that relate to the matter being litigated between them. Without such an exception, it would be virtually impossible to establish the facts necessary to prove any alleged breach of duty.

Answer (A) is incorrect because if an exception applies, the holder has no privilege to claim.

Answer (B) is incorrect because if an exception applies, there is no privilege even if the client still exists.

Answer (D) is incorrect because the attorney-client privilege does not apply here. Also, where the privilege does apply, it covers both confidential communications to the attorney and the attorney's confidential communications to the client.

258.   **Answer (C) is correct.** Lay opinion testimony is admissible if it is "(a) rationally based on the perception of the witness and (b) helpful to a clear understanding of the witness's testimony or the determination of a fact in issue." The opinion in answer (C) depends on more than the witness's "rational . . . perception." It probably requires expertise to determine whether the water seepage really caused the damage. Thus, a lay witness's testimony is not likely to be "helpful" to the trier of fact.

     Answer (A) is incorrect because a lay witness can describe the impressions of her senses, such as appearance, sound, or smell. There is, in fact, hardly any way to describe the smell without giving an opinion.

     Answer (B) is incorrect because lay witnesses are probably capable of rendering opinions as to the speed of automobiles from their everyday experience. The jury would be helped by this testimony much more than from hearing a vague factual description about the car's movement.

     Answer (D) is incorrect for the same reasons as in answer (A). From our real-world experience, we tend to be able to recognize the outward effects of intoxication. In addition, we tend to develop a holistic sense of a person's state of sobriety; it isn't any one thing as much as a combination of factors that lead us to conclude that another person might be intoxicated. The jury would be helped by this testimony.

259.   **Answer (B) is correct.** Though the court is unlikely to sustain the objection, W arguably lacks personal knowledge of her relationship to D. That knowledge is second-hand, raising a possible violation of FRE 602 ("A witness may not testify to a matter unless evidence is introduced sufficient to support a finding that the witness has personal knowledge of the matter.").

     Answer (A) is incorrect. At least on the surface, W is stating a fact, not an opinion. Naturally, all statements of fact are actually statements of one's opinion about the fact (when a person says, "the light was green," she is really saying that in her opinion, the light was green), but the opinion rule is designed to exclude only statements that would be considered opinions in a more narrow sense. Even so, this answer does have some merit.

     Answer (C) is incorrect because W is not *testifying* about an out-of-court statement. True, W is basing her testimony on what she's been told, but she does not testify directly to the out-of-court statement. Some courts have found that the hearsay rule is violated in situations such as this, but that conclusion does not seem to be supported by the language of FRE 801(c), which strongly suggests that hearsay is *testimony about* an out-of-court statement, offered to prove the truth of the matter asserted, and not merely *testimony based upon* an out-of-court statement offered to prove the truth of the matter asserted. (Note that if W had testified, "my mom told me D is my father," that testimony would be hearsay.)

It is also possible, though unlikely, that W's testimony, even if hearsay, fits within the exception established in FRE 803(19), which concerns testimony in the form of reputation evidence concerning personal or family history. That evidence can be community reputation, but can also be reputation among family members. Here, W has not testified in terms of reputation, so the exception might not apply.

Answer (D) is incorrect because FRE 601 provides that "[e]very person is competent to be a witness" except as specifically provided. There is no specific provision making children incompetent. In some jurisdictions, children under a certain age are presumed incompetent, but an eight-year-old is not covered by that presumption.

260.   **Answer (C) is correct.** Though "erratically" is an opinion, it is closer to a statement of fact than the other answers. "Erratic" behavior can be defined as wandering behavior, that which lacks a fixed course, consistency, or regularity. These are descriptive terms, and though they embody opinions, they are less removed from the witness's actual observations than are the other answers.

Answer (A) is incorrect because "carelessly" is more clearly an opinion. In addition, the jury will not be helped meaningfully by hearing a witness testify that D drove "carelessly." The jury would want to know what led W to reach this conclusion. (A court might still allow this opinion, however, if it believes the jury would benefit from hearing it.)

Answer (B) is incorrect because "negligently" is a legal conclusion. Even though FRE 704(a) permits a witness to testify to an opinion that "embraces" an ultimate fact, courts generally have not interpreted that rule to allow such a bald statement of opinion on an ultimate issue, especially when the term used carries specialized meaning in the law. In addition, W's use of the term "negligence" might not accord with the legal definition. It is the court's job to instruct the jury as to the meaning of legal terms. Finally, the jury is helped by evidence of what D did, not of the witness's opinion about whether D's actions amounted to negligence.

Answer (D) is incorrect for the same reasons as answer (B). "Recklessly" is also a technical term in the law, and W's statement that D was driving "recklessly" is not particularly useful to the jury; the jury should hear facts instead.

261.   **Answer (C) is correct.** P's witness is an orthopedic surgeon. Her expertise does not extend to engineering questions involving the strength of the structures surrounding automobile passengers.

Answers (A), (B), and (D) are incorrect because each states an opinion that an orthopedic surgeon probably would be permitted to give. Under answer (A), an orthopedic surgeon is most likely qualified to assess the cause of a bone fracture as well as know how to treat it.

The opinion in answer (B) would be permitted because it relies on the witness's expertise about the force necessary to fracture limbs, something an orthopedic surgeon probably understands.

The opinion in answer (D) would be permitted because an orthopedic surgeon is probably qualified to render an opinion about any permanent impairment that might result from a leg fracture.

262.   **Answer (D) is correct.** Neither objection is well-taken.

   Answer (A) is incorrect because W is very likely qualified as an expert. FRE 702 provides that a person may qualify as an expert if she has obtained "knowledge, skill, experience, training, or education." There is no general requirement that a person have become an expert through formal education. (Obviously, some fields require formal training. One may not be an expert physician without having completed the necessary formal education, for example.)

   Answer (B) is incorrect because FRE 703 provides that an expert witness may base an opinion on otherwise inadmissible evidence (including hearsay) *as long as experts in the field reasonably rely on such information.* Here, W based her opinion, in part, on hearsay—the out-of-court statements of eyewitnesses. The facts state that in doing so, W was using techniques learned through experience. This strongly suggests that expert arson investigators reasonably rely on bystander statements in drawing conclusions about the origins of fires.

   Answer (C) is incorrect because, as discussed above, the court should overrule both objections.

263.   **Answer (B) is correct.** W's testimony is admissible to demonstrate the underlying basis for W's conclusion that the fire was arson-caused. This is necessary to assist the jury in deciding how much credit to give W's testimony. If, for example, other admissible evidence persuades the jury that the bystander statements were accurate (suppose the bystanders testify to what they saw), the jury is likely to give greater credit to W's conclusion. But if the prosecution's admissible evidence does not persuade the jurors that the facts relied on by W actually occurred, the jury is likely to ignore W's conclusion that the fire was arson-caused. Answer (B) is correct because the proposed instruction would inform the jury that it may only consider the bystander statements to explain the basis of W's testimony. As will be shown next, the statements are not admissible to prove the truth of the matters asserted.

   Answer (A) is incorrect because most courts hold that FRE 703 does not establish a hearsay exception. This means that the bystander statements are not admissible to prove the truth of the matters asserted—that the fire proceeded as the statements describe. Answer (A) violates that rule.

(Note that the distinction between admissible only to show the basis of the expert's opinion and admissible to prove the truth of the matters asserted in the statements is very likely to be lost on the jury. Even so, the law draws the distinction.)

Answer (C) is incorrect because the bystanders' beliefs about how the fire proceeded are not relevant. This is not a valid argument to avoid the hearsay rule. What matters is what happened, not what the bystanders believed happened.

Answer (D) is incorrect because, pursuant to FRE 105, when evidence is admissible for one purpose but not another purpose, the court "*shall* restrict the evidence to its proper scope and instruct the jury accordingly" (emphasis added). This has been interpreted to mean that if a party asks for a limiting instruction in such a situation, the court *must* issue it.

264.   **Answer (B) is correct.** FRE 704(b) provides that "[n]o expert witness testifying to the mental state or condition of a defendant in a criminal case may state an opinion or inference as to whether the defendant did or did not have the mental state or condition constituting an element of the crime charged or of a defense thereto." This rule was intended to prohibit an opinion as to whether the relevant test is met or not. In the case of the insanity defense (the matter the drafters chiefly had in mind), the rule was designed to forbid an opinion as to whether the test for insanity was met. Answer (B) states the federal test for insanity and gives the opinion that D satisfied that test. The opinion is therefore inadmissible.

Answer (A) is incorrect because the disease of paranoid schizophrenia is not a mental state that forms an element of a crime or defense. **Answer (D) is incorrect** for the same reason.

Answer (C) is incorrect for much the same reason: it does not specify a particular mental state that is an element of the defense, and thus does not violate the rule stated in FRE 704(b).

265.   **Answer (D) is correct.** According to FRE 703, an expert may base her opinion on any source that is reasonably relied upon by experts in the field. Certainly, a psychiatrist often bases her conclusions on tests and observations she conducts personally. At times, a psychiatrist certainly uses tests performed by other mental health professionals. And a hypothetical question is a common way to convey facts to the expert. FRE 705 makes clear that the hypothetical need not be asked of the witness while she is on the witness stand. Therefore, **answers (A), (B), and (C) are incorrect** because each states a proper source of the facts or data upon which the expert may rely in forming an opinion.

266.   **Answer (A) is correct.** In *Frye v. United States*, 293 F. 1013 (D.C. App. 1923), the court held that an expert opinion based on a scientific technique is not admissible unless it is "generally accepted" in the relevant scientific community: "Just when a scientific principle or discovery crosses the line between the experimental and demonstrable stages is difficult to define. Somewhere in this twilight zone the evidential force of the principle must be recognized, and while courts will go a long way in admitting

expert testimony deduced from a well-recognized scientific principle or discovery, the thing from which the deduction is made must be sufficiently established to have gained general acceptance in the particular field in which it belongs." This standard, which placed a great deal of faith in the scientific community to determine the validity of novel scientific theory or technique, was the prevailing standard for many decades, and some courts continue to adhere to that standard today.

Answer (A) is correct because it embodies the *Frye* test. **Answers (C) and (D) are incorrect** because they do not state the *Frye* standard. **Answer (B) is incorrect** because, although it states a correct basic standard, it incorrectly assumes that the question involved is one of conditional relevancy under FRE 104(b). The question must be decided by the judge under FRE 104(a).

267. **Answer (C) is correct.** In *Daubert v. Merrell Dow Pharmaceuticals, Inc.*, 509 U.S. 579 (1993), the Supreme Court held that the Federal Rules had abolished the *Frye* general acceptance test and replaced that test with one requiring the court to assess the reliability and relevance of scientific testimony. Reliability is to be shown according to a flexible standard that looks at several factors including peer review and publication, error rates, and general acceptance, with no single factor serving as a *per se* test. In addition, the court must find a fit between the expert's testimony and the facts of the case—that the testimony is relevant to an issue in the case (here, causation). FRE 702 was later amended to essentially codify the basic principles of *Daubert*. Answer (C) states the general test.

Answer (A) is incorrect because it states the *Frye* test. Although many states still apply that test (or a version of it), the federal courts no longer do so, as explained above.

Answer (B) is incorrect because it allocates the fact-finding authority largely to the jury. *Daubert* and FRE 702 do not do this. The judge is to be the "gate-keeper," and the jury will only hear purported scientific testimony if the judge finds (by a preponderance of the evidence) that it is reliable and relevant.

Answer (D) is incorrect because publication and peer review is only one factor in the test for determining admissibility. It is not a *per se* factor. As explained above, the test is flexible.

268. P's chances on appeal are not good. In *General Electric Co. v. Joiner*, 522 U.S. 156 (1997), the Supreme Court held that the "abuse of discretion" standard applies to trial court *Daubert* rulings. That standard gives the trial court broad discretion, and appellate courts usually show substantial deference to such decisions. The court will typically affirm the trial court's decision even if it would have reached a different conclusion, as long as the trial court's conclusion is within the broad range of its discretion.

Even if the court finds that the trial court has erred in excluding the evidence, the court will not reverse unless exclusion affected "a substantial right of the party" (FRE 103(a)). In this situation, exclusion of P's expert was probably fatal to P's case, making causation difficult or impossible to prove. Thus, if there was error, reversal probably would be required.

269. **Answer (C) is correct.** The document asserts that the interview took place at a certain date and time, and it is being offered to prove the truth of that statement. Thus, it is hearsay. However, the document appears to satisfy the requirements of FRE 803(8), the public records exception. Because the document is being offered by, rather than against, the criminal defendant, the exclusions from the exception in parts (B) and (C) of the rule do not apply.

Answer (A) is incorrect because the witness did not profess to a loss of memory that the document refreshed. **Answer (B) is incorrect** for a similar reason. FRE 803(5) (recorded recollection) only applies when the witness does not remember a fact to which she has been asked to testify. **Answer (D) is incorrect** because the document is admissible as a public record.

270. **Answer (A) is correct.** The statements in the article are the act over which the suit has been brought, so they are not hearsay. (They fall into the category of words of independent legal significance; they are the libel itself.) However, when a party wishes to prove the contents of a writing, the best evidence rule (FRE 1002) requires that the writing itself be produced. It was not, and no reason was given, nor does any exception apply.

Answer (B) is incorrect because the evidence is not hearsay. **Answer (C) is incorrect** because the testimony does violate the best evidence rule. **Answer (D) is incorrect** because the testimony is inadmissible.

271. **Answer (B) is correct.** When "other crimes, wrongs, or acts" are offered to prove a relevant fact, those acts might be admissible under FRE 404(b) if their relevance does not depend on an inference of the actor's character. Here, the prosecution is using another very similar bank robbery to show that D committed the current robbery, and the theory is *modus operandi*. That theory only applies when the events are both very unusual and very similar. That requirement is probably satisfied here because of the dance the robbers forced the tellers to perform. **Answer (D) is incorrect** for this reason.

This does not mean the evidence will be admissible, however. The court first must determine whether there is evidence sufficient to support a finding that the actor did engage in the uncharged act. This is a FRE 104(b) test. **Answer (C) is incorrect** because it assumes the applicable test is that set forth in FRE 104(a), under which the court decides the existence of the preliminary fact. Even if the court decides that the FRE 104(b) test is met, the court must still determine whether the evidence is relevant (which it is here, because D denies involvement in the bank robbery), and whether the probative value of the evidence is substantially outweighed by the danger of unfair prejudice.

For the evidence to be admissible, the court must also examine its relevance to the crime for which D is charged and determine whether it should be excluded by FRE 403. **Answer (A) is incorrect** because it assumes that the evidence is automatically admissible without consideration of these issues.

272. **Answer (D) is correct.** W's statement is hearsay because it asserted that D robbed the bank, and it is offered to prove that fact. D's laughing response might, however, amount to an adoption of W's statement, and if so the statement and D's response will constitute non-hearsay under FRE 801(d)(2)(B). **Answer (A) is incorrect** because the facts do not support a conclusion that W was speaking while under the stress of excitement caused by a startling event. **Answer (B) is incorrect** because W's statement reflected on an event that had occurred an hour earlier, which is too long to qualify the statement as a present sense impression under the circumstances. **Answer (C) is incorrect** because FRE 804(b)(3), the declaration against interest exception, only applies if the declarant is unavailable, and D is available.

273. **Answer (A) is correct.** D1 and D2 admit possession of V's wallet, but claim lack of intent to steal. Evidence that D1 and D2 had possessed two other wallets for a period of several weeks is intuitively strong on the issue of intent because one would think it extremely unlikely that D1 and D2 would innocently find three wallets on the street in a matter of a few weeks. Thus, the evidence is admissible to prove intent on doctrine of chances reasoning.

    Answer (B) is incorrect because identity is not an issue here. D1 and D2 admit possession but deny intent to steal. Even if identity were an issue, the facts state that the method allegedly used is common among pickpockets. This makes the *modus operandi* theory inapplicable.

    Answer (C) is incorrect because a few similar incidents do not rise to the level of habit. Undoubtedly, D1 and D2 do not steal wallets on the street far more often than they do. Moreover, the level of conscious deliberation needed to steal wallets in this way argues against characterizing the behavior as habitual. Though a conscious act may be classified as a habit, the more conscious it is, the less likely it will qualify.

    Answer (D) is incorrect because, as discussed above, the evidence is admissible to prove intent.

274. **Answer (A) is correct.** P's statement to her doctor is not hearsay because it is a party admission under FRE 801(d)(2)(A). It is also not subject to the physician-patient privilege because of the patient-litigant exception. By bringing the personal injury action against D, P waived her physician-patient privilege with respect to relevant aspects of her medical condition.

    Answers (B), (C), and (D) are incorrect for the reasons just discussed.

275. **Answer (D) is correct.** D's own statement is not a party admission if D offers it. Thus, it is inadmissible hearsay when offered to prove that V attacked D with a moose

head. The statement is not admissible as a prior consistent statement under FRE 801(d)(1)(B) because D made the statement at a time when he had a motive to lie (he was about to go to trial for assault with a deadly weapon). Thus, D cannot offer the statement to support her credibility.

Answer (A) is incorrect because D's statement does not qualify for admission as a prior consistent statement, and thus may not be used to prove D's self-defense claim. **Answer (B) is incorrect** because a prior consistent statement may not be offered for any purpose unless it satisfies the requirements of FRE 801(d)(1)(B). **Answer (C) is incorrect** for the same reasons that answers (A) and (B) are incorrect.

276. **Answer (D) is correct.** This is a direct application of the Supreme Court's holding in *United States v. Zolin*, 491 U.S. 554 (1989). **Answers (A), (B), and (C) are incorrect** because they do not correctly state the holding of that case.

277. **Answer (B) is correct.** Under the Federal Rules definition of hearsay, an utterance is not classified as hearsay unless it makes an assertion of fact and is offered to prove that fact. X's statement does not assert a fact; it is a request to do something. The request is relevant because it is circumstantial evidence that X was planning to set a fire. Because it is offered for that purpose, but does not assert that fact, it is not hearsay.

Under a declarant-based definition of hearsay, an utterance can be classified as hearsay if its value depends on the credibility of the declarant. Here, there might be significant credibility issues. Most importantly, we might not understand what X meant by the request; X might not have been trying to convey anything about a possible fire (thus raising issues of ambiguity). Also, X might have misperceived some fact that led X to make the statement (raising issues of perception), or X might have been insincere, or have had a faulty memory. Because of these concerns, a declarant-based definition of hearsay probably would characterize the utterance as hearsay. **Answers (C) and (D) are incorrect** for this reason.

Answer (A) is incorrect because X is not a party. Thus, her statements cannot constitute party admissions.

278. **Answer (A) is correct.** This question raises the privilege for confidential communications between spouses. Generally, both spouses are holders. This means that if D does not want W to testify about what D told W in confidence, D may prevent W from testifying. **Answer (C) is incorrect** because it fails to recognize that D is also a holder of the privilege for confidential communications between spouses. **Answer (B) is incorrect** because D's statement, offered by the prosecution, is a non-hearsay party admission. **Answer (D) is incorrect** because a privilege does apply in this case.

279. **Answer (B) is correct.** The evidence of V's violent character is relevant because it makes it more likely that V did in fact attack D first, causing D to respond in self-defense. The idea is that a person with a reputation for violence is more likely to have an actual character for violence than is one without such reputation. From that, one

may infer that the person is more likely to start a fight than is one who is not violent. On the facts of this case, this evidence is relevant even though D was unaware of V's reputation for violence, because the evidence is being offered to show V's behavior, not D's. (Note that if D's theory of self-defense was that she feared V, the reputation evidence in question would not be relevant unless D had heard about it.)

The next question is whether the evidence is *admissible* to prove that V attacked D. Under the FRE 404(a)(2) exception to the general ban on character to prove conduct, a criminal defendant may offer evidence of a pertinent trait of the character of the alleged victim. FRE 405(a) permits the use of reputation and opinion evidence. Thus, this evidence is admissible to prove that V attacked D. **Answer (A) is incorrect** for this reason.

Answer (C) is incorrect because the evidence is not being offered to impeach V. V was not a witness, nor were any statements by V offered into evidence.

Answer (D) is incorrect because, as explained above, the evidence fits into an exception to the general ban on character evidence to prove conduct.

280. **Answer (A) is correct.** If this statement is to be admissible, it will be as an authorized admission under FRE 801(d)(2)(C). For that to be the case, X must have been authorized to speak for D Corp. about this matter. Under the Federal Rules, authorization is a question to be decided by the court under FRE 104(a) because the statement will be relevant even if the declarant was not authorized to speak. (In other words, this is not a case of conditional relevancy.)

      Answer (B) is incorrect because the statement can be non-hearsay even if X is not a party. As noted above, the statement might be admissible as an authorized admission, which is not hearsay under the Federal Rules.

      Answer (C) is incorrect because in making its ruling, the trial court is permitted to take into account any non-privileged information, even inadmissible evidence, and even the very evidence at issue. Here, that evidence (X's statement) contains an assertion of authority to speak for C Corp. The trial court may use that assertion as part of its basis for finding that X was authorized to speak for D Corp.

      Answer (D) is incorrect because it assumes authority is a question of conditional relevancy to be treated under the standard of FRE 104(b). As explained above, it is not.

281. **Answer (C) is correct.** The Supreme Court has held that if evidence satisfies a "firmly rooted" hearsay exception, it generally also satisfies the confrontation clause without additional inquiry. *See, e.g.,* Ohio v. Roberts, 448 U.S. 56 (1980). Given its age and adoption in practically every jurisdiction, the dying declarations exception almost certainly would be classified as "firmly rooted." **Answers (A), (B), and (D) are incorrect** because they fail to recognize this rule. (Note: In *Crawford v. Washington*, 2004 WL 413301 (Mar. 8, 2004), the Supreme Court signaled its dissatisfaction with

the *Roberts* test, though it did not overrule *Roberts* as to what it called "non-testimonial" hearsay. In this hypothetical, the dying declaration would be classified as "non-testimonial," so technically, *Roberts* remains good law as to that statement.)

282.   **Answer (D) is correct.** X's statement about the accident is relevant, of course, to prove what happened. It is also hearsay, but might fit within the excited utterance exception. The foundational facts necessary to establishing applicability of the excited utterance exception are to be decided by the court pursuant to FRE 104(a). That is because the statement will be relevant even if the foundational (preliminary) facts are not true. (In other words, this is not an example of conditional relevancy.) Thus, the court must decide whether X's statement about the accident was made under the stress of excitement caused by the accident. **Answer (A) is incorrect** because it is not clear that X's statement fails to satisfy the requirements of the excited utterance exception. **Answer (B) is incorrect** because it assumes that the standard of FRE 104(b) applies. As discussed above, FRE 104(a) applies.

X's earlier statement, about the weather, is not offered to prove the truth of the matter asserted (what the weather was like), but as circumstantial evidence that X was not experiencing the stress of the accident. Thus, it is not hearsay. That statement is relevant not because of what X said about the weather, but because it suggests that the so-called excited utterance should not be given as much weight as otherwise. The theory here is that if excited utterances tend to be trustworthy because they are made under stress and before the declarant has an opportunity to reflect, evidence that the person was not suffering from the stress of the accident, and that some time had passed after the event, would tend to undercut its probative value. The jury is therefore entitled to learn that X might not have been under quite as much stress as it seems from hearing only the second statement. (Of course, the assumptions about the reliability of excited utterances are not sound, but the rule persists.)

Answer (C) is incorrect because the fact that X spoke about the weather is still relevant even if the other statement qualifies as an excited utterance.

283.   **Answer (B) is correct.** The declarant-based definition of hearsay will classify utterances as hearsay when their value depends on the credibility of the declarant. There are meaningful issues concerning the credibility of the declarants in this hypothetical. For example, they might not have understood the nature of D's establishment, or they might have been trying to frame D. Thus, there is a very good chance that these utterances would be classified as hearsay under a declarant-based definition of hearsay.

The assertion-based definition will not classify an utterance as hearsay unless it is a statement, which is defined as an assertion, and unless the statement is being offered to prove the truth of the matter asserted. These utterances are relevant because they suggest that the callers believed D was running a house of prostitution, but the utterances did not assert that fact. Thus, most courts applying the assertion-based definition of hearsay (the definition in the Federal Rules) would not characterize these utterances as hearsay.

Answers (A), (C), and (D) are incorrect because they do not apply the principles stated above correctly.

284. **Answer (A) is correct.** This is a leading question because it suggests the answer P wants the witness to give. Thus, **answer (C) is incorrect.** However, it is proper to lead an adverse witness on direct examination. D is obviously adverse to P. Thus, P may lead D. **Answer (B) is incorrect** for this reason. **Answer (D) is incorrect** because the question does not assume a fact not in evidence; it asks about a fact, though in a leading way.

285. **Answer (D) is correct.** FRE 404(a)(2) permits an accused (which most courts interpret to mean a criminal defendant) to offer evidence of a pertinent trait of the character of an alleged crime victim. V is the alleged victim. Thus, **answer (C) is incorrect.** D has offered evidence of V's violent reputation, which is pertinent to whether V would have attacked another person. FRE 405(a) provides that on direct examination, character may be proven by reputation or opinion. This was reputation evidence. The evidence is admissible.

Answer (A) is incorrect because, as explained above, the evidence does relate to whether V might have attacked D. A person with a violent character is more likely to act violently than is one without such a character. **Answer (B) is incorrect** because the evidence, although hearsay, satisfies FRE 803(21), which creates an exception for evidence of reputation about a person's character.

286. **Answer (C) is correct.** In *Luce v. United States*, 469 U.S. 38 (1984), the Supreme Court held that in order to preserve for appeal the question of whether the court committed error in allowing the prosecution to offer evidence of defendant's prior conviction to impeach, D must subject herself to that impeachment by testifying at trial. Because D did not take the stand, he did not preserve the issue for appeal. Note, as well, that **Answer (A) is incorrect** for another reason: a prior conviction for burglary is not automatically admissible because it is not a crime involving dishonesty or false statement.

Answer (B) is incorrect because it is not true that appellate courts may not review trial court decisions admitting or excluding prior conviction evidence. The problem here is that D did not properly preserve the issue for appeal, not that an appellate court may not review this type of ruling.

Answer (D) is incorrect because the prosecution has no due process right to offer prior convictions to impeach.

287. **Answer (A) is correct.** Except where defendant offers evidence of her character to prove her innocence, and in sexual assault and child molestation cases, and where defendant offers evidence of the victim's character, the prosecution is not permitted to offer evidence of defendant's character to prove action in conformity therewith on a particular occasion. Thus, the evidence is not admissible to prove that D had a character that would lead her to embezzle. Thus, **answer (B) is incorrect.**

A conviction for misdemeanor perjury is admissible, however, to impeach D's credibility under FRE 609. Because perjury is a crime involving dishonesty or false statement, the conviction is admissible regardless of the balance of probative value and prejudice. In fact, the trial court *must* admit the evidence; it has no discretion to exclude it under FRE 403. This is why **answer (C) is incorrect. Answer (D) is incorrect** because, as noted above, the evidence is admissible to impeach D's credibility.

288.   **Answer (B) is correct.** This is a prior inconsistent statement, and it is relevant both to impeach W's credibility as a witness and to show that W's employer sometimes set back odometers.

The evidence is admissible to impeach simply because it is inconsistent with W's trial testimony. W has been given an opportunity to explain or deny making the statement, as required by FRE 613(b).

The statement is also admissible to prove the truth of the matter asserted at the deposition because W testified at the trial, was subject to cross-examination concerning the statement, the statement is inconsistent with the trial testimony, and the statement was made under oath, subject to penalty of perjury (at the deposition). Thus, the requirements of FRE 801(d)(1)(A) have been satisfied.

Answer (A) is incorrect because the evidence is admissible both to impeach and to prove that odometers sometimes were set back (and that by implication, the odometer on the car P bought might have been tampered with). **Answer (C) is incorrect** because unavailability is not a precondition for admission of prior inconsistent statements. **Answer (D) is incorrect** because a prior inconsistent statement made under oath and subject to the penalty for perjury may be admitted substantively even if the declarant was not cross-examined when she made the statement.

289.   **Answer (D) is correct.** The evidence concerning D's theft of office supplies from D's employer is relevant to impeach D if D testifies or if out-of-court statements of D are offered into evidence. Thus, **answer (B) is incorrect.** Here, there is no indication that either has occurred. Thus, D is not subject to impeachment.

Even if D has testified or is otherwise subject to impeachment, the method used here is impeachment by bad character for truthfulness. Under FRE 608(b), only acts probative of truthfulness or untruthfulness may be used. That requirement has been satisfied because an act of theft is probably minimally probative of untruthfulness. However, the rule forbids the use of extrinsic evidence, and D's personnel record is extrinsic evidence. The prosecution would have been allowed to ask D about the theft on cross-examination if D testified, but that is not what happened.

Note that the requirements of the business records exception are probably satisfied here (meaning that **answer (C) is incorrect**), but that does not matter because the evidence is inadmissible, as explained above. Thus, **answer (A) is incorrect.**

290.   **Answer (D) is correct.** The prosecutor has simply used the document to refresh V's recollection. A party may use anything to refresh a witness's recollection. All that is required before the witness testifies to the facts after the device is used is that the witness testifies that she now remembers the facts. The thing used to refresh recollection is not evidence, and is not read to the fact-finder.

Here, because V has stated that she now remembers the other items she found missing after the break-in, V may state what those items were.

Answer (A) is incorrect because the prosecution was not using the past recollection recorded doctrine (FRE 803(5)) here.

Answer (B) is incorrect because the document was not being used; the witness's memory was being used. (Even if the document were being used, no rule prohibits the use of all documents against a criminal defendant.)

Answer (C) is incorrect because the prosecutor was not attempting to lay the foundation for the business records exception. The document need not be a business record or any specific kind of record. Because it is not evidence, no evidence rules restrict what can be used to refresh recollection.

291.   **Answer (B) is correct.** W's testimony at the first trial is hearsay when offered at the second trial. The reporter's transcript is also hearsay in that it is the statement of the reporter that W gave certain testimony, offered to prove that W gave that testimony. The transcript itself easily satisfies FRE 803(6), the business records exception to the hearsay rule. The former testimony exception (FRE 804(b)(1)) will cover W's testimony: D was a party to the earlier civil action, D had an opportunity to cross-examine W at that trial, D's motive in cross-examining W at the second trial would be the same as at the first (to show that W was wrong when she stated that D ran a red light and struck V in a crosswalk), and, finally, W is unavailable under FRE 804(a)(2) because she refuses to drop her unsupported privacy claim even when ordered to do so by the court.

Answer (A) is incorrect because the importance of particular evidence is not a reason to admit it if it violates a rule of evidence. Thus, this is not a reason to admit the evidence.

Answer (C) is incorrect because W is unavailable, as explained above.

Answer (D) is incorrect because under the reasoning of the Supreme Court in *Crawford v. Washington*, 2004 WL 413301 (Mar. 8, 2004), "testimonial" hearsay that fits within an exception satisfies the demands of the confrontation clause is admissable against a criminal defendant if the defendant had an opportunity to cross-examine the declarant, and if the declarant is unavailable. Both conditions are satisfied here.

292.   **Answer (D) is correct.** Messon's public relations officer is undoubtedly authorized to speak for the company. That is, in fact, the primary job of a public relations officer.

Thus, authorization, the key requirement of FRE 801(d)(2)(C), is satisfied. Of course, the statement is also being offered against Messon, the party.

Answer (A) is incorrect because unavailability is a requirement of the declaration against interest exception (FRE 804(b)(3)), and Messon is not unavailable.

Answer (B) is incorrect because there is no indication this was an excited utterance. Even if the officer sounded excited, there is nothing in the facts to suggest that she was speaking while under the stress of excitement caused by a startling event or condition. Almost certainly, she was just doing her job of selling her company's point of view.

Answer (C) is incorrect for a rather technical reason: The statement is a direct statement of Messon's "state of mind." That is, it directly states Messon's beliefs about the state of the bay. (From that, of course, it may be inferred that it saw no reason to engage in more cleanup, which is why the statement is relevant.) Because the officer's utterance is a direct statement of her employer's beliefs, it is hearsay when offered to prove those beliefs.

293. **Answer (B) is correct.** Evidence that D and W1 are lovers tends to impeach W1 by showing a motive to testify in D's favor. This form of impeachment is not explicitly regulated by the Federal Rules. Therefore, it is not limited by any specific rules such as one forbidding the use of extrinsic evidence.

Answer (A) is incorrect because merely being D's lover does not show that W1 has a bad character for truthfulness.

Answer (C) is incorrect because the evidence does not contradict anything about which W1 testified. W1 never denied being D's lover.

Answer (D) is incorrect because, as explained above, the evidence is admissible to impeach W1 by showing a motive to testify favorably toward D.

294. **Answer (A) is correct.** The tape recording is relevant only if it actually was a recording of D's voice. Thus, whether it was D's voice would be a case of conditional relevancy even without a specific rule making it so. But such a rule exists: FRE 901(a) sets forth the FRE 104(b) standard for authentication issues. Thus, the court's task is to determine whether there is evidence sufficient to support a finding that the voice on the tape was D's. **Answer (B) is incorrect** because it sets forth a FRE 104(a) standard under which the judge makes the determination of preliminary fact.

Answer (C) is incorrect because the evidence is not hearsay. Rather, it constitutes words of independent legal significance. If the recording contains D's voice, it is not evidence of the slander. It is the slander itself. (The machine recording does not add a level of hearsay; the machine's workings are questions of relevance and probative value, not hearsay.)

Answer (D) is incorrect because voice identification does not require an expert witness. The jury may hear the voice on the tape, compare it to D's voice, and make its own determination whether the voices are the same.

295.   **Answer (D) is correct.** The right to jury trial includes the right not to be retried because the judge believes the jury reached the wrong decision. Put another way, a jury's acquittal is final. Also, retrial would violate the double jeopardy clause. Thus, **answer (A) is incorrect**; the court may not order a new trial.

         Answers (B) and (C) are incorrect for a second reason. The jury's failure to consider crucial evidence and its disregard of the judge's instructions are not the type of juror behavior that can be the subject of testimony to impeach the verdict. FRE 606(b) forbids juror testimony or affidavits to impeach the verdict unless the testimony or affidavit would show that "extraneous prejudicial information was improperly brought to the jury's attention or whether any outside influence was improperly brought to bear upon any juror." What happened in this case does not fall into either category.

296.   **Answer (B) is correct.** Whether this constitutes a habit under FRE 406 is a close question, but the fact that D rode with "no hands" for part of each of the 20 rides W observed creates at least a decent argument for habit.

         Answer (B) is incorrect because being a careless bicycle rider is probably character evidence, and character may not be offered in this situation to prove D acted in conformity with her character on a specific occasion. (None of the exceptions in FRE 404(a) apply.)

         Answer (C) is incorrect because W's testimony does not contradict D. D did not claim she never rode with "no hands"; she only testified that she did not do so on this occasion.

         Answer (D) is incorrect because D's intent to ride with "no hands" is not relevant. What is relevant is whether D in fact did so. Even if one might argue that intent to do so makes it more likely D did in fact do so, the character rule still would bar the testimony. That is because the conclusion that D would intend to ride with "no hands" is made possible by inferring from D's past conduct that she is a careless rider who would ride carelessly on this occasion. As explained above, character evidence is not admissible in this situation to prove D acted in conformity with her character on a specific occasion.

297.   **Answer (A) is correct.** This is a leading question because it suggests the answer the prosecutor wants the witness to give. FRE 611 provides that generally, leading questions may not be asked on direct. However, the rule specifically allows leading questions "as may be necessary to develop the witness's testimony." That is the situation here. The prosecutor is using a leading question to help the witness provide her testimony.

         Answers (B) and (C) are incorrect for the reasons just given. **Answer (D) is incorrect** because the question is not argumentative nor is it compound. It is simply leading.

298.   **Answer (D) is correct.** The evidence is relevant because it has a tendency to narrow the universe of possible perpetrators to that small group (of which D is a member)

that knows how to use this technique to crack safes. Thus **answer (A) is incorrect.** **Answer (B) is incorrect** because considerations of unfair prejudice do not make evidence irrelevant. They only lead to the exclusion of relevant evidence.

FRE 404(b) permits the use of other crimes, wrongs, or acts to prove a relevant fact other than through an inference as to the person's character. That evidence is relevant on such a basis does not mean it is admissible, however. The Supreme Court in *Huddleston v. United States*, 485 U.S. 681 (1988), made clear that the court should still determine whether the probative value of the evidence is substantially outweighed by the danger of unfair prejudice. That is why **answer (C) is incorrect** and **answer (D) correct.**

299. **Answer (D) is correct.** Though it is unusual to call a witness to testify about another person's trial testimony, nothing in the rules prohibits a party from proving the testimony this way. The best evidence rule does not apply because P is not using X to prove the contents of a writing (the transcript). Rather, P is trying to prove what W said, something X knows from personal knowledge. Thus, **answer (A) is incorrect.**

Though W's testimony at the first trial is hearsay when offered to prove its truth (that W caused the collision by running a red light), FRE 804(b)(1), the former testimony exception, applies here. The evidence was offered at the first trial against D. (It does not matter that W was an adverse witness; W's testimony was still being offered by P against D. Thus, **answer (B) is incorrect**.) At the first trial, D would have had a motive to cross-examine W in the hope of showing that W did not in fact run the light. That is the same motive D would have in the second trial. Thus, X's testimony is admissible.

Note that **answer (C) is incorrect** because it gets the matter exactly backward. One way to test the application of the rules of evidence is to take a step back and think about the fairness of applying them in certain ways. Here, *not* permitting P to prove W's testimony at the first trial would be unfair to P because it would make it more difficult to prove P's case for reasons beyond P's control, and under circumstances where the adverse party had an opportunity and a good reason to try to repair the damage caused by W's testimony. This fairness test will not work in all cases, of course; some evidence rules exist to promote values other than fairness and require rulings that seem unfair. But it cannot hurt to consider such matters as fairness in testing the application of the rules.

300. **Answer (A) is correct.** Under the "Morgan/McCormick" theory of presumptions, a presumption shifts *both* the burden of production *and* the burden of persuasion to the opponent. If the proponent produces sufficient evidence to meet a burden of production on the foundational facts, the presumption comes into existence and is not dispelled (rebutted) merely by offering evidence sufficient to meet a burden of production on the non-existence of the presumed facts. Instead, the presumption persists.

Here, if P has offered sufficient evidence to meet a burden of production on the existence of the foundational facts (the child was born within ten months of the last date on which a male and female were cohabiting), the presumption came into existence. This shifted to D the burden of persuading the jury that he was not the child's father (the presumed fact). This means the court should issue the instruction noted in answer (A).

Answer (B) is incorrect because it places the fact-finding role in the court's hands rather than the jury's. This is improper. The court's only role is to determine whether there is evidence sufficient to support a finding that the foundational facts are true.

Answer (C) is incorrect because, as explained above, under the Morgan/McCormick view of presumptions, evidence contradicting the presumed fact does not destroy the presumption.

Answer (D) is incorrect because, as in answer (B), it places the fact-finding role in the court's hands rather than the jury's. It is not up to the court to decide whether D's blood test evidence proves he was not the father. The court should decide only whether there is sufficient evidence to permit such a finding.

301. **Answer (D) is correct.** FRE 703 provides that "[t]he facts or data in the particular case upon which an expert bases an opinion or inference may be those perceived by or made known to the expert at or before the hearing." The only limitation is set forth in the second sentence of the rule: "If of a type reasonably relied upon by experts in the particular field in forming opinions or inferences upon the subject, the facts or data need not be admissible in evidence."

Looking at the choices in light of this rule, all meet the test of FRE 703: A psychiatrist may base her testimony on things she learned while treating the defendant. These facts were made known to the psychiatrist before the hearing. Thus, **answer (A)** sets forth a permissible source of knowledge. **Answer (B)** also sets forth a permissible source of information. This is information another expert gathered. It seems reasonable to assume that psychiatrists frequently rely on psychological tests performed by other experts. (If there is an objection on this ground, the party calling the expert will have to show that psychiatrists do indeed rely on this source of data.)

Hypothetical questions are still permitted, as well, as long as they are based on facts supported by testimony in the record. FRE 703 abolishes the common law requirement that the facts in the hypothetical question be supplied while the expert is on the stand. Thus, **answer (C)** also sets forth a permissible source of the expert's knowledge.

302. **Answer (D) is correct.** FRE 602 states that every person is competent to be a witness except as provided in the rules. There is no rule making children below a certain age incompetent. Thus, **answer (C) is incorrect**.

At the same time, there is no rule prohibiting the judge from asking questions of a prospective witness as the judge did here. It is possible that a person's mental condition would make her testimony so useless that it is a waste of time to allow the person to testify. Though this situation would be very rare, the judge could exclude the witness on the ground that the probative value of the witness's testimony is substantially outweighed by the waste of time involved. Thus, **answer (A) is incorrect**.

The court's determination of all preliminary facts under FRE 104(a) is made on a "preponderance of the evidence" standard. In deciding whether to allow W to testify, the judge should not apply a stricter standard. Thus, **answer (B) is incorrect**.

303.   **Answer (A) is correct.** The evidence is relevant because it shows that the ride acted in the same way alleged by P on another occasion close in time to P's injury, and that the person involved on that occasion was nearly thrown out of the car even though he was seated properly. Thus, the evidence tends to show that inadequate maintenance could have been the cause of the accident.

   Answer (B) is incorrect because this not a situation in which character evidence may be offered to prove action in conformity therewith on a particular occasion. None of the exceptions to the character ban in FRE 404(a) apply.

   Answer (C) is incorrect because two incidents are not sufficient to establish a "habit" to maintain the ride poorly.

   Answer (D) is incorrect because, as shown above, the evidence is relevant and admissible "similar accidents" evidence.

304.   **Answer (A) is correct.** Under FRE 104(a), the court has the authority to determine the "qualification of a person to be a witness. . . ." **Answer (C) is incorrect** because it assumes the jury has the ultimate authority to decide this question.

   The trial court has made its ruling after arguments on the issue. At this point, only that much is on the record for possible appeal. P must also give the appellate court a basis for determining the effect of the error, if indeed the trial court's ruling was erroneous. This requires P to place on the record what the witness would have testified if permitted to do so. *See* FRE 103(a)(2). With that information, the appellate court can determine whether the error affected "a substantial right of the party." **Answer (B) is incorrect** because, as just shown, P has not preserved the point for appeal.

   Answer (D) is incorrect because there is no crying in trial advocacy.

305.   **Answer (C) is correct.** The issue here is one of authentication of the signature on the letter as that of D. Under FRE 901(a), authentication is an issue ultimately for the jury, as long as the court determines that there is "evidence sufficient to support a finding that the matter in question is what its proponent claims."

   A party wishing to authenticate a signature is not required to call an expert witness. In fact, FRE 901(b)(2) envisions non-expert testimony on handwriting from a person familiar with the individual's handwriting (as long as the familiarity was not acquired for purposes of litigation). The methods of authentication in FRE 901(b) are "illustrative only," meaning that there is nothing to prohibit the court from allowing the jury to do the comparison of D's admitted handwriting sample with the writing on the allegedly libelous letter. The court need only look at the two items to decide whether there is evidence sufficient to support a finding that they were made by the same person. Thus, **answer (A) is incorrect.**

Answer (B) is incorrect for the same reason as well as because it assumes the court must decide that the letter was written by D rather than simply determine whether there is sufficient evidence for the jury to find that the letter is authentic. **Answer (D) is incorrect** for the same reason: it also appears to assume that the court must determine whether D wrote the letter.

306.   **Answer (C) is correct.** Because P is basing her claim against D on D's own negligence in retaining the guard, an issue in the case is whether the guard was, in fact, unreliable. That places the guard's character for reliability "in issue." (In the words of FRE 405(b), this is a situation in which character is "an essential element of a . . . claim.") Because the guard's character is in issue, FRE 405(b) allows evidence of character in the form of specific instances of conduct in addition to reputation and opinion as allowed under FRE 405(a). Thus, answer (C) is correct because the prior incidents are offered to show that the guard was in fact unreliable.

The evidence is also relevant on another basis: It shows possible notice to D of the guard's unreliability. In this negligence case, is it not enough to show that the guard was unreliable; P must also show that reasonable school officials would have discovered his unreliability. Evidence that the guard had been absent twice in the past month would tend to show notice. **Answer (D) is incorrect.** It starts out correctly, but goes wrong when it suggests that the incidents have low probative value which is substantially outweighed by the danger of unfair prejudice the evidence carries. That conclusion is incorrect on the facts because the jury will certainly use the evidence of the guard's absences for their proper purpose. Though there is some danger the jury will use the evidence to prove that the guard was absent on this occasion (see discussion of answer (A) below), that danger is very unlikely to substantially outweigh the legitimate probative value of the evidence.

Answer (B) is incorrect because a jury is entitled to determine that two absences in the month prior to the accident should have put D on notice of the guard's unreliability. There is no need to prove a "pattern" per se; it is enough to raise suspicion of unreliability in reasonable school officials.

Answer (A) incorrect because the evidence may *not* be used to prove the guard was absent on the day of P's accident. That would be an improper use of character evidence to prove action in conformity on a particular occasion. Though character evidence is admissible in this case as explained above, it is not admissible to prove action in conformity.

307.   **Answer (D) is correct.** If W has sued D's spouse, W might be biased against D, which might lead W to shade her testimony improperly in P's favor. No specific rules govern bias impeachment, but the Supreme Court in *United States v. Abel*, 469 U.S. 45 (1984), made clear that that form is still permitted.

Answer (A) is incorrect because, as shown above, the evidence is relevant to the witness's possible bias. **Answer (B) is incorrect** because there is no prohibition on the use of extrinsic evidence to impeach by showing bias. **Answer (C) is incorrect** because there is no prohibition on the use of a witness's specific instances of conduct to show bias.

308.   **Answer (C) is correct.** V's utterance is hearsay because it asserts, among other things, that V was on the sidewalk, and it is offered to prove that fact. The statement would qualify as a dying declaration under FRE 804(b)(2) if the following requirements are satisfied: this is a civil action or homicide prosecution (it is a civil action); the declarant is unavailable (V is unavailable because he is dead); the declarant believed death was imminent when he made the statement (see below); and if the statement concerned the cause or circumstances of what the declarant believed to be his impending death (that is clear here).

The issue here is whether V believed he was about to die when he made the statement. This preliminary fact (along with the others) must be decided by the court under FRE 104(a) because this is *not* a case of conditional relevancy. (The statement is relevant even if V did not believe she was about to die.) The court will apply the "preponderance of the evidence" standard to deciding this question.

Answer (A) is incorrect because the evidence is hearsay. **Answer (B) is incorrect** because the statement does concern the cause or circumstances of what V believed to be his impending death (where he was located when the crane hit him is part of the circumstances of the accident that killed V). **Answer (D) is incorrect** because it assumes that the disputed preliminary fact is to be decided according to the conditional relevancy standard of FRE 104(b), rather than the standard of FRE 104(a).

309. The court should grant D's motion and instruct the jury to disregard W's testimony. Unless W's testimony satisfies the requirements of FRE 801(d)(1(C), the "prior identification" rule, it is inadmissible hearsay. In this case, the rule's requirements are not satisfied.

First, X's statement, "He's the one who robbed V" is offered to prove that D is the one who robbed V. So, too, is X's act of pointing, which qualifies as a "statement" under FRE 801(a) because it was "intended by [X] as an assertion." It is therefore hearsay unless it fits into an exemption or an exception. No exceptions apply here. (It is not a present sense impression because it describes an event that took place some time earlier, not one taking place at the moment or immediately before.) The statement satisfies most of the requirements of the prior identification rule, but not all: The prosecution has failed to call X to testify as a witness at the trial. Thus, X was not "subject to cross-examination concerning the statement."

310. In *Daubert v. Merrill Dow Pharmaceuticals, Inc.*, 509 U.S. 579 (1993), the Supreme Court held that when the issue concerns the admissibility of purported scientific testimony, the court must determine whether the opinion represents scientific knowledge that will assist the trier of fact. FRE 702 was later amended to incorporate this basic idea. This test means that the court must decide both whether the evidence is reliable and whether it is relevant to the facts of the case. Reliability is not to be decided according to a categorical test of "general acceptance," as was the case under the *Frye* test. Rather, the court should look at such matters as whether W's theory has been subjected to peer review and publication, whether it has an error rate and whether the error rate is known, and indeed whether the theory is generally accepted. Relevance is not a difficult issue in this case. It is clear that the evidence concerns the disputed issue of causation.

If the court decides that the theory underlying W's proposed testimony is reliable and that it is relevant to the facts of the case, the court should admit the evidence. Otherwise, the court should exercise its "gate-keeping" function by excluding the evidence.

311. At common law, witnesses were generally not allowed to give an opinion on an ultimate issue in the case. FRE 704(a) changes that rule by providing that "[t]estimony in the form of an opinion or inference otherwise admissible is not objectionable because it embraces an ultimate issue to be decided by the trier of fact." That rule does not completely abolish the common law practice. If a witness's proposed opinion testimony is given in the form of technical terms of a legal rule, the testimony invades the province of the court to instruct the jury about the meaning of legal terms. Here, the terms "aided and abetted" and perhaps other terms of the statute have special legal meaning, and

it is the court's job to instruct the jury about the meanings of those terms, not the job of a witness. W can probably testify in another form that does not invade this judicial function. The court should sustain D's objection.

312.   The court should overrule P's objection and allow D to ask the question. D's question is an attempt to impeach W by contradiction. The fact on which D is to be contradicted is collateral because its only value to the case is in contradicting W. Though the Federal Rules do not contain the common law rule that it is impermissible to impeach a witness by contradiction on a collateral matter with extrinsic evidence, most federal courts would exclude evidence that fits within the rule under FRE 403 because it is a waste of time. Thus, the rule was not violated, and the court should overrule P's objection.

313.   The court should sustain D's objection because the testimony violates the hearsay rule. The testimony is not simply that D twice committed similar crimes. It is that someone (the police chief) *told* W that D had done so. The police chief's statement is hearsay because it asserts that D committed these crimes, and it is offered to prove that fact. No exception applies in this situation.

If the prosecution offered the evidence in a way that did not violate the hearsay rule (such as by offering testimony of one who has personal knowledge of D's two prior crimes), it probably would be admissible to prove identity through *modus operandi*. All three of the burglaries were committed in the same rather unusual way. It is likely that the same person committed all three. If D committed the two uncharged acts, D is more likely to have committee the charged crime.

314.   The court should sustain the objection on both grounds. First, the bystander's statement in the police report is hearsay within hearsay. The "inner" layer is the bystander's statement that D ran the red light. This is offered to prove the truth of the matter asserted: that D ran the light. The "outer" layer is the report itself, which is the officer's statement that the bystander made this statement. It, too, is hearsay. FRE 803(8)(C), part of the public records exception, covers the officer's statement (the shell of the report, in essence), but there is no exception covering the bystander's statement. FRE 805 states that hearsay within hearsay is admissible if each part fits within an exception. Because the "inner" part does not fit within an exception, the part of the report containing the bystander's statement is inadmissible hearsay.

P's proposed testimony also violates the best evidence rule, FRE 1002. P is testifying about what the report contains. This is testimony about the contents of a writing. The best evidence rule provides that to prove the contents of a writing, the writing must be produced. P has not produced it, and has not shown that an exception applies.

315.   The court must overrule D's objection and allow the prosecution to ask W about the conviction. Under FRE 609(a)(2), a witness's conviction for a crime involving dishonesty or false statement is admissible to impeach the witness. Courts have held that admission is always permitted; FRE 403 may not be used to exclude it. The crime of filing a false federal income tax return is a crime involving dishonesty or false

statement. It is therefore admissible automatically. The passage of seven years since conviction or the end of confinement (whichever is later) is not long enough to change the answer. The relevant period under FRE 609(b) is ten years.

316. The court should sustain D's objection to W's testimony about what D said to W, but should overrule the objection to W's testimony about the cat hair.

Both spousal privileges are implicated here. The privilege for confidential communications between spouses generally belongs to both spouses. Thus, D may prevent W from testifying about D's statement, which appears to have been made in confidence.

In federal court and many state courts, the privilege not to testify adversely to a spouse belongs to the testifying spouse. Thus, D may not prevent W from testifying about D's appearance if W wishes to do so.

317. The court should overrule D's objection. X's statement is hearsay because it was made other than while testifying at the trial, and is offered to prove the truth of the matter asserted (that D robbed the bank). FRE 804(b)(6) provides an exception for statements offered against a party when the party procured or acquiesced in the procurement of the declarant's unavailability. That is the case here. X's absence from the country qualifies as unavailability under FRE 804(a)(5). If the court concludes that D's threat procured X's unavailability, X's statement will be admissible under FRE 804(b)(6).

318. The court should overrule D's objection. FRE 404(a)(2) allows a criminal defendant to offer evidence of a pertinent character trait of an alleged crime victim. Dishonesty in business dealings is a pertinent trait because it makes commission of fraud more likely. FRE 404(a)(1) allows the prosecution, in this situation, to offer evidence concerning the same trait of the defendant's character. That was the purpose of W2's testimony. The evidence thus fits within FRE 404(a)(1), and because it took the form of reputation testimony, it complies with FRE 405(a).

INDEX

INDEX